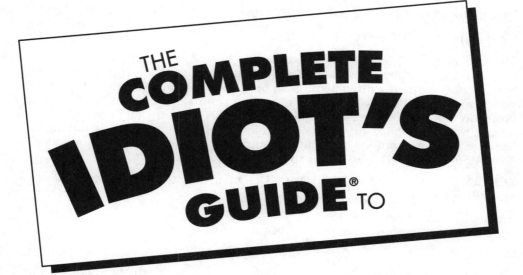

THE COMPLETE IDIOT'S GUIDE® TO

Saving the Environment

by Greg Pahl

alpha books

Macmillan USA, Inc.
201 West 103rd Street
Indianapolis, IN 46290

A Pearson Education Company

I want to dedicate this book to the world's children and grandchildren.

Copyright © 2001 by Greg Pahl

International Standard Book Number: 0-02-863982-0
Library of Congress Catalog Card Number: Available upon request.

03   02   01   8   7   6   5   4   3   2   1

Interpretation of the printing code: The rightmost number of the first series of numbers is the year of the book's printing; the rightmost number of the second series of numbers is the number of the book's printing. For example, a printing code of 01-1 shows that the first printing occurred in 2001.

Printed in the United States of America

The Complete Idiot's Reference Card

Basic Environmental Checklist

Here are some of the most important points to remember to help save the environment and create a sustainable world for our children and grandchildren.

➤ **Our over-consumption of resources is one of the most serious threats to the environment.** We need to learn to live within the Earth's ability to meet our needs, yet also without compromising the ability of future generations to meet their own needs.

➤ **The Three Rs of the Environmental movement are Reduce, Reuse, and Recycle.** The Three Rs are the key traditional strategies for being an environmentally responsible citizen. You can practice all of them in your daily life at home and at work.

➤ **Reduce your use.** Source reduction is the best way to cut waste, help the environment, and save money at the same time. It's also the hardest of the Three Rs to achieve because it affects our lifestyles.

➤ **When it comes to reducing waste, there's no place like home.** Replacing older, worn-out appliances with new, energy-efficient models, using compact fluorescent light bulbs, and improving the insulation in our homes can save a lot of energy and help reduce global warming.

➤ **Reuse saves.** Reuse is an old strategy that has become hot again in recent years. Reuse saves money and resources while cutting pollution and waste.

➤ **Reuse at home.** Choosing reusable home products over their throwaway alternatives is a beneficial—and money-saving—strategy to help improve the environment.

➤ **Recycling is the least effective of the Three Rs, but it's still important.** Once you get used to recycling, it's not a big deal. A few minutes a day—at the most—is all it takes.

➤ **You're not really recycling unless you're buying recycled.** The most important part of recycling is buying products that contain as much post-consumer recycled content as possible. Look for it and ask for it when you go shopping.

➤ **Help create a sustainable world.** In order to create a sustainable future for our children and grandchildren we need to reduce our over-consumption of resources, shift to renewable forms of energy, work for a more balanced transportation system, stop urban sprawl, and deal with overpopulation—among other things.

➤ **Your efforts really do matter.** There's so much that needs to be done that it's easy to feel there is nothing you can do that will make a difference. But everyone has a productive role to play in working for a sustainable future. Figure out where you can do the most good, and get involved.

alpha
books

Top-Ten Most Useful Environmental Web Sites

There are hundreds of environmentally related Web sites on the Internet. I've put together this list of my 10 favorites for you. Keep this list handy as a quick reference tool. Feel free to add your own favorites:

1. **www.awea.org** is the site of the American Wind Energy Association, which promotes wind energy as a clean source of electricity for consumers around the world.

2. **www.newdream.org** is The Center for a New American Dream, a nonprofit membership-based organization that helps individuals and institutions reduce and shift consumption to improve the quality of life and protect the environment.

3. **www.communities-by-choice.org** is a national network of individuals and communities committed to learning and practicing sustainable development.

4. **www.oldgrowth.org/compost** is The Compost Resource Page, a great source of information about composting that includes basic and advanced composting information, tips, and products.

5. **www.coopamerica.org** features a national nonprofit organization that provides the economic strategies, organizing power, and practical tools for businesses and individuals to address today's social and environmental problems.

6. **www.eaaev.org** is The Electric Auto Association, a nonprofit educational organization that promotes the advancement and widespread adoption of Electric Vehicles.

7. **www.igc.apc.org/frugal** is the Frugal Living Resources section of EcoNet's Web site, which provides information sources for better, healthier, more satisfying living with less.

8. **www.rri.org** is the Resource Renewal Institute Web site, providing a lot of useful information about green plans in this country and around the world.

9. **www.simpleliving.net** is a great site for those who are serious about learning to live a more conscious, simple, healthy, and earth-friendly lifestyle.

10. **www.ucsusa.org** is The Union of Concerned Scientists, an independent nonprofit alliance of 50,000 concerned citizens and scientists across the country committed to build a cleaner, healthier environment, and a safer world.

Publisher
Marie Butler-Knight

Product Manager
Phil Kitchel

Managing Editor
Cari Luna

Senior Acquisitions Editor
Randy Ladenheim-Gil

Development Editor
Kris Simmons

Production Editor
JoAnna Kremer

Copy Editor
Jan Zunkel

Illustrator
Jody P. Schaeffer

Cover Designers
Mike Freeland
Kevin Spear

Book Designers
Scott Cook and Amy Adams of DesignLab

Indexer
Lisa Wilson

Layout/Proofreading
Angela Calvert
Mary Hunt
Ayanna Lacey
Heather Hiatt Miller
Stacey Richwine-DeRome

Contents at a Glance

Contents

Introduction

For better or worse, the twenty-first century is going to be the Environmental Century. Activists in the environmental community have been warning of impending ecological ca-tastrophe for years. Whether their dire predictions come true or not largely depends on our actions in the next few decades. Though we have made progress in some areas, we are un-fortunately losing ground in many others. That's why I decided to *The Complete Idiot's Guide to Saving the Environment.*

But I didn't write this book for long-time environmentalists. That would be like preach-ing to the choir. I've written it for the vast majority of Americans who generally understand that there is a connection between our over-consumption of resources and the many envi-ronmental problems we face—but fail to make the direct link to their own individual lifestyles.

In a 1995 study prepared for the Merck Family Fund, 86 percent of those surveyed said they were concerned about the quality of the environment. Yet only 51 percent agreed that their *own* buying habits have a negative effect on the environment. This disconnection between environmental reality and our own personal behavior is one of the biggest remaining obsta-cles to making serious progress toward saving the planet—and ourselves.

But there are other difficulties. With all the claims and counter claims made by the many special-interest groups involved in environmental debates, it's often hard to know whom to believe. What's more, a large part of the scientific information is so technical that many people just can't seem to get a handle on it. And many scientists and academics aren't very good at explaining these things in language that you and I can easily understand.

Another problem is that many of these issues are so interrelated that it's hard to figure out what to do. It's often difficult to fix one problem without causing another one. But though we should not underestimate the environmental challenges we face, we also should not un-derestimate our abilities to deal with them.

One encouraging sign is that an increasing number of individuals, groups, and organiza-tions, as well as businesses and even governments, are beginning to realize that dealing with the environmental crisis offers some remarkable opportunities along with the chal-lenges. And if these groups can find ways to cooperate—some already are—there is good reason for optimism.

The fact that you are reading this right now is another reason for optimism. If you're like most people, you probably really do care about our future—and your children's future. But, like many folks, you may not have been a long-time environmental activist. And you may not have studied environmental subjects much in school, either. But that doesn't have to be a problem. If you really want to learn about these issues and understand how they affect us—and the Earth—this book can help.

What You'll Learn in This Book

But you still might be tempted to ask, "I'm just one person; what can I possibly do that will make a difference?" Actually, there are lots of things you can do. And you'll find many of them right in your own home. Or in your garage. Or at work. Or in your community.

And that's where this book comes in. I'm going to give you the information you need to help save the environment while you also take care of your daily household chores or go through your busy schedule at work. Or even when you're on vacation. In many cases, you'll be able to accomplish this while saving money at the same time. That's a pretty good deal if you ask me. Here's how the book is organized to help you do this.

Part 1, "The Environment and You," looks at the many environmental challenges we face. I start by explaining basic environmental terms and principles so you can better understand the larger issues. I'll also include some historical background to help put things into perspective. Then, I'll cover the many problems related to the air we breathe, the water we drink and use every day, and the land we live on. Finally, I'll introduce you to the Three Rs of the environmental movement: reduce, reuse, and recycle, and the Big S—sustainability.

Part 2, In "Reduce Your Use," I focus mainly on solutions to the many problems covered in Part 1. I'll go into more detail about reducing, the most important of the Three Rs. I'll explain the many different ways you can use this strategy in your daily life and why it's so important for the environment—and you. I'll also explore a number of lifestyle changes that involve some interesting types of reduction.

The second most important R is reuse. In **Part 3, "Reuse It,"** I'll explore a wide array of money-saving reuse strategies that cut your living expenses while at the same time helping to save the environment. I'll offer many reuse suggestions that you can employ at home, at work, and many other places as well.

The third of the Three Rs is recycling. In **Part 4, "Recycle It,"** I'll explain all the basics as well as the current status of this highly visible—and controversial—strategy. You'll learn which materials are easily recyclable and which ones aren't. Then we'll look at nature's original recycling program, composting, and check out an old family recipe or two. I'll also explain how to close the recycling loop with money-saving ideas for buying recycled products.

Part 5, "A Sustainable Future," explains the concept of sustainability and how it can help us save the planet. We'll explore the hot new markets for renewable energy resources and how they can supply your future energy needs. We'll also look at transportation issues, living patterns, and population. In addition, I'll explain the exciting growth of "green plans" and why they are the wave of the future. Finally, you'll learn even more ways to get involved in creating a sustainable world.

Plus, you get appendixes that include an environmental timeline to help you see the "big picture," a glossary of terms to help you with all the jargon, a list of books and publications for further reading, and groups, organizations, and other resources you can turn to for more information.

Along the way you'll find these helpful boxes offering tips, definitions, warnings, and some interesting bits of information:

Earth Education

You'll find interesting or useful background information about the environment and related issues in these boxes.

Eco-Explanations

These boxes contain definitions that will help you learn environmental terms quickly without having to reach for a dictionary.

Green Tips

Check here for helpful hints that may save you time or money or make things better or easier.

Planetary Perils

Look here for environmental warnings and safety tips.

Acknowledgments

I would like to thank the many editors and assistants at Macmillan Publishing who helped to bring this book to completion. In particular, Randy Ladenheim-Gil, my acquisitions editor whose commitment to this project never failed, and JoAnna Kremer, my production editor, who really helped pull things together.

I would also like to acknowledge the many people in the environmental community who were so generous with their time and advice. This book would not have been possible without people like Eric Brown and David Tilford, Center for a New American Dream; Vivian Fong and Janet Overton, World Resources Institute; Liz Hitchcock, PIRG; Jera Duff, Environmental Media Services; Bill Bryant, Leif Skoogfors, Greenpeace USA; Arthur Weissman, Green Seal; Sherry Binette, Environmental Choice Program; and Vanessa Mercer, Center for Resource Solutions.

I also want to thank Professors Ray Coish, John Elder, Frank Winkler, Richard Wolfson, Associate Professors Helen Young, Christopher Klyza, Daniel Bedford, Assistant Professor Timothy Billings, Associate College Librarian Hans Raum, and Science Librarian Louise Zipp, all from Middlebury College; and Associate Professor Craig Shinn from Portland State University, for their advice, comments, and assistance.

Other individuals who helped in many different ways were Dorothy Schnure, Green Mountain Power; Martha Staskus, Vermont Environmental Research Associates; Laura Routh, Addison County Solid Waste Management District; Gary Weiss, Computer Alternatives; Amanda Loomis, IGO Mobile Technology Outfitter; Jo McGettrick, Collectible Flea Mart; Katherine Wheatley; and Georgene Lockwood. I also offer my sincere thanks to anyone else I may have forgotten to mention.

Last, but by no means least, I want to thank my wife, Joy, for her help in chasing down obscure facts, proofreading, making suggestions, and generally putting up with me while I was trying to meet some very tight deadlines.

Special Thanks to the Technical Reviewer

The Complete Idiot's Guide to Saving the Environment was reviewed by an expert who double-checked the accuracy of what you'll learn here, to help us ensure that this book gives you everything you need to know about the environment. Special thanks are extended to Yuri Horwitz.

Yuri Horwitz received a degree in both environmental studies and government from The College of William and Mary class of 2001. He is currently pursuing a career in environmental policy, and hopes soon to enter politics and produce environmental legislation. He has worked for some time in the environmental field as both a teacher and researcher, and is dedicated to continuing his work to improve the environment throughout his life.

Trademarks

All terms mentioned in this book that are known to be or are suspected of being trademarks or service marks have been appropriately capitalized. Alpha Books and Macmillan USA, Inc., cannot attest to the accuracy of this information. Use of a term in this book should not be regarded as affecting the validity of any trademark or service mark.

Part 1

The Environment and You

You keep hearing in the media about how we're ruining our environment. Unfortunately, most of those reports are true. If you're like most folks, you'd probably like to try to help fix things. But do you really understand the issues? Or even the terms? How can you help if you really don't know what's going on—and why it's happening?

So, before you waste a lot of time and energy spinning your wheels, let's start with the basics. I'll explain the terms and how all of this stuff is interrelated and why it's so important to you. And because it's hard to know where you are going unless you know where you came from, we'll take a look back at the past before we stumble blindly into the future. Then, I'll tell you about the many environmental problems we face.

But along the way we'll also pause to drink some cold, clear water, take a whiff of the fresh morning breeze, and stroll through a lush green forest filled with wildflowers, birds, and animals. Then we'll try to imagine what the world would be like without these things. It could happen. Finally, I'll introduce you to some actions you can take to keep this from happening.

Chapter 1

It's Our Home

> ## In This Chapter
>
> ➤ The lessons of Earth Day
>
> ➤ How your future depends on the environment
>
> ➤ What we've forgotten since kindergarten
>
> ➤ The biggest global threats
>
> ➤ Why we need to change our habits

What a beautiful picture! Our lovely blue and green Earth with its swirling white cloud patterns set against the stark blackness of space. It's simply breathtaking. These now-familiar views of our home planet taken from the moon have caused a lot of people to change their thinking about our society—and their place in it. From space there are no visible political boundaries. There are just huge interconnected mountain ranges, forests, rivers, and oceans. And one big, interdependent global community.

But back down on Earth, things aren't so pretty. Radioactive emissions, oil spills, toxic chemical leaks; strip-mined landscapes; clear-cut rainforests; vanishing plants, birds, and animals; huge killer storms and mudslides; increasing competition for dwindling resources; famine, disease, and poverty—the unhappy list goes on and on.

All of these events are connected to a variety of environmental issues, especially over-consumption of limited resources. What's more, these issues are all related to each other in one way or another. It can get confusing pretty quickly. While you might be tempted to stand there and scratch your head in bewilderment, you don't need to hold an advanced degree in environmental studies to grasp this stuff. Actually, if you understand a few simple lessons that you probably learned in kindergarten, most of this becomes pretty clear. We'll get to those lessons a bit later in this chapter.

First, we're going to pause briefly for a birthday party. Then, I'll introduce you to the basic issues we'll be seeing throughout the rest of the book. I'll also explain some environmental lingo and show you why all of this is so important.

Happy Birthday, Earth Day!

Earth Day 2000 was quite a bash. All over the planet millions of people celebrated the 30th anniversary of what started out as an environmental teach-in on college campuses in the U.S. back in 1970. Since then, Earth Day has expanded across the country and around the world. This year it was marked by events, both large and small, almost everywhere.

During the month of April 2000 there were speeches and parades, and demonstrations that featured alternative energy technology, and lots of other imaginative new products, programs, and ideas to help save the environment. Many participants looked fondly back over the past three decades at the many environmental success stories that have taken place. But participants also were faced with the sobering realization that while we've made progress in some areas, we're losing ground in many others.

Earth Education

Former U.S. Senator Gaylord Nelson from Wisconsin came up with the idea for the first Earth Day during a plane flight to the University of California at Berkeley in 1969. Shortly thereafter, he announced that he would help initiate a nationwide environmental "teach-in" the following spring. It worked.

In this country, the original Earth Day ultimately led to strengthened national Clean Air and Clean Water legislation, among many other positive things. We've cleaned up some of our worst toxic waste sites, improved the quality of the water in many of our rivers and lakes (the Cuyahoga River in Ohio doesn't catch fire anymore), banned the use of many dangerous chemicals and pesticides, increased environmental awareness, and much more. But we've still got a long way to go—especially in the realm of over-consumption because it relates to so many other environmental issues (more on that later). So, we can't pat ourselves on the back too quickly.

In Western Europe, Earth Day participants had quite a lot more to celebrate. A number of European countries have moved far ahead of us in environmental protection, alternative energy generation, and in establishing comprehensive environmental "green plans" (more on them in Chapter 26, "Green Plans"). On the other hand, in parts of Eastern Europe, and especially in Russia, the situation is grim, but not hopeless.

But the biggest challenges of all are probably in many parts of the Third World, where huge numbers of impoverished people are struggling to simply survive. And in many cases, they're stripping what few natural resources remain to try to do that. This, of course, makes survival even harder. So, on a global level it's a real mixed bag. Consequently, Earth Day was both a celebration and a call for redoubled efforts to tackle the many difficult environmental problems that remain.

The Environmental Century

At the very least, the Earth Day anniversary has helped to refocus our attention on the continuing damage we're causing to the very resources that provide us with our food, clothing, shelter, and fuel. And we're beginning to run out of time to make the fundamental changes needed to reverse these trends.

Although environmentalists have been warning about this situation for decades, many other people are finally beginning to realize that if we don't act soon it will be too late. The good news is that more and more businesses and governments are beginning to understand that without a healthy environment the global economy and everything that depends on it will be seriously endangered. And they are beginning to take positive action. We'll focus on the good news later on in the book.

One way or another, this is unquestionably going to be the Environmental Century. We'll either tackle these problems head on and begin to resolve them, or Mother Nature will do it for us. And, as you've probably heard, it's not a good idea to mess with Mother Nature. But that's exactly what we have been doing for a very long time. Now she's beginning to get really irritated.

Planetary Perils

Most observers agree that if we continue to gobble up natural resources and pollute the planet at our current rate, the environmental support system that we depend on may begin to collapse sometime during this century.

What's All This Environmental Stuff?

Okay, so things could be better. And we need to get to work on these problems as soon as possible. But before we grab our emergency repair kits and other tools, we need to know what we are dealing with—and how it works. You wouldn't try to fix a complicated piece of machinery without understanding its parts and how they interconnect. The same applies to the environment, which in many ways functions like a huge—and very complex—machine. So, let's take a closer look at the environment and some of its most important parts.

The Environment

Almost everything in the natural environment is interrelated. You can't really understand one part without looking at the other parts. But let's start with the basics. Just what, exactly, is an environment? Simply stated, it's all of the external factors that affect any organism (including you and me). These factors can be other living organisms or nonliving variables like water, soil, light, oxygen, and climate, to name just a few. Now for a little environmental lingo. We'll be using most of these terms again, so let's get them sorted out now.

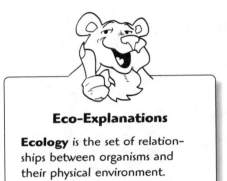

Eco-Explanations

Ecology is the set of relationships between organisms and their physical environment.

Ecology

You probably have heard the term *ecology* used quite a bit. It's often confused with environmental science. But that's not really correct. Ecology has two related meanings. Ecology is the branch of biology that deals with the interaction of organisms (individual life forms) with their environment. It's also the set of relationships between organisms and their physical environment. In other words, it's how you and I (and all other living organisms) interact with each other and our environment. Okay? On to the biosphere.

The Biosphere

Our planet's entire living environment is known as the biosphere. It includes a relatively thin zone of air, soil, and water that is capable of supporting life. This zone extends up about six miles into the atmosphere and down to the bottom of deepest ocean. Life in this zone depends upon the sun's energy and on the circulation of heat and nutrients.

Within the biosphere are a number of large categories of living communities that are called biomes, which are normally characterized by their main vegetation patterns such as forests, shrub lands, grasslands, deserts, tundra, and so on. Don't worry too much about the term "biome." Just remember that this is the part of the biosphere where we tend to hang out rather than six miles up in the sky or at the bottom of an ocean. Got it? Good. On to ecosystems.

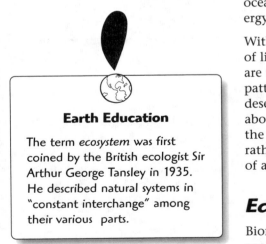

Earth Education

The term *ecosystem* was first coined by the British ecologist Sir Arthur George Tansley in 1935. He described natural systems in "constant interchange" among their various parts.

Ecosystems

Biomes, in turn, are made up of ecosystems. An ecosystem includes living parts, such as plants, animals, and bacteria found in the soil, which are known as a community. The physical surroundings of an ecosystem are known as the environment or habitat. An ecosystem could be something as small as an aquarium in your living room, or as large as a tropical rain forest.

Biodiversity

The last bit of lingo for now is "biodiversity." This is actually another way of saying "biological diversity." Biodiversity is the variety of living organisms in a particular habitat or geographic area. We normally measure biodiversity as the number of species of plants, animals, and microorganisms found in a particular area. Diversity of species is usually important to the functioning of ecosystems, and that's why it's considered an indication of the health of an environment. Major declines in biodiversity usually mean environmental trouble.

Why Is This Important?

As you can see from these descriptions, our global environment is made up of systems within systems within systems. And they all form an interconnected whole that has been described by some as the Web of Life. If you muck around with one part, it's likely that there will be a reaction in another part. And these reactions can have bizarre ripple effects that are sometimes hard to predict.

But why is all of this so important? It's really quite simple. Think of the environment as your life-support system. Because that's exactly what it is. If you are a diver—say—your scuba gear is your life support system. If your scuba equipment is damaged somehow (especially if you're under water), you're in trouble. The more the damage, the deeper the trouble. If your scuba gear stops functioning, you're done for. Get the picture? It's the same general idea with our environment.

But with our increasingly technological society, people are becoming more and more detached from the natural environment and less aware of what is going on with it. And many people seem to have forgotten that, despite our technological sophistication, our modern civilization is totally dependent on its ecological foundations. Without those foundations, our civilization would collapse into chaos. And that would be a bummer.

Yet we continue to consume huge quantities of natural resources as if there is no tomorrow (and if we're not careful, there may not be a tomorrow). Unfortunately, this consumption is the most excessive right here in this country. The United

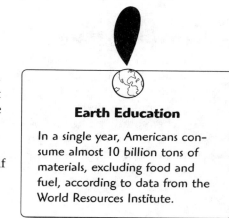

Earth Education

In a single year, Americans consume almost 10 billion tons of materials, excluding food and fuel, according to data from the World Resources Institute.

States, with just 4.5 percent of the world's population, consumes about 33 percent of the world's materials today, according to the United States Geological Survey. The other 95.5 percent of the global population gets what's left over.

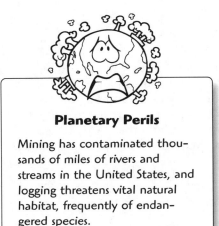

Planetary Perils

Mining has contaminated thousands of miles of rivers and streams in the United States, and logging threatens vital natural habitat, frequently of endangered species.

Not only is this unfair, it's also unsustainable. Especially if the rest of the world decides to try to copy our lifestyle. And that's what is beginning to happen in many parts of the world. You can't really blame them. Unfortunately, it would take three planets like Earth to supply the resources necessary for everyone to live a lifestyle like ours. It's simply impossible.

This kind of over-consumption is very destructive for the environment. It results in excessive and unsustainable mining; logging; quarrying; coal, oil, and gas extraction; and similar activities on a colossal scale. And it results in the dumping of huge quantities of industrial and consumer wastes that have to go somewhere. Often they end up in the air, in our drinking water, on the land, or in the oceans, where they pollute our remaining precious resources and cause even more problems.

Lessons from Kindergarten

While the potential solutions to these problems can get rather complicated—and painful—there are some very simple guidelines that you might recall from your childhood that put these issues into their proper perspective. Robert Fulghum lists them in his wonderful 1993 book *All I Really Need to Know I Learned in Kindergarten: Uncommon Thoughts on Common Things.* These simple suggestions were: share everything, clean up your own mess, and flush. Let's look at each of them.

Share Everything

If the members of the global community could just adopt this simple strategy, we would eliminate many of the causes of international unrest and discord. This idea, of course, is fairly popular in the poorer countries where they would welcome any improvement in living standards. Not surprisingly, this strategy is not so popular in the richer countries, like our own, because it means giving up some of our privileged lifestyle. But considering how wasteful we are as a society, if we just cut back on *some* of our extravagant habits we could live just as comfortably on a lot less stuff. Maybe even better. We'll revisit this issue throughout the book, but especially in Chapter 11, "Help, I Wanna Get Off!"

Clean Up Your Own Mess

If everyone, including individuals, small businesses, large corporations, and governments followed this advice, the world would be a much better place to live in. Unfortunately, this has not been the practice, and we are still faced with cleaning up the terrible mess left behind by prior generations—to say nothing of the awful mess we're *still* making in many parts of the world.

Quite a few people in this country have begun to take this simple advice to heart and are beginning to make a difference at the local and state levels with a wide variety of programs and initiatives. But we still have a long, long way to go here. In some other countries, however, especially in the Netherlands and New Zealand, "cleaning up your own mess" has taken on a whole new national dimension. I'll tell you more about this exciting development in Chapter 26.

Flush

I suppose you could view this one as a variation on the previous suggestion. But if everyone would just properly dispose of his or her own waste, it would go a long way toward making for a cleaner environment. Now, I'm not suggesting that you should dump all of your household waste in the toilet. Not at all. That could cause some messy problems. And depending on what you flushed, it might lead to serious groundwater pollution. But the idea of putting our waste, whatever it is, in its proper place is important in a world that is drowning in garbage. We'll look at this issue in more detail in Chapter 5, "The Land We Live On."

These are admittedly simplistic solutions to complicated issues, but they do cut right to the heart of many of the environmental problems we face today. Do you wish you were back in kindergarten? Sometimes I do, too.

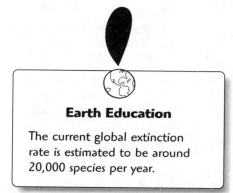

Earth Education

The current global extinction rate is estimated to be around 20,000 species per year.

The "Big Three" Global Threats

Although the problems I have mentioned already are bad enough, it gets worse. We face three additional major threats: the decline of biodiversity, the thinning of the ozone layer, and global warming. Let's look at each of them. These aren't much fun, but they're important to understand.

Decline in Biodiversity

As I mentioned earlier in this chapter, biodiversity is considered an indication of the health of an environment. And any time there is a decline in biodiversity it usually means that there is an environmental problem of some sort. Many scientists around the world have become increasingly alarmed in recent years by the massive declines in large numbers of plant and animal species.

For example, huge flocks of songbirds have traditionally migrated from Mexico to the United States every spring. But since the 1960s, their numbers have fallen by as much as 50 percent. Many other animals have been vanishing as well. The reasons for some of these disappearances are still not entirely clear. But most of these declines are directly or indirectly linked to the huge changes humans have made to the planet—especially the clearing of forests for agriculture and ranching, as well as massive urbanization, all of which have had a significant impact.

One of the leading experts on biodiversity, Harvard University's biologist Edward O. Wilson, estimates that the world could lose 20 percent of all existing species by 2020. And not just one by one, but in large groups in what he calls mass extinctions. We have some evidence that this is already happening to some species in various locations around the world. Disturbing? You bet. But that's not all.

Thinning of the Ozone Layer

There's another problem. And it's over our heads—literally. What's the ozone layer? Well, it's a section of the atmosphere about 12 to 30 miles above the Earth. It involves some complicated chemistry, but basically ozone forms from the action of sunlight on oxygen. And this process has been going on for millions of years. Recently, though, things have changed.

Back in the 1970s, scientists discovered that chemicals called chlorofluorocarbons, or CFCs (that had been used as refrigerants and as aerosol spray propellants), posed a threat to the ozone layer. Additional chemicals that damage the ozone layer were soon added to the list. Then, in the 1980s, other scientists working in Antarctica discovered a thinning or "hole" in the ozone layer above them during the Antarctic spring. A similar phenomenon was later found to be developing in the arctic region as well. Things seemed to be going from bad to worse.

Planetary Perils

A damaged ozone layer allows more of the sun's ultraviolet rays to pass through the atmosphere, causing skin cancer, cataracts, and many other serious problems.

But why worry about an invisible hole in the sky? The problem is that the ozone layer protects life on Earth from the full effects of the sun's cancer-causing ultraviolet radiation. And destruction of the ozone layer means more skin cancer, cataracts, and damage to some crops, as well as parts of the marine food chain (if the marine food chain collapses, goodbye fish). Ultimately, after years of controversy and debate, CFCs were banned in this and many other countries. It's too soon to tell how successful this strategy has been. We'll look at the ozone issue again in Chapter 3, "The Air We Breathe." But there's still one more big global threat.

Global Warming

The most serious problem of all is global warming, an increase in the Earth's temperature due to the use of fossil fuels (coal, oil, natural gas, etc.) and other industrial and agricultural processes. This causes a buildup of so-called "greenhouse gases" in the atmosphere. These gases—especially carbon dioxide and methane—tend to keep some of the Earth's infrared radiation from escaping into space, helping to maintain our planet's relatively warm temperatures. This is called the *greenhouse effect*. While it's nice to stay warm, too warm can be a problem.

Most scientists agree that the human burning of fossil fuels has finally started to have an effect on our climate. As greenhouse gases increase, so does the average global temperature. However, there is still a lot of disagreement on how much and how fast our climate will warm.

But why should you worry about the rise in global temperatures by just a few degrees? Do you have a beachfront home somewhere along the coast? If you do, you should be concerned. The increased melting of the polar ice caps caused by global warming could raise the level of the world's oceans enough to cause even more severe flooding during heavy storms than we're already experiencing.

But even if you don't live in a low-lying coastal area, global warming is going to cause greater fluctuations in weather patterns, with more severe storms and more intense droughts. These changes could in turn cause disease patterns to shift and other problems, and some of the most productive areas in the world, such as the Midwestern U.S., will probably not be able to provide the food they do presently. We've already begun to see graphic evidence of this pattern in recent years.

As bad as all this sounds, it could be worse. While not all scientists agree, some have warned that if greenhouse gases are allowed to continue to build up, there is the potential for a "runaway" greenhouse effect sometime after 2050 that could turn areas such as the Amazon basin and southern Europe into virtual deserts.

We'll be looking at global warming repeatedly throughout this book because it's such an important issue. And I'll explain global warming in even greater detail in Chapter 3. But for now, the main thing to remember is that this phenomenon is caused primarily by our reliance on fossil fuels, as well as consumption in its many forms—especially over-consumption.

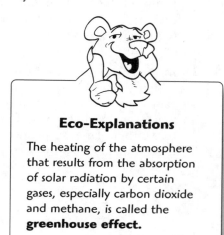

Eco-Explanations

The heating of the atmosphere that results from the absorption of solar radiation by certain gases, especially carbon dioxide and methane, is called the **greenhouse effect.**

Crisis? What Crisis?

Despite all these serious environmental problems we are facing, many people in the United States still don't seem to get it. Without a healthy environment we cannot expect to continue to maintain the kind of lifestyle we have become accustomed to. Yet, if we continue to live this way, there won't be a healthy environment. Especially if the rest of the world tries to copy what we're doing. And they already are.

Deep down, most of us realize that there are some problems. But we like to think of them as someone else's problems. Meanwhile, we continue to drive our huge, gas-guzzling sport-utility vehicles, build huge trophy homes with enough room in them to house several large extended families, and blindly accumulate so much stuff that we don't know what to do with all of it. We are a nation that is increasingly addicted to consumption for its own sake. And like it or not, we definitely are part of the problem.

There's one more unhappy scenario I must mention before we start to look on the bright side (and I promise we will). If current rates of unsustainable consumption (and its associated pollution) were to continue on a global level too much longer, there is a possibility of what some scientists call "system collapse." Simply stated, this is when the fabric of the Web of Life I mentioned earlier becomes so seriously damaged that one ecosystem after another begins to unravel, causing interrelated systems to fall like a series of dominoes. This does not mean that all life on the planet would end. But it does mean that the creatures that survive would have a miserable existence. It's not a very attractive prospect. But, remember what I said about Mother Nature?

There's Still Time

While all the environmental problems we face are challenging, the good news is that there still is time to deal with them before things get completely out of hand. But not too much time. So, we need to get to work, because escape from our problems is not an option.

Although we do have the technical capability for limited space travel, as a practical matter we're still very much Earth-bound. There is no realistic possibility for us to escape from our planet in the event of a systems collapse. Consequently, we need to do whatever we can to avoid that scenario. So, the next time you see that beautiful picture of our planet suspended against the blackness of space, just remember, the Earth is our home. Our only home.

The Least You Need to Know

➤ Today, most people realize that we're one big, interdependent global community.

➤ For better or worse, this is going to be the Environmental Century.

➤ Although we've made some progress in cleaning up our own mess, we still have a long, long way to go.

➤ We need to take global warming seriously and do whatever we can to reduce it.

➤ We still have some time to deal with our many environmental problems.

Chapter 2

Something Old, Something New

In This Chapter

➤ Environmental problems are nothing new

➤ What happens when you hit the limits

➤ A quick look back at our past

➤ How the environmental movement got started

➤ New problems around the world

At the start of the third millennium we move toward an uncertain future. We're surrounded by mounting evidence of widespread environmental deterioration and are faced with increasing pressure to do something about it. But if we don't understand how we got into this mess in the first place, how can we expect to know what to do next?

To help put all of this in its proper historical perspective, it's useful to look back to the past. As you may have heard, those who do not learn from the lessons of history are doomed to repeat them. Let's try to avoid that.

In this chapter, we'll see how some of our own distant ancestors interacted with their environment and what happened when they got out of balance with it. After that, we'll look briefly at the history of this country to help you understand the roots of our current environmental problems. All set? Let's take a trip back in time. Way back.

An Old Problem

Trying to maintain a healthy relationship with the environment is not a new problem for humans. Our earliest hunter-gatherer ancestors managed to be fruitful and multiply mainly by adjusting their economic and living patterns constantly to stay in balance with their natural environment. Although it was usually a challenge, it was obviously a successful strategy, or we wouldn't be here today.

Things got a little more complicated, however, when folks started to settle down and build cities in the ancient Middle East. For one thing, they became more vulnerable to sudden environmental changes because they couldn't just pack up and leave on a moment's notice as they had in the past.

The ancient Akkadian Empire is a case in point. Around 2200 B.C.E., some archeologists claim that an abrupt dry spell parched the northern region of the Mesopotamian valley, causing the downfall of the entire empire that stretched 800 miles from parts of what is now Turkey to the Persian Gulf border of Iraq and Iran.

At the other end of the climate spectrum, an early Babylonian story from 1700 B.C.E. describes the great flood (later told in the Noah story in Genesis) as the gods' efforts to control the overpopulation of the land. Similar events (and stories) have been repeated throughout history in many parts of the world.

Earth Education

"For the first time since cities were built and founded, the great agricultural tracts produced no grain...the irrigated orchards produced neither syrup nor wine. The gathered clouds did not rain ... people were flailing at themselves from hunger ...."

—The "Curse of Akkade," taken from Mesopotamian clay tablets from about 2000 B.C.E.

Our ancient ancestors tried (but often failed) to stay in harmony with their natural environment. They frequently blamed their failures on the displeasure or whims of the gods. They probably should have looked a little closer to home for answers. It's significant to note that ancient farmers and herders turned the so-called Fertile Crescent, where the first cities developed, into a virtual desert.

By the fifth century B.C.E., the ancient Greeks, especially the Athenians, had become concerned with the delicate balance between food supply and population. The Greek philosophers Plato and Aristotle kept these concerns in mind when they outlined their ideal size for a city-state of their day. They often warned of the dangers of overpopulation and were strong supporters of zero population growth. We'll come back to the issue of population growth later in the book. For now, just remember that trying to stay in harmony with the environment has been on people's minds for a very long time.

One of the strange statues on Easter Island.

(Credit: AMS Press)

Hitting the Limits in the Past

Now let's fast-forward in time and place to Easter Island. This tiny, isolated Pacific island, now known locally as Rapa Nui, has been shrouded in mystery ever since a Dutch explorer landed there on Easter Day in 1722. The giant, enigmatic stone statues (known as moai) and other monuments he found there have puzzled people ever since.

Much of Easter Island's early human history is also unclear. In one local legend, a great Polynesian chief and his family sailed there about 1,500 years ago. Others insist that the early inhabitants came from the coast of South America, 2,300 miles to the east. Whatever the truth may be, the island has recently given up one of its most compelling secrets.

When the first settlers arrived, luxuriant palm forests covered the island. From about 1000 to 1680 C.E. the island's population expanded rapidly. Some estimate that the population may have peaked at 9,000. The carving and transport of the huge stones was most active during the last part of this period.

What happened next is based on evidence from recently taken core samples from the island.

Planetary Perils

When a society overshoots the carrying capacity of its environment, the results can be catastrophic. We are in danger of repeating the mistakes made by some of our ancestors if we do not change many our destructive habits.

Gradually the lush palm forests disappeared, the soils became depleted, and erosion set in. The population had exceeded the carrying capacity of its environment, and the society quickly descended into chaos and probably even cannibalism, according to a recent Nova series on the island broadcast on PBS. There were perhaps 2,000 impoverished inhabitants remaining on the island by 1722. This is a graphic example of how nature can adjust the imbalances caused by overpopulation and human environmental damage.

Limitless Resources?

Okay, now it's time to check out our own history. What sort of relationship have we had with our environment in this country? When early settlers first arrived in America they found a land rich with seemingly limitless resources. There were vast stands of old-growth forests, teeming with wildlife, extending as far as the eye could see; there were rivers and streams filled to overflowing with fish, enormous deposits of minerals, all just waiting to be exploited. It seemed too good to be true. And maybe it was.

The New World created a new problem. The sheer quantity of natural riches that this country originally offered helped to establish the idea of unlimited resources in the American psyche, where it has remained long after many of those original resources were gone.

Most of the early settlers brought their economic habits and other traditions with them from the Old World, where the Biblical view of wilderness as an evil place, and the idea of man subduing nature, were long established. Consequently, the wilderness needed to be conquered. And most of its natural resources were viewed simply as inputs for the economic system. If resources were economically useful, they were valued and exploited. If they had no economic use, they were ignored, damaged, or eliminated if they got in the way. This philosophy migrated to the New World, where it was put into action with a vengeance.

America's original inhabitants, of course, had a very different view of the environment and their place in it. But Native Americans, their traditions, and their concerns, were brushed aside. We'll come back to them and their views later in the book.

From Sea to Shining Sea

After the American Revolution ended, there was a brief pause while the new nation caught its breath and got itself organized. At about this same time, the Industrial Revolution, which had started in England in the last half of the eighteenth century, began to spread to this country. The development of large-scale industry in America was about to have a profound effect on the nation's economy and environment.

Then, beginning in 1803 with the Louisiana Purchase, the United States set out to acquire and colonize the rest of the continent. This process continued until 1867, when Alaska was added to the already considerable territorial collection for $7 million—quite a bargain at just two cents per acre. The popular concept of *Manifest Destiny* had firmly taken hold of the nation.

As the nation included more and more territory within its boundaries, it became increasingly important to populate these wild new lands. But how to persuade large numbers of people to leave the relative comfort and security of the settled eastern part of the nation to start a new life in the middle of nowhere? The members of Congress and the president put on their thinking caps.

Eco-Explanations

The widely held belief that the territorial expansion of the United States was not only inevitable but divinely ordained became known as **Manifest Destiny.**

First Homestead Act of 1862

The idea they finally came up with was simple but effective: Free land. Although this suggestion had been floating around for some time, prior to the Civil War the South resisted the idea because it feared that homesteaders would be opposed to slavery. But the secession of the southern states left the door wide open for the legislation, which was signed into law in 1862 by President Abraham Lincoln.

Under the new law, any citizen who was head of a family, 21 years old, or a veteran, could obtain a tract of federally owned land up to 160 acres. The only requirement was that he or she had to settle on or cultivate the land for five years. Not surprisingly, the offer was wildly popular.

It should also come as no great surprise that all this free land did nothing to dispel the growing myth of limitless resources. The frontier mentality of taking advantage of all this endless bounty was, by now, firmly established.

Mining Laws of 1866 and 1872

But the federal government wasn't just interested in attracting settlers. The Gold Rush of 1849 in California had already proven that there was lots of gold in them thar hills. Folks just needed a little more incentive to get out there and find more of it—and copper, and silver, and other treasure, while they were at it. Congress and the president put their thinking caps back on. What they came up with was legislation guaranteeing free access to

Earth Education

The Mining Law of 1872, as amended, encouraged miners to explore for and extract minerals on public lands for as little as $2.50 per acre with no additional payments or royalties. Essentially, the law is still in effect.

federal lands, with very few strings attached. The Mining Law of 1866 was born. It seemed like a good idea at the time.

Not entirely satisfied with the first attempt, Congress modified the law several times and eventually came up with the now-infamous General Mining Law of 1872, which was signed into law by President Ulysses S. Grant.

This law regulates the mining of hardrock minerals (non-fuel minerals such as gold, copper, and silver) in this country. Like the earlier Mining Law of 1866, it was designed to entice miners to explore for and exploit the vast mineral riches of the West. The law did not (and still does not) address the environmental impact of mining on the environment.

The Gold Rush mentality that had developed in California now spread throughout the West with mining and logging interests competing to see who could take the most resources, in the shortest amount of time, at the lowest possible cost. Subsequent legislation opened public lands to ranching and oil interests as well. The environmental consequences of all of this were (and still are) devastating.

Voices in the Wilderness

While many Americans were busily carving up the nation's natural resources for profit, there were a few lonely individuals who held very different views on humanity and nature.

➤ John James Audubon (1785–1851), noted for his stunning bird drawings and paintings, was one of this country's first naturalists. Others soon followed in his footsteps to try to raise the national consciousness about the beauties and importance of nature.

➤ Henry David Thoreau (1817–1862), the American writer and philosopher, is probably best remembered for his observations of his natural surroundings while he lived for two years on Walden Pond in Concord, Massachusetts. But he also wrote stinging attacks on the wasteful and arrogant environmental behavior of his fellow citizens.

➤ George Perkins Marsh (1801–1882), a native of Woodstock, Vermont, was appointed as the first U.S. minister to Italy by President Lincoln. Marsh went on to become the so-called "fountainhead of the conservation movement." His landmark 1864 study of Western civilization's terrible environmental record, *Man and Nature*, remains relevant to this day.

➤ John Muir (1838–1914), the American naturalist, explorer, and writer, became an influential conservationist who worked to preserve wilderness areas and wildlife from commercial exploitation and destruction.

The efforts of these and many other like-minded early environmentalists gradually began to have an effect on the national conscience. Eventually this shift in thinking was translated into action.

Taking Action

The most important tangible step taken toward preserving natural resources in this country was the creation of Yellowstone National Park in 1872. Images of the region made by photographer William Henry Jackson and artist Thomas Moran during an 1871 expedition were instrumental in convincing the American public and the federal government to preserve the area. President Ulysses S. Grant signed the bill for the park in 1872, and Yellowstone became the first jewel in the crown of the national park system.

In 1891 President Benjamin Harrison added another jewel to the crown when he signed the Yosemite act, creating Yosemite National Park. In the same year, Congress authorized President Harrison to create forest preserves from public lands with the Forest Preserve Act.

In 1892, John Muir founded the Sierra Club, an organization that has gone on to play a key role in the ongoing environmental debate. In the years that followed, more and more national legislation and additional environmental organizations gradually slowed the plundering of America's natural resources.

Earth Education

Yellowstone National Park was the first national park in the world. Located in northwestern Wyoming, and parts of Montana and Idaho, Yellowstone, with its 2.2 million acres, is known for its spectacular geysers, hot springs, deep canyons, and fossilized forests.

The Rise of the Consumer Society

As we entered the twentieth century, the battle between development and conservation continued. In the first half of the century, the American environmental movement became a national political force by building a structure of laws to protect our public lands.

But the emergence of a consumer society based upon mass-produced goods added a whole new dimension to the picture. A growing American preoccupation with material possessions began to compete with environmental considerations.

Earth Education

A total of 195 million acres of forestland was eventually set aside under the provisions of the Forest Preserve Act. Today, these forests can be found in 44 states, Puerto Rico, and the Virgin Islands.

The rise of advertising, packaging, and mass merchandising whetted our national appetite for more and more consumer goods. Automobiles, trendy new clothing, housewares, and many other items flowed out of factories around the country, while the industrial wastes and byproducts of those same factories fouled the air, contaminated the land, and poisoned our rivers and streams worse than ever.

World War I

World War I temporarily sidetracked the fast-rising consumer economy. During the conflict, the idea of conservation was promoted as a patriotic duty. Everyone pitched in. Recycling and reusing old materials became second nature. Old clothing was cut down and refitted for younger family members. People saved and reused twine from packaging, turned old sheets into pillowcases and handkerchiefs, and made old oilskin table covers into shelf lining.

Eco-Explanations

Frugal means not wasting things. By the time you finish reading this book, you may decide that being frugal makes a lot of sense.

Eco-Explanations

Rationing is the restriction of the consumption of products and supplies, often during war time. The Office of Price Administration directed rationing in the United States during World War II.

When the war ended, Americans quickly abandoned their *frugal* ways and enthusiastically jumped into the Roaring Twenties. The economy, consumer consumption, and consumer debt, spiraled to dizzying new heights.

The Great Depression

The stock market crash of 1929 brought the Roaring Twenties to an abrupt end. Americans suddenly faced the stark reality of an economy in ruins, and little or no work. By 1933, the low point of the Great Depression, more than 15 million Americans—one-quarter of the total workforce—were out of work.

Once again, being careful with resources and allowing nothing to go to waste became a cruel necessity. The depression affected the people who survived it in different ways. Some developed frugal saving and spending habits, while others focused on accumulating material possessions to create a comfortable life that was in stark contrast to their depression experiences.

World War II

The onset of World War II helped to lift the U.S. economy out of the lingering effects of the depression. But the need to channel resources into the war effort meant that recycling and *rationing* again became a way of life. A rubber shortage at the beginning of the war made the recycling of tires, inner tubes, and boots a necessity. Families saved tin cans, newspapers, textiles, and even grease drippings from the kitchen. Groups of volunteers went door to door to collect recyclables as part of the national war effort. Meanwhile, U.S. industry was churning out huge quantities of armaments and other war materials. Environmental considerations were not a top priority.

When the war ended, rationing was discontinued, and recycling quickly fell out of favor, along with anything else that reminded people of the enforced frugality that they had endured since the depression.

Out of Control!

As Americans put the war behind them, they embarked on a new wave of consumerism. Any suggestions for conservation of any kind tended to remind people of the painful depression era and war years—something they desperately wanted to forget. And besides, they wanted to celebrate their new-found peace and prosperity. Furthermore, increased consumption was essential to continue the production levels of the 1940s. These levels produced large profits for many companies and spurred the economy.

But by the 1950s, the accumulation of damage from the Industrial Revolution in this country finally reached the point where people could no longer ignore it. Pollution of every kind was so out of control that clearly a coordinated national effort was going to be needed to resolve it.

Getting Our Act Together

In 1955 Congress passed the Clean Air Act and President Dwight D. Eisenhower signed it into law. The Water Pollution Act of 1956 followed. When the Solid Waste Disposal Act of 1965 was signed into law by President Lyndon B. Johnson, the first round of national environmental legislation was complete. These laws have since been amended or replaced by more comprehensive legislation. We'll look at the many issues surrounding air, water, and land pollution in the next three chapters.

The passage of environmental legislation was one thing, but actually making serious progress on environmental issues was another matter. Frustrated by the lack of action, a number of environmentalists organized a national demonstration to be held in the spring of 1970.

Earth Day and the EPA

As I mentioned in Chapter 1, "It's Our Home," Earth Day was originally created to dramatize the need for conservation of the world's natural resources. An estimated 20 million people across the nation participated in the first Earth Day, held on

March 21, 1970. It met its organizer's goal of sending a clear message to the country's political establishment that the concerns of the environmental community needed to be taken seriously. Now celebrated annually on April 22, Earth Day has become a major environmental educational and media event.

Another landmark event in 1970 was the foundation of the Environmental Protection Agency. The EPA is an independent government agency that is responsible for protecting the environment and helping to maintain it for future generations. The agency's primary aims are to control and reduce air and water pollution, noise pollution, and pollution by radiation, pesticides, and a variety of other toxic substances. More recently, the agency expanded the scope of its mission to include issues related to global warming and environmental change.

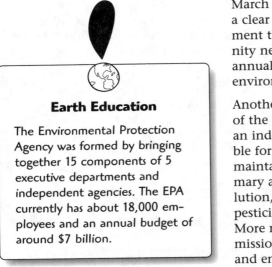

Earth Education

The Environmental Protection Agency was formed by bringing together 15 components of 5 executive departments and independent agencies. The EPA currently has about 18,000 employees and an annual budget of around $7 billion.

More Progress

In subsequent years, we have made efforts in this country to address a wide variety of environmental issues on the national, state, and local levels. Recycling programs have been set up across the country with varying degrees of success. New solid waste management initiatives have been launched to try to resolve serious land pollution problems. Environmental groups nationwide have focused attention on endangered species, forestry management, and many other areas of concern, to try to ensure clean water, fresh air, and healthy communities for both humans and animals. Despite all these efforts, our relationship with our environment remains troubled.

The Throwaway Society

Some of our biggest problems are related to our consumption habits, which are deeply rooted in our past. Our frontier mentality, the idea of limitless resources and the freedom to exploit them to satisfy our desires, has become so ingrained in our thinking that it's going to be difficult to change course.

This conspicuous consumption, encouraged by a constant barrage of promotional advertising in the media, has extended to just about every part of our modern consumer economy, where convenience and immediate gratification have replaced quality and durability as primary objectives. The resulting waste of natural resources is enormous. That's bad enough. But it gets worse.

A Global Problem

The emergence of the United States economy as the most powerful and successful economic system on the planet, following the fall of Communism and the breakup of the former Soviet Union, has raised a whole series of new environmental challenges. As the largest consumers of natural resources on the planet, our wasteful habits are setting a terrible example.

The main problem, of course, is that the rest of the world—especially the underdeveloped world—sees our economic success and wants to copy it. Unless we are willing to change our ways, and we learn to live in balance with our environment, we can hardly ask them to do the same.

But time is running out to shift to a more sustainable approach. The American model of conspicuous consumption is already spreading throughout the new global economy like wildfire. If we don't learn from the mistakes of our past, we're doomed to repeat them—but this time on a global scale.

The Least You Need to Know

➤ Early humans adapted their lifestyle to stay in harmony with their natural environment.

➤ Ancient societies that misused their environments suffered severe consequences.

➤ Americans have become accustomed to the (false) idea of limitless resources.

➤ Many Americans are still operating under a "frontier mentality" long after the frontier was closed.

➤ Our throwaway economic model is spreading across the planet.

Chapter 3

The Air We Breathe

There's nothing quite like a breath of fresh mountain air first thing in the morning. Here in Vermont, we tend to take that sort of thing for granted. But in recent years, oven-like daytime temperatures have replaced that cool, fresh air in a series of record-breaking summer heat spells. And, of course, this isn't just taking place in New England, it's happening nationwide and around the world.

And it's not just my imagination, either. The 1990s was the hottest decade on record, breaking the previous record—held by the 1980s—according to a report by the National Climate Data Center. And the 1980s was the warmest decade of the twentieth century. So, what's going on here? What's happening is global warming.

Now, if this was just a matter of higher summer temperatures, you might be tempted to take a cold shower, jump in the pool or maybe a cold mountain stream, and forget about it. Unfortunately, it isn't that simple. Global warming has the potential to affect just about everybody and everything on the planet in one way or another—year 'round.

That's why we'll focus mainly on global warming in this chapter. I'll begin by explaining what global warming is in greater detail. Then we'll look at what's causing it and why it's so important. I'll also explain the growing problem with the ozone layer and how it's related to global warming. We'll look briefly at acid rain, and then explore some of the long-term implications of all of these problems.

Up in the Air

The air we breathe is such a basic ingredient of life that we tend to take it for granted. We shouldn't. For hundreds of years we've been pumping huge amounts of pollutants into the atmosphere without giving much thought to what the long-term effects might be. But now the effects of this activity are beginning to catch up with us in strange and potentially devastating ways.

You may recall that I mentioned global warming briefly in Chapter 1, "It's Our Home" (along with biodiversity and the ozone layer). But global warming and its related issue of the thinning ozone layer are so important that I'm going to discuss them both in even greater detail here. And the reason they're so important is that they are directly or indirectly related to just about every other issue you will read about in this book. And those issues are going to affect you.

And this is where things begin to get a little more complicated. As you will see, it's hard to decide where one issue ends and the next one begins when we talk about these things. Remember the Web of Life? It's all interconnected. And you're going to begin to see examples of that shortly.

Global Warming

For years, *climatologists* and other members of the scientific community have debated whether global warming was actually happening. While the debate goes on, the majority has come to accept the fact that it's actually taking place. The main disagreement now is about what the impact on us and on the planet will be, and how we should respond.

There is also general agreement that global warming presents us and the rest of the world with one of the most challenging dilemmas we have ever faced. In order to deal with this problem, we're going to have to fundamentally change our habits, as well as much of our current economic system, from one of exploitation to one of sustainability. That's a tall order. But it begins to put this issue in its proper perspective.

Eco-Explanations

A **climatologist** is a scientist who studies climate conditions and phenomena.

What Is It?

As you may recall from Chapter 1, global warming is an increase in the Earth's temperature due to the use of *fossil fuels* and other industrial and agricultural processes. This causes a buildup of so-called "greenhouse gases" such as carbon dioxide and methane in the atmosphere. There are other gases involved, too, but we'll stick with the main culprits. Like a one-way filter, carbon dioxide lets energy from the sun pass through, but it absorbs the longer wavelength radiation from the Earth and traps it. This is called the "greenhouse effect."

Without the greenhouse effect, the Earth's temperature would be about 60 degrees colder, which would result in unbearably frigid conditions. Consequently, the greenhouse effect is very important to life as we know it on Earth. However, since the nineteenth century our massive use of fossil fuels, along with extensive deforestation (trees absorb carbon dioxide), has caused greenhouse gases to flow into the atmosphere in huge quantities, turning the Earth into a giant hothouse.

The burning of fossil fuels has raised the concentrations of carbon dioxide in the atmosphere by about 30 percent since the preindustrial era. And the levels of carbon dioxide are now at their highest point in 160,000 years, according to recent studies. And if these trends continue, higher average global temperatures are almost certainly going to follow, somewhere between 2 and 6 degrees Fahrenheit by 2100. This warming will be focused in the mid-latitudes, and will be especially apparent at night and in the winter. Now, 2 to 6 degrees may not sound like much, but as you will soon see, even a few degrees' increase can cause huge problems.

Eco-Explanations

A **fossil fuel** is an energy-rich substance formed from the long-buried remains of prehistoric life. These fuels mainly consist of hydrocarbons, which are compounds composed of hydrogen and carbon.

Fossil Fuels

The fossil fuels that are the main contributors to global warming are coal, oil, and natural gas—the primary energy sources of our modern economy that account for around 75 percent of commercial use. In addition to causing air pollution, the burning of coal and oil also results in the production of carbon monoxide (a colorless, odorless, poisonous gas) and tiny particles that have been linked to lung cancer and other health problems. Other byproducts cause urban smog and acid rain (more about acid rain in a moment). Although natural gas is cleaner, it still gives off greenhouse gases when burned.

That's bad enough. But there's more bad news about fossil fuels—and this is where the interrelationships of these issues really start to show up. The mining or extraction of these fuels, their transport, and their processing, also causes other environmental damage from oil spills, refining operations, and water and ground pollution. And none of these fuels is renewable. Once they're gone, they're gone. But the many environmental problems associated with fossil fuels will probably cause us to abandon them long before the supplies run out.

Why Is It Important?

Okay, you know what's happening and what's causing it. But why is this such a big deal? In Chapter 1, you may recall that I mentioned a worst-case scenario of a "runaway" greenhouse effect that turns vast sections of the Earth, which are currently productive, into deserts. While that's unlikely, even the possibility should give us pause. A number of other more likely scenarios are almost as bad, however.

Weird Weather

One of the most likely effects of global warming is the disruption of normal weather activity, including a shift in the world's wind and rainfall patterns. The extraordinary heat in recent years has led to a series of bizarre weather-related occurrences.

The highly publicized—and destructive—series of *El Niño* events in recent years is probably one of them. While not all scientists agree, many say that global warming is altering El Niño patterns significantly, causing more intense and possibly more frequent activity.

El Niño aside, more intense storm activity around the globe is almost certainly going to accompany global warming. This is because warmer oceans and higher temperatures increase water vapor evaporation, fueling more precipitation and causing more storm damage from flooding, erosion, and mud slides.

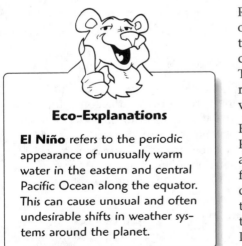

Eco-Explanations

El Niño refers to the periodic appearance of unusually warm water in the eastern and central Pacific Ocean along the equator. This can cause unusual and often undesirable shifts in weather systems around the planet.

Researchers at the Massachusetts Institute of Technology have calculated that an increase in tropical ocean temperatures of only 3.6 degrees Fahrenheit could increase hurricane intensity by as much as 40 percent. The huge killer hurricanes we've been experiencing in recent years would seem to lend weight to that observation.

But it's not just giant storms we have to worry about. Record heat has also caused severe drought conditions around the globe. The rash of rare fires in subtropical forests from Indonesia to Mexico, and even the recent devastating wildfires in Florida, are all associated with the deadly heat waves that have affected many countries and regions from the United States to Europe to India, to name just a few.

Most recently, record dryness was seen in the Northeast, Mid-Atlantic, and Ohio Valley as a result of the drought of 1999. The April-to-July period was the driest (or second driest, depending on the state) ever in all states from West Virginia to Maine. Ironically—and significantly—the drought was followed by record rainfall from hurricanes Dennis and Floyd along the East Coast. Floods, fire, windstorm; you'd think it couldn't get much worse. But it does.

Rising Sea Levels

Another unfortunate effect of global warming is the melting of the polar ice caps. That may not sound like such a big deal, but it doesn't take much of an increase in ice melt to start to make some dramatic changes elsewhere. When this ice melts in large enough quantities, it raises the levels of the oceans around the world. And even a slight rise in ocean levels puts low-lying coastal areas at risk for flooding or for going underwater altogether.

Depending on the future pace of global warming, sea levels may rise somewhere between 2 inches and 37 inches by 2100, according to recent estimates. That's up to five times the increase of the past 100 years. And if the melting of the ice caps should accelerate, these figures could increase substantially.

In recent years huge sections of the Antarctic ice sheet have been breaking off and falling into the ocean, increasing concerns about a massive thaw. Iceberg B-18, which broke off from the Ross ice shelf in April 2000, measured 4 miles wide and 11 miles long—twice as wide and almost as long as Manhattan Island. That's a big berg.

You may have noticed that this discussion about global warming has shifted from the atmosphere to the subject of oceans. And icebergs. It's all connected, remember?

Earth Education

About 69 percent of the world's fresh water is locked up in glaciers and permanent snow and ice fields, located mainly in Antarctica and Greenland. If all the ice on the planet melted, it would raise sea levels by more than 250 feet.

A Hole in the Sky

But there's another problem hanging over our heads related to global warming—the thinning of the ozone layer. You'll recall from Chapter 1 that in the 1970s scientists discovered that chlorofluorocarbons (CFCs) and other gases could damage the ozone layer that protects us and most other life forms from dangerous ultraviolet rays. Other scientists later discovered a "hole" in the ozone layer over Antarctica and a thinning over the arctic region. Eventually, CFCs were banned in most countries, in accord with the 1987 Montreal Protocol. This international treaty calls for a global phaseout by 2006.

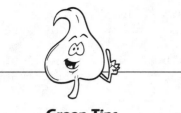

Green Tips

The Montreal Protocol, originally signed and ratified by 36 nations (now over 100 nations), is an important early example of countries cooperating to solve a global environmental problem. The production of CFCs ended in developed nations at the end of 1995.

Nevertheless, the long, cold arctic winter of 1999–2000 resulted in one of the most massive ozone losses on record, according to scientists from NASA and the European Union. Measurements taken by researchers aboard NASA's high-flying ER-2 plane showed that ozone in the arctic region decreased by about 60 percent between January and mid-March. Other data collected by satellites confirmed their findings.

Since the production of CFCs has been dramatically reduced, the amount of human-made–chlorine-bearing pollutants in the atmosphere is not increasing. But because CFCs are so chemically stable, they may remain in the atmosphere for more than 100 years. They can also take as long as 15 years to make their way into the stratosphere. Once there, they become trapped because of the lack of air circulation. Consequently, it's going to be many decades before the ozone layer begins to recover.

What It Means for Us

The most obvious danger from the thinning of the ozone layer for us is the increased likelihood of skin cancers and cataracts caused by increased ultraviolet radiation. This is especially true for people living in Northern Europe, Canada, the arctic, as well as southern parts of South America, Australia, and other localities in extreme southern regions.

Eco-Explanations

Photosynthesis is a process by which plants and other organisms use light to convert carbon dioxide and water into a simple sugar. This provides the basic energy source for almost all organisms.

... And for Plants and Animals

The implications for many plants and animals could be more severe. Increased levels of ultraviolet radiation have been penetrating the oceans recently. This has affected *photosynthesis* and the growth of algae and tiny marine organisms that are part of the marine food chain.

But this problem isn't limited to simple organisms. Increased ultraviolet radiation also harms the early development of shrimp, crabs, and some fish. This is double trouble, because it harms these species when they are most vulnerable and threatens their food supply simultaneously. And that could mean big trouble for the world's fisheries.

Again, I'd like to point out that we've gone from talking about invisible problems high up in the atmosphere to potential damage to fish in the oceans. The Web of Life again.

Ouch—Acid Rain!

The burning of fossil fuels that is causing global warming is also responsible for the emissions of compounds causing another problem—acid rain. The main culprits are sulfur dioxide and nitrous oxides. These byproducts of combustion come mainly from coal and oil-fired industries, cars, and trucks.

Once they are released into the atmosphere, these compounds can be carried by the prevailing winds for long distances until they come back to the ground in the form of acid rain, snow, fog, or even dust. The resulting acid can damage fish and wildlife, lakes and forests, even crops. Acid rain also plays a large role in the deterioration of stone buildings and monuments.

Acid rain has long been a problem around the country and even in relatively remote places like Vermont, where it has caused noticeable damage to lakes and ponds, as well as portions of forests in the Green Mountains. Most of this pollution has been coming from the Midwest, especially coal-fired utilities, for many years.

Earth Education

The annual costs in the United States for respiratory and other health-care problems due to contaminated air is estimated to be more than $1 billion.

A coal-fired and nuclear electrical generation plant in Pennsylvania.

(Greenpeace)

On the international level, the United Nations Economic Commission for Europe negotiated a treaty to curb acid rain by strengthening pollution laws in the northern hemisphere in 1978. Additional protocols in the mid and late 1980s tightened the laws even further. One of the main arguments in favor of combating global warming is the interrelationship between the greenhouse effect and other forms of atmospheric pollution such as acid rain.

Long-Term Consequences

Okay, we've looked at global warming from a number of different angles already. But we need to explore some additional long-term issues. There's good news and there's bad news. The good news is that some of the climate changes caused by global warming might actually improve some conditions in certain parts of the planet. The bad news is that this will come at a cost to other regions. There will be winners and losers.

Unfortunately, this may tend to pit one region or nation against another in the debates about how and when to deploy the political and economic resources to deal with the problems caused by global warming. These kinds of debates already exist around the globe even without significant global warming disruptions, so the outlook for the future is not real encouraging.

Deep Trouble

I've already mentioned one of the most serious threats of global warming—rising ocean levels. This will not cause much of a problem for lands that are high and dry. But for low-lying, poorly-drained coastal regions, even slight increases could be catastrophic. In this country, think: the coasts of Louisiana, Florida, Georgia, and the Carolinas. Even New York City could be in trouble with a 36-inch rise in the Atlantic Ocean, which would submerge the subway system and the major airports. Seventy-five percent of all residents within the United States live on the coast. According to the EPA, the areas most vulnerable to rising seas are found along the Gulf of Mexico and the Atlantic Ocean south of Cape Cod. Although there are also large low areas around the San Francisco Bay and the Fraser delta (British Columbia), most of the Pacific coast is less vulnerable than the Atlantic and Gulf coasts. But the largest potential problems are in other parts of the world. The low coastal regions of Thailand, Indonesia, Egypt, China, India, and Bangladesh are especially vulnerable, to say nothing of countless low-lying islands around the globe.

Eco-Explanations

A **typhoon** is a hurricane in the western Pacific and China seas. Because of the huge numbers of people who live in low-lying coastal areas in this region, the threat of death and injury from typhoons is substantial.

The destruction and heavy loss of life from storms in India and Bangladesh in recent years may be a terrible preview of things to come. The *typhoon* that hammered the eastern Indian state of Orissa in October 1999 was one of the worst modern disasters in that country's history. Ten million people lost their homes, livestock, or livelihood. An estimated 10,000 lost their lives. And in a 1991 typhoon, a staggering 138,000 people lost their lives in Bangladesh.

These are countries that are already struggling just to provide basic support to their impoverished populations. Yet they are likely to be the most heavily affected by rising sea levels. And they are the least able to afford to cope with it. Admittedly, these countries have been suffering these kinds of disasters for generations, but that doesn't alter the fact that things could get worse. A lot worse.

The Moving Farm Belt

If you think I've run out of global warming problems, think again. Another likely effect of global warming is the migration of productive agricultural regions to the north in many regions, following shifting annual precipitation patterns.

In this country, that would mean a shift from states like Ohio and Iowa to Michigan and Minnesota, according to a report prepared for the 1992 United Nations environmental summit in Brazil. It is even possible that much of the productive land currently in the Midwest could migrate into Canada.

Some of the southern states in this country could see their land go out of agricultural production completely. In Europe that could mean losses for Spain and France, and gains for Denmark and Sweden. You get the picture—some lose, some gain. This same sort of scenario could be repeated around the world.

Food

The potential disruptions to agriculture in this country caused by global warming, while serious, would probably not threaten our food supply. One study found, in fact, that we could probably absorb crop losses of up to 36 percent and still be able to feed ourselves.

But crop losses in certain regions could be substantial. And the effect this would have on farmers in those regions would be severe. The corn yield in states such as Georgia, North Carolina, and Mississippi might decline as much as 50 percent, according to projections made by the Environmental Protection Agency. In other states, corn yields might drop anywhere from zero to 30 percent.

Earth Education

The drought of 1999 in the Northeast caused more than $1 billion in crop damage (most of it uninsured) and put a strain on municipal and private water supplies from West Virginia to Maine.

But in states like Michigan and Minnesota, corn production might actually increase by 30 percent. Similar patterns were found for soybeans. It's likely that many other crops would also be affected.

Water

For the states that come out on the short end of the temperature and precipitation stick, about the only realistic solution for this problem would be irrigation. And even in a relatively conservative temperature and rainfall projection, this could require some additional irrigation in 39 states. But irrigation is not a simple fix because it uses water so inefficiently. The implications for our water supply in this case would be substantial (more on water issues in the next chapter).

Planetary Perils

Global warming can lead to species extinction as ecosystems move north faster than life can adjust within these systems. A northward movement of ecosystems will also lead to the spread of diseases such as malaria and West Nile Disease, traditionally associated with tropical regions.

Developing Countries

Although we in this country could probably manage to survive farm losses due to global warming, this is not the case for many less-developed nations in Asia, Africa, and South America. In these countries as much as 50 percent of the population still works on farms, and agriculture is the backbone of the economy.

If you add major crop losses caused by global warming on top of the other environmental stresses to fisheries and forests in countries that can barely feed their current populations, it's easy to understand why they might be worried (more on fisheries in Chapter 4, "Water: Our Most Precious Resource," and forests in Chapter 5, "The Land We Live On"). For countries like these, food supply questions quickly become major political concerns.

Time Out

Okay, you can relax. I've run out of global warming problems—until the next chapter. Sorry. But I want to pause long enough to help you get a little perspective on this.

If you come away from this chapter with nothing more than a sense of just how interconnected all these issues are, then it's been worth the effort. At the very least, I hope you can see that what starts out as a global warming concern about the atmosphere can quickly become a weather problem, which in turn can change into a food issue, which then becomes a major political concern. More interconnections.

If you're beginning to feel a bit overwhelmed by all of this, I don't blame you. I feel overwhelmed, too, sometimes. But once we've gotten through all the challenges in

Part 1, "The Environment and You," I promise I'll offer lots of suggestions for making things better. You might even come away with a great idea for making some money in the new sustainable economy I'll be talking about in Part 5, "A Sustainable Future." I'm saving the best for last. And that's not just a bunch of hot air.

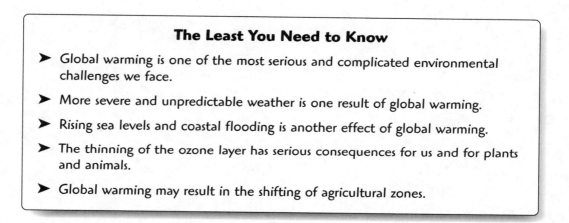

The Least You Need to Know

➤ Global warming is one of the most serious and complicated environmental challenges we face.

➤ More severe and unpredictable weather is one result of global warming.

➤ Rising sea levels and coastal flooding is another effect of global warming.

➤ The thinning of the ozone layer has serious consequences for us and for plants and animals.

➤ Global warming may result in the shifting of agricultural zones.

Chapter 4

Water: Our Most Precious Resource

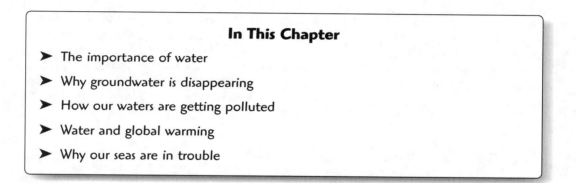

In This Chapter

➤ The importance of water

➤ Why groundwater is disappearing

➤ How our waters are getting polluted

➤ Water and global warming

➤ Why our seas are in trouble

"Water, water, everywhere, nary any drop to drink." You've probably heard these familiar lines from *The Rime of the Ancient Mariner* by the English poet Samuel Taylor Coleridge. First published in 1798, these words may yet prove to be prophetic.

I've already said that, for better or worse, this is going to be the Environmental Century. And one of the main reasons for this can be summed up in just one word: water. More specifically, the scarcity of fresh water. This is probably the most underestimated basic resource issue that we face this century. But it won't remain that way for long.

I'll begin this chapter by explaining why water is so important. Then we'll look at the shocking disappearance of our water supply and see where it's going. I'll also go through the unhappy list of things that are in our water that shouldn't be there. Then I'll explain the connection between water problems and—you guessed it—global warming. Finally, we'll take a sea cruise and explore some very troubled waters.

Water 101

Water is our most important resource. Life would simply be impossible without it. Our bodies are made up of about 65 percent water. And it's difficult to survive without it for more than a few days. We use it to brush our teeth, wash our clothes and dishes, take baths and showers, wash our cars, water our lawns; and, of course, we drink it. But, overall, personal use only accounts for about 10 percent of total water use worldwide. Twenty percent is utilized by industry, and the other 70 percent is consumed by agriculture.

Planetary Perils

In India, 500 million to 600 million people—about 10 percent of the world's population—depend on river systems that could run dry in 50 years. Trying to figure out how to meet the needs of these people will present major challenges in the future.

And, at first glance, there's plenty of it. The oceans contain over 322 million cubic miles of water. That's an awful lot of water. But the oceans contain 97 percent of the water on the planet. That leaves only 3 percent of fresh (non-salty) water for us. And of that fresh water, about two thirds is locked up in glaciers and permanent snow pack at the poles and on Greenland. That means that only about a third of the fresh water on the planet is readily available for our use. And as you're about to see, a lot of that isn't fit to drink.

Going, Going, Gone?

It's important to remember that water is a limited resource. There's only so much of it to go around. And unfortunately, for many people, it's not distributed equally. Not even close. Two thirds of the global population lives in areas that receive only a quarter of the world's rainfall. China, with 20 percent of the world's people, only has 7 percent of its fresh water. The United States, on the other hand, with only 4.5 percent of the world's population, is fortunate to have 8 percent of the planet's water.

About 300 million people currently live in areas of serious to severe water shortage. Twenty-five percent of the developing world remains without clean water. And, the world's population, presently at 6 billion, is expected to exceed 10 billion sometime this century. You don't have to be a genius to figure out that these trends mean big trouble. We've fought many wars over oil, a resource that is replaceable with alternative energy sources. Water is irreplaceable, and even more basic for survival.

Falling Aquifers

It gets worse. The challenges related to water for China and India, for example, are huge. Both depend on irrigation to produce at least half of their food supply for their enormous populations. The water table on most of China's flat agricultural lands, which produce nearly 40 percent of the country's grain, is falling at a rate of 5 feet per year. As you might expect, this is a matter of some concern to the Chinese government.

In India, the situation may be even worse. Twice as much water is being removed from India's *aquifers* as is being naturally recharged. As a result, the fresh water level in those aquifers is dropping between 3 and 10 feet *a year*. That's staggering. It's also unsustainable. Sooner or later (but probably sooner) this strategy will collapse, with terrible consequences.

The situation in India and China is not unique. And this problem is not limited to agricultural areas either. Cities worldwide face similar challenges. However, urban areas also have some distinct water issues of their own. Many cities suffer severe groundwater loss when gutters, pipes, pavement, storm sewers, and other manmade structures channel water away from the ground before it has a chance to sink in. As a result, the land may subside, causing structural damage to buildings, roads, water pipes, and other utilities. Parts of Mexico City have sunk about 30 *feet* in the last 100 years due primarily to overpumping of the groundwater.

A Pinch of Salt

But the overpumping of groundwater can lead to other problems. One of the most serious is the infiltration of salt water from the oceans. This is especially true for large urban areas on or near the seacoasts of the world.

Here in this country, there are many illustrations of this phenomenon all along the Atlantic coast from Cape Cod, Massachusetts, to the southern tip of Florida. A similar scenario can be found along the Gulf and West coasts as well. But the situation in Florida is a good example of the problem.

The increasingly heavy demands that the state's growing population and industry have put on Florida's supplies of fresh water have caused the water table to fall in many areas, resulting in the infiltration of salt water into freshwater aquifers in coastal areas.

Eco-Explanations

An **aquifer** is a layer of rock, gravel, or sand that contains or conducts underground water. The flow of water in and out of aquifers is part of the water cycle.

Earth Education

Salt-tolerant mangrove forests have been moving inland as salt water infiltrates the groundwater in Florida. As long as the over-pumping of the state's underground aquifers continues, this movement of the forests will persist.

Projected future population growth along the coastal areas of the United States and other countries will almost certainly increase the stress on coastal aquifers and ecosystems in the years ahead.

Similar Problems

Generally speaking, in this country we face the same water issues that the rest of the world is struggling with. The unequal distribution of water is one. The western half of the country generally suffers from a shortage of water, while the eastern half generally does not.

The water tables in the Great Plains and many other parts of the country are falling steadily from overuse. In the Southwest the Colorado River rarely reaches the Gulf of California. States such as Texas, Florida, Nevada, Arizona, and California all face serious water shortage issues. And many states have been arguing over water rights for years.

And, like the rest of the world, our water resources are suffering from the ill effects of pollution from a wide range of materials and sources:

➤ Thousands of toxic chemicals

➤ Gasoline and other petroleum products

➤ Agricultural fertilizers

➤ A witch's brew of pesticides

➤ Animal wastes from agriculture

➤ Road salt

➤ Sediment

The list goes on and on. While progress has been made to clean up some of this mess, much remains to be done.

Earth Education

The ancient Egyptians first developed irrigation along the Nile River around 5000 B.C.E. By 2100 B.C.E. there was an elaborate system for irrigation of agricultural lands in Egypt, including a 12-mile channel that diverted Nile floodwaters to a lake.

Irrigation

Although I've already mentioned irrigation briefly, it's an important issue that deserves another look because it uses such a huge proportion of the world's water resources.

Irrigation is the main strategy used to bring water to agricultural crops that don't receive enough rainfall. Irrigated fields often produce twice the crop yields of nonirrigated lands.

Although irrigation does ensure the continued growth of crops in locations that would not otherwise be productive, it is not without its drawbacks. Chief among them is that if proper drainage is not provided, the soil can become waterlogged, or worse yet, can be degraded by a buildup of salts that eventually damage or destroy crops. About a third of all irrigated lands around the world suffer from this dilemma.

Another problem associated with irrigation is that it has traditionally been a very inefficient use of water. The sheer quantity used demonstrates this fact. Currently, 70 percent of all water diverted from rivers or pumped from underground sources is used for irrigation. While more efficient irrigation techniques such as sprinkler, drip, or trickle strategies can bring moisture to crops with less waste, these methods are not appropriate for all crops or locations. And they tend to be expensive to install.

As the battle over water use intensifies around the globe, the agricultural sector will gradually lose out because industrial use generates far more output in dollar terms than farms do. Water-use growth statistics for the past 100 years bear this out. Since 1900 the municipal use of water worldwide has grown about 19 times, industrial use by 26 times, but agricultural use has only increased by 5 times. The long-term trends are clear. We should not look to irrigation to bring large new areas of marginal land under cultivation when we are already having problems finding enough water to supply current irrigation schemes.

It's likely that the most serious limiting factor on the expansion of food production in this century will be the shortage of water for irrigation, rather than land shortage. And you don't have to be a *hydrologist* to understand that this means water scarcity equals food scarcity.

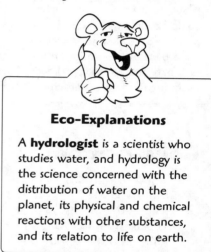

Eco-Explanations

A **hydrologist** is a scientist who studies water, and hydrology is the science concerned with the distribution of water on the planet, its physical and chemical reactions with other substances, and its relation to life on earth.

Global Warming

But one of the most challenging aspects of all of these issues is the probable impact global warming will have on our fresh water supplies. And I'll bet you knew this was going to pop up again.

The uneven distribution of water worldwide leaves about half of the globe with a natural scarcity of water resources. And while climate change is expected to have a significant impact on the water supply of all regions, this will be a particular problem where water is already scarce.

Hydrologists have calculated that higher temperatures could increase the risk of flooding or drought on river systems with low water-storage capacity. In this country, rivers in New England and the mid-Atlantic states fall into this category. On the other hand, rivers in the west with higher reservoir capacity, such as the Colorado system, will be far less vulnerable to flooding or droughts than rivers in the east.

There are additional likely consequences:

➤ Regions with high water consumption in relation to total water supply can expect significant pressures on their existing storage capacity.

➤ Regions that presently rely heavily on hydroelectricity for their electric power should anticipate substantial cuts in generation.

➤ Regions that rely on groundwater for fresh water can expect their sources to decrease.

➤ Regions that currently have highly variable and unpredictable water flows can expect things to get worse.

It's clear from all of this that global warming has the potential to aggravate already-serious water problems worldwide.

Planetary Perils

Global warming will almost certainly make our serious water problems even worse. Droughts could become more severe and prolonged, leading to famine in some parts of the world—an unfortunate pattern that is already occurring in some countries.

Conservation

If global warming does put additional strains on our supplies of fresh water, we're obviously going to have to figure out ways of making better use of what we have. And one of the best ways of stretching our available water resources is conservation. This is because water has not been widely subjected to the same pressures for efficiency gains as other resource sectors. The good news is that there is lots of room for improvement.

Many cities around the world could save huge amounts of water simply by repairing their water systems. It is estimated that Manila, in the Philippines, loses a staggering 60 percent of its water due to leaky pipes and theft. In this country, Boston reduced its water demand substantially a number of years ago by fixing leaky pipes, installing water-saving fixtures, and educating the public about water conservation.

Another important way to conserve is to remove incentives for the excessive use of water. The installation of water meters, raising extremely low prices, and eliminating volume discounts are all useful strategies to help encourage households to conserve. And because, in many countries, the residential sector uses around 50 percent of municipal water, additional conservation measures in the home can make substantial reductions in water demand, from around 10 to 40 percent. In this country, we tend to waste vast amounts of water, so demand-management strategies could be extremely effective.

The capture and use of rainwater is another conservation strategy that also offers flood control benefits. Rooftop collection tanks in some cities are already being used to supply essentially free water for a wide variety of non-drinking water purposes. You can expect to see a dramatic increase in this approach in the future. We'll look at many additional water conservation ideas later in the book.

An Ocean of Trouble

Our exploration of water issues would not be complete without a look at the oceans, which cover nearly three quarters of the Earth's surface. These vast bodies of salt water, which stretch to the horizon and beyond, have been the subject of human wonder, curiosity, and superstition for as long as we have walked the Earth. In fact, the oceans are the very cradle of life.

For thousands of years, we have viewed the sea as a mysterious but inexhaustible source of food and other valuable resources. Many civilizations have grown up along the seacoasts around the world, taking advantage of the supply of fish and other marine life, as well as the trade routes that the oceans provided.

Unfortunately, for almost as long, we have also viewed the oceans as a limitless dumping ground for every kind of filth and garbage imaginable. This time-honored human habit hasn't gotten much better in recent years. And the accidental pollution of the oceans and beaches, in incidents like the now-infamous 1989 Exxon Valdez oil spill off the coast of Alaska, just make an already bad situation even worse.

More recently, we have begun to push the limits of the sea's ability to supply us with resources or to deal with our wastes. We do this at our peril, because, in addition to being the source of a wealth of economic activity, the marine environment also performs essential functions such as the production of oxygen, the recycling of nutrients, and the regulation of our climate. It's easy to take these things for granted. But we shouldn't, because we depend on the oceans for life itself.

Earth Education

For around 3.2 billion years, all life on this planet was limited to the oceans. For much of that time, "life" mainly consisted of algae and other tiny soft-bodied organisms. It wasn't until relatively recently, around 345 million years ago, that the first amphibious creatures began to crawl out of the oceans and onto land.

Earth Education

Total world economic activity related to the oceans is estimated to be around $600 billion. More than half of world trade travels on ships, and that figure is expected to rise dramatically in the next few decades. The value of all marine goods and services is estimated to be around $21 trillion annually.

View of the 1989 Exxon Valdez oil spill, where 11 million gallons of oil leaked from the ship after it ran aground on a reef in Prince William Sound, Alaska.

(AP/Wide World Photos)

Threats to Our Oceans

In Chapter 2, "Something Old, Something New," you will recall that I mentioned the problems associated with the frontier mentality related to the exploitation of natural resources. This attitude is not confined to this country, however, and has its roots in Old World beliefs and practices. In fact, the application of these beliefs to the world's oceans predates the founding of our nation by hundreds of years.

The idea that the oceans provide limitless resources, and are something to be conquered and controlled by humankind, goes back at least to the fifteenth century. Unfortunately, these outdated notions still persist today. Despite the enormous importance of the oceans to almost every aspect of human life, we have continued to abuse this most important resource with a variety of unfortunate practices.

The main threats to the oceans today are interrelated and human-induced:

➤ Overfishing

➤ Pollution

➤ Habitat degradation

➤ Climate change

Let's take a look at each one of these problem areas.

Gone Fishing

It's hard to overstate the importance of fish in our lives. Around the world, people on average get about 16 percent of their animal protein from fish. In Asia that figure is around 30 percent. Yet in many parts of the world fish stocks have been exploited to the point where fisheries have declined dramatically or even collapsed altogether. Most of this has been caused by the technologically sophisticated, but otherwise short-sighted, activities of the world's industrialized fishing industry.

Eleven of the world's 15 most important fishing areas are fully exploited or overexploited, according to the United Nations Food and Agriculture Organization. The once-great Atlantic cod fisheries off the coast of New England and Canada, for example, are only a shadow of what they once were, and competition for the remainder of this highly valued species is intense. Tuna and swordfish are in the same boat, so to speak.

As the fishing industry has depleted the most valuable species, it has begun to work its way down the marine food chain to exploit less popular, smaller varieties. This is obviously a self-defeating strategy that can't last for long. Yet much of the world's fishing industry has been in denial for decades about these problems.

Overfishing also creates serious biological problems for marine ecosystems. The reduction in genetic diversity makes it more difficult for various species to adapt to changing environmental conditions in the future. And the sudden decline of one species can disrupt the delicate predator-prey relationship, causing a severe imbalance in marine ecosystems.

Planetary Perils

The overexploitation of one marine species can result in an invasion by another species, which can damage fragile ecosystems. The overfishing of triggerfish and pufferfish in the Caribbean (for souvenirs) has led to an explosion in numbers of sea urchins that the fish used to eat. The sea urchins, in turn, have damaged coral reefs.

Down the Drain

But overfishing isn't the only problem. The long-term effects of industrialization have disrupted and damaged the fragile ecology of many of the world's coastal regions with the indiscriminate dumping of industrial and municipal wastes. The pollution of the marine environment by oil spills, toxic chemicals, insecticides, plastic debris, medical waste, human sewage, and other noxious and dangerous products has had a severe impact on coastal wildlife, fish, and other marine species.

This is especially significant because the coastal zone is so valuable from a biological as well as commercial perspective. The majority of marine biological activity takes place along the coasts, where the sunlit surface waters are fed by the rich runoff from the land by rivers and streams. This mixes with nutrient-rich water currents from the cold depths of the oceans to produce an abundance of marine life. These coastal areas, in fact, account for between 80 and 90 percent of the world's commercial fish catch.

Yet the damage from the many forms of pollution continues to the point where some of the ecosystems of the coastal zone are collapsing, as marine life declines or disappears under the weight of all these problems. And the marine-based industries that depend on that life suffer as well. More than half of the world's coastlines are threatened by human activities, especially intensive coastal development and pollution.

Unhappy Habitat

The pollution of our oceans with toxic substances, especially the highly vulnerable coastal regions, is one of the primary causes of habitat degradation. But there are other reasons as well.

Eco-Explanations

The **continental shelf** is the part of a continent that is submerged in relatively shallow seas and extends an average distance of 43 miles offshore.

Another major problem relates back to commercial fishing. The practice of trawling, especially by huge, modern trawling vessels, is particularly destructive of marine habitat on the *continental shelves*. Trawlers drag enormous nets with chains attached across the bottom of the coastal fisheries, which basically sweeps up everything in its path, leaving a trail of ecological devastation behind.

But I don't want to leave you with the false impression that it's only huge corporate fishing practices that are to blame for habitat damage. Believe it or not, some fishermen actually use cyanide poisoning or dynamite to kill or stun fish. Although these methods are generally illegal, they have been popular in parts of the western Pacific, especially around Indonesia. The devastation this causes to *coral reefs* and their fragile ecosystems is enormous.

Eco-Explanations

A **coral reef** is a ridge or part of a shallow area of sea floor near the sea's surface made up of the calcium-containing remains of millions of tiny coral animals, red algae, and mollusks.

Currently, around 60 percent of the world's coral reefs are threatened by a variety of human activities. There are many other reasons for habitat destruction, but I think you get the general idea.

Global Warming—Again

I know, we talked about global warming already in this chapter. But the effects of global warming on the oceans are different enough that they need a separate discussion.

Because the oceans play such a key role in how the other elements of our environment function, anything that alters marine ecosystems will have an impact on everything else. And global warming has the potential for dramatic changes in our oceans. I've already covered the rise in ocean levels predicted due to global warming, so I won't repeat myself.

In Chapter 3, "The Air We Breath," I already mentioned the damage to marine organisms caused by increased ultraviolet radiation associated with the thinning of the ozone layer. I just want to add that since these organisms act as the main natural "safety valve" for excess global warming because they remove excess carbon dioxide from the atmosphere, any damage to them poses the risk of increasing the pace of global warming even more.

Another early warning sign of global warming of the oceans is the phenomenon of coral bleaching. When a coral reef is subjected to the stress of warmer water temperatures (among other possible stresses), it expels tiny plants, which gives the reef a bright white bleached appearance. Bleached corals are slow to recover; it can often take years. And if bleaching recurs, the corals may not be able to recover at all.

There have been numerous bleaching incidents in recent years from Easter Island to Okinawa, and from the Caribbean to the Great Barrier Reef of Australia. In 1998 scientists discovered massive bleaching throughout the tropics, and for the first time on reefs in the Indian Ocean. The problem is definitely spreading.

Global warming has implications for fisheries, too. Some bodies of water may become too warm for the fish that are there. On the other hand, some fish in cold ocean waters might actually grow more quickly. But one of the biggest potential problems is the possible decline in the amount of oxygen in the water, with an accompanying increase in pollution and salt levels. But overall, global warming will probably affect inland and coastal fisheries more negatively than deep ocean fisheries.

A Watershed

It should be pretty clear by now that we have reached a watershed or turning point in the way we think about our water resources. At the very least, we're going to have to start using water more efficiently. We also need to redouble our many efforts to clean up and protect all of our water resources on land as well as at sea.

And to help you remember just how important all this is, the next time the sweat is running down your back on a record hot summer day, and you reach for a cold glass (or bottle) of refreshing water (or your other favorite beverage), imagine what it would be like if there were nary "a drop to drink."

The Least You Need to Know

➤ There's only so much water available.

➤ We're using our groundwater faster than it can be replaced.

➤ We need to clean up our fresh water supplies.

➤ There is a serious need for water conservation.

➤ We are severely damaging our oceans and their resources.

Chapter 5

The Land We Live On

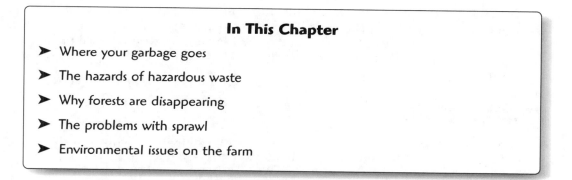

In This Chapter

➤ Where your garbage goes

➤ The hazards of hazardous waste

➤ Why forests are disappearing

➤ The problems with sprawl

➤ Environmental issues on the farm

So far we've looked at the many environmental problems we face in the air and in our waters. But one of the reasons why some of these issues are so hard to get a handle on is that they are more or less invisible. Now it's time to shift our focus to the land we live on.

Although many of the environmental dangers associated with the land are also out of sight, many more are dramatically obvious. And since this is where we live, rather than in the upper atmosphere or at the bottom of the ocean, many of these problems are harder to ignore. Unfortunately, we've been trashing our immediate neighborhood just as badly as the rest of the planet. And damage to the land has the same sort of negative impact on the Web of Life as elsewhere.

In this chapter, we'll take a hard look at how we treat the land we live on. We'll begin by following the garbage truck to see what happens to your trash after you toss it. Then we'll put on our protective clothing and explore the problems that hazardous wastes pose to the land. After that I'll take you on a walk through a magical forest.

Then we'll go for a long, long car ride to check out the spread of suburban sprawl. Eventually, we'll end up down on the farm, where we'll find more than cows and chickens.

The Garbage Barge Incident

One of the most serious ways we have been trashing our environment is our indiscriminate dumping of waste material for many, many years. The now-infamous "garbage barge" incident of 1987 brought this issue to the attention of most Americans. A barge loaded with over 3,000 tons of garbage from New York State cruised for weeks from port to port along the eastern seaboard in a vain attempt to find somewhere to dump its load. After sailing all the way to the Caribbean without success, the barge returned to New York, where the foul-smelling cargo was unloaded and eventually burned.

This highly publicized incident brought the issue of solid waste disposal into sharp focus for many people, and created an unforgettable image of the problem. Shortly after the barge incident, a large quantity of filthy medical waste washed up on New York's beaches, and the issue of waste disposal has been a matter of public concern ever since.

Talkin' Trash

So, just how big a problem is this? It's huge. You and I (and 275 million of our fellow citizens) tossed out more than 442 billion pounds of garbage in 2000.

Earth Education

Every man, woman, and child in the United States tosses about 1,600 pounds of waste in the garbage every year. That's a lot of apple cores, cereal boxes, disposable diapers, junk mail, old shoes, and whatever else you put in your garbage cans or bags.

But that's not all. Industry contributes its share with over 2.5 billion pounds of nasty toxic waste that ends up in the air, water, or ground as well. But for now we'll focus on the nontoxic stuff. So, what's this garbage composed of and where does it go? Let's follow the garbage truck and find out. Hold your nose.

What's MSW?

All lumped together, our garbage is called municipal solid waste, or MSW. According to 1996 statistics, this includes a wide array of items such as paper and paperboard (38 percent), yard trimmings (13 percent), food (10.4 percent), plastics (9.4 percent), metal (7.7 percent), glass (5.9 percent), wood (5.2 percent), rubber, leather, textiles, and other miscellaneous items (about 10 percent). Although these items are part of the problem, they are also part of the solution, so we'll run into them again later in the book.

According to the Environmental Protection Agency ...

➤ This country generated a total of 221 million tons of MSW in 2000, an increase of 9 million tons from 1995.

➤ Recycling (including composting) recovered 31.5 percent of MSW in 1999, an increase of almost four times the rate of 10 years ago.

➤ Garbage incinerators burned 7.5 percent of MSW in 1999, down from 17 percent in 1996.

➤ Landfills took in 61 percent of MSW generated in 1999, up from 57 percent in 1996.

These statistics show some interesting trends. The total amount of MSW has generally continued to increase in recent years, along with the amount that is recycled or composted. The amount that is burned has declined dramatically, while the quantity that is landfilled has increased. More recent (but incomplete) statistics, however, seem to indicate that recycling rates may have peaked or are even declining in some areas.

Out of Sight, Out of Mind

Still, huge amounts of garbage—116 million tons—were landfilled in 1996. And contrary to media reports of the late 1980s and early 1990s, this country is not in any imminent danger of running out of landfills in the near future. That's because so many huge new landfills were built following those reports. And now a lot of municipalities and private companies want to maximize the return on their very large investments.

This is not to say that landfills are good for the environment. They're not. Despite significant improvements in landfill design and siting, they still pose a long-term threat to groundwater supplies. And burying this much garbage represents a huge waste of potentially valuable resources. The main advantage of landfills is that they are still the cheapest way of getting rid of our garbage, or at least getting it out of sight. More on landfills later in the book.

Planetary Perils

Landfills produce large amounts of methane (a greenhouse gas that contributes substantially to global warming) and also pose a long-term threat to groundwater supplies, especially in the case of older, unlined landfills. It has been estimated that landfills in the U.S. are responsible for about a third of this country's total methane emissions.

Hot Stuff!

You've probably heard how we're all going to live better lives, thanks to modern science—especially modern chemistry. I'm not convinced. Neither are a lot of other people these days. It's time to put on our protective clothing, because we're going to take a look at some wonders of modern science that aren't so wonderful.

Hazardous Waste

We'll start with hazardous waste. Just what, exactly, is hazardous waste? There are four main categories:

➤ Ignitable—can burn or cause a fire

➤ Corrosive—can corrode steel or harm organisms

➤ Reactive—may explode or create toxic gases

➤ Toxic—contains poisonous substances

There's a lot of hazardous waste on the planet. Worldwide, there are about 400 million tons of the stuff generated *each year*. And 250 million tons of it are produced right here in our own country. That's almost a ton for every man, woman, and child in the United States. Next year, add another ton. And so on. In fact, there are some 40,000 locations in this country that have been listed as hazardous waste Superfund sites by the EPA. And cleanup of just 1,400 of the worst ones is projected to cost $31 billion.

Mining operations tend to be big generators of all kinds of waste, but especially of hazardous waste. In 1998, mining facilities released 3.5 billion pounds of toxics into the U.S. environment, according to the EPA. Mining companies use a variety of toxic chemicals such as cyanide, mercury, and sulfuric acid to separate metal from the ore. Mine tailings, the material left over once the metal has been removed, are highly toxic, and often are just dumped on the land or into rivers and streams. The environmental consequences can be disastrous.

But even when mining wastes are contained in holding ponds, there can be serious problems. In one of Europe's worst environmental disasters in years, huge amounts of cyanide overflowed a dam at the Baia Mare gold mine in the Romanian town of Oradea in January 2000. Within a few weeks, the pollution had flowed downstream into neighboring Hungary and Yugoslavia where almost all aquatic life in the Tisa and Danube rivers was poisoned. The Tisa, for all practical purposes, was biologically dead after the incident.

Terrible Toxics

But toxics have lots of other potential problems. Somewhere around 80,000 chemicals are in common use today. Some of them are like time bombs just waiting to go off. And many of these chemicals have the potential to affect the genetics of people and animals a generation or more after they have been exposed to them.

Some of the worst are known as persistent organic pollutants, or POPs. These highly toxic substances can be carried by the winds and have even been ending up in remote Arctic locations—and in the indigenous people who live there. Dioxin is one of the most poisonous POPs known to science. Remarkably, there isn't enough information for even a partial health assessment of 95 percent of the chemicals in the environment, according to the U.S. National Academy of Sciences.

Many other toxic chemicals are known as *pesticides*. Unlike other chemicals, pesticides are designed specifically to alter or kill living organisms. If we're not careful, that can include us. Remarkably, most Americans were largely ignorant of these hazards until Rachel Carson published her now-classic book *Silent Spring* in 1962, which questioned the widespread use of chemical pesticides. Practically no one has any doubts about the dangers of pesticides anymore. The EPA has ranked pesticides as the third most important environmental problem in this country in terms of cancer risk. In fact, the National Academy of Sciences has concluded that pesticide contamination of our foods may be responsible for up to 20,000 cancer deaths each year.

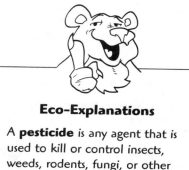

Eco-Explanations

A **pesticide** is any agent that is used to kill or control insects, weeds, rodents, fungi, or other organisms. More than half of the pesticides used in this country are herbicides designed to control weeds.

Pesticides have also seriously contaminated our groundwater. And worst of all, contrary to what you may hear in the advertising that promotes their use, pesticides have simply made many pest problems even worse. In response to heavier pesticide use, many insects have become more resistant, requiring heavier use of even more potent pesticides. The same phenomenon has occurred with plants, and a whole new crop of "super weeds" has been created by Mother Nature in response to our chemical assaults. Thousands of pesticide products are currently used in this country.

The list of hazardous and toxic substances goes on and on. The improper disposal or accidental discharge of any of these hazardous substances can cause serious environmental problems for us and for many generations yet to come.

Nuclear Nemesis

Now we're going to look briefly at some hot stuff—nuclear waste. Although radioactive materials are frequently used for beneficial medical and other purposes, trying to figure out what to do with the contaminated wastes can be a puzzle. Low-level nuclear waste, including radioactive materials from research activities, medical wastes, and so on, are normally disposed of in low-level nuclear waste dumps. Trying to find dump sites, even for these low-level materials, has become more difficult in recent years.

However, the really hot stuff—spent fuel from nuclear power plants and materials from nuclear weapons—are so toxic that they must be placed in special containers and then stored in incredibly expensive, specially designed underground sites. The lack of sufficient underground storage facilities has forced utilities and military installations all over the country to store their spent fuel rods and other radioactive materials in holding facilities that were never designed for such long-term use. The government-designed site for nuclear storage is Yucca Mountain in Nevada, yet construction of the facilities at this location are decades behind schedule, and local environmental factors may not be favorable to long-term storage.

Environmentalists and some scientists have warned of this impending dilemma for decades. Now the problems—like the proverbial chickens—are coming home to roost. No easy or cheap solutions are likely to be developed.

But the continuing threat of a major nuclear meltdown and the release of radioactive debris is probably the most serious pollution issue of all. The now-infamous Chernobyl nuclear accident in the former Soviet Republic of Ukraine on April 26, 1986, was the worst nuclear accident in history. Large areas of several former Soviet republics were contaminated and 200,000 people had to be evacuated and resettled. Around 4.9 million people in the former Soviet Union were ultimately affected.

The enormous environmental and financial costs of nuclear power, nuclear weapons, and their wastes are simply too high to continue pursuing their development and use.

A 1986 aerial view of the Chernobyl nuclear plant in the Ukraine shows damage from an explosion and fire in reactor four on April 26, 1986.

(AP/Wide World Photos)

Where Have All the Forests Gone?

Okay, it's time to take a break from all of this and go for a nice, restful walk in a magical forest. All set? Let's go. The lush green canopy of leaves rustling over our heads protects us from the hot summer sun. Sweet bird songs echo through the trees.

Colorful wildflowers and green ferns carpet the forest floor. A small, clear brook gurgles around moss-covered rocks, and chipmunks and other small creatures scurry away as we approach. It's a little piece of heaven. Now close your eyes. I'm going to count from one to three. When I reach three, open your eyes again. Ready? One, two, three!

Uh-oh, our magic forest has disappeared! And so has everything else. In its place is a wasteland of stumps, and a tangle of branches and treetops. The ground is scarred with deep, muddy ruts, the stream is clogged with silt, and the broiling sun is beating down on our heads mercilessly. It looks like hell. And it is.

Unfortunately, this isn't just a fantasy. This sort of thing is happening every day in countries all across the planet. In the past 50 years, the natural forests of the Philippines, Thailand, Haiti, and El Salvador have been virtually destroyed by excessive logging and by the spread of migrant farming. Similar devastation is taking place in many other nations as well. Logging for wood products, in fact, imperils more than 70 percent of the world's remaining virgin forests, according to the World Resources Institute. If current trends continue, half of the planet's remaining tropical forests may have vanished by 2050.

Earth Education

The world has lost about half—almost 7.5 billion acres—of the forests that once covered the earth. Every year, at least 40 million additional acres disappear as a result of logging or conversion of forests to other uses. Almost 10 percent of the world's tree species are at risk of extinction, and tropical deforestation alone is taking place at more than 33 million acres per year.

An Axe to Grind

Andif you think this sort of thing is limited to poor, money-hungry nations, think again. Most of our own old growth forests were cut down early in our history. By the end of the nineteenth century they were mostly gone. But huge areas of the Pacific Northwest in Canada and in this country have been clear-cut in recent decades as well. And the destruction continues. The environmental impact of clear-cutting is severe.

Healthy forests provide a wide range of benefits. Not only do trees remove carbon dioxide from the atmosphere through the process of photosynthesis—helping to combat global warming—they also add pure oxygen to the air. In addition, forests provide habitat for a wide variety of plants and animals, store large amounts of moisture, and prevent erosion of the soil. But clear-cutting removes all the trees at once, and leaves the remaining land vulnerable to severe erosion because the moisture just runs off instead of being absorbed by the forest.

And the economic impact of indiscriminate logging can be just as bad. For example, in Idaho in the 1960s, lumber companies cut forests along the Salmon River. They made a profit of $14 million. But the silt that they left behind from the eroded land ended up costing the salmon fisheries over $100 million in damages. Does this make economic sense to you? Not to me, either.

The sad thing is that it doesn't have to be this way. Although the clear-cutting of forests generally maximizes the short-term financial gain for logging companies, (which is why it is so popular), sustainable, selective logging practices offer far better long-term advantages for both loggers and the environment.

Deforestation Disaster

The devastating floods that China suffered in 1998 are another sad example of the consequences of indiscriminate logging practices. Massive deforestation in the headwaters region of the Yangtze River left areas downstream vulnerable to the worst flooding in 40 years. As a result, the Chinese government belatedly began to enforce a logging ban in the headwaters region, where a staggering 85 percent of the forest cover had been cut down. It also began to institute reforestation of the affected area. The government decided that the forests were far more valuable for water storage than for saw logs.

Even where the forests have not been completely cut down, a new and terrible phenomenon has emerged in recent years—*defaunation*—also referred to as "the empty forest." From Asia to Africa, and many other places around the globe, impoverished people desperate to find food are killing anything that moves. Many tropical forests have essentially been picked clean by subsistence hunters. Now there are large areas of habitat with few birds or mammals to populate them. Talk about massive species decline.

Eco-Explanations

Defaunation is the removal of large segments of bird and mammal populations from forests by local hunters looking for food to feed their families.

A Developing Dilemma

Although the empty forest phenomenon is found mainly in countries or regions with poor populations, the same general trends can be seen across the planet where a growing world population—rich and poor alike—consumes more and more of our limited resources. Of course, the rich are consuming more than the poor, and this only intensifies the problems and makes it that much harder to find ways to bridge the ever-widening gap between these two groups.

People Pressure

The world population, now over six billion and counting, continues to grow at a staggering rate—especially in the poorer nations that can least afford the increase. The implications of this population explosion for the planet are staggering—especially the mad rush to develop a globalized economy capable of supporting this population. We need to remember that the Earth has a limited "carrying capacity" or ability to provide us and other life forms with adequate food, water, shelter, and habitat for an acceptable quality of life.

And the world's ballooning human population is definitely straining the planet's carrying capacity to the limits. Many of the environmental problems that we have already looked at in earlier chapters are clear warnings of our approach to those limits. These problems are particularly graphic in many of the world's cities.

One of the key trends of this growth is the increasing urbanization of the planet. In 1900, only 16 cities had a population of a million or more. At that time, about 10 percent of humanity lived in cities. Now, 326 cities have populations of a million or more, and 14 of these are enormous megacities of 10 million or more residents. If these trends continue, more than half of the global population will be living in cities by 2010, according to the World Watch Institute.

The Spread of Sprawl

Although this growing population strains the resources of the entire planet, the expansion and development of the huge urban areas worldwide present enormous problems for urban citizens and governments alike. Just trying to bring basic services such as clean water and electricity to their inhabitants can be a major challenge for some cities in many countries.

But that's just part of the problem. As they grow, urban areas swallow up surrounding countryside—frequently prime agricultural lands or forests—at a phenomenal rate. This is known as *urban or suburban sprawl.* Huge population increases in the cities of developing countries will account for 90 percent of the 2.7 billion people projected to be added to the world's population between 1995 and 2030. Consequently, cities can be expected to have a profound impact on the global environment because they are projected to consume 75 percent of its resources, the World Watch Institute says.

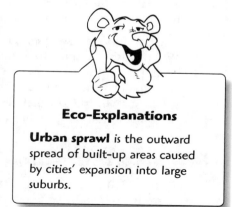

Eco-Explanations

Urban sprawl is the outward spread of built-up areas caused by cities' expansion into large suburbs.

Unfortunately, we can find the worst examples of urban sprawl right here in this country. For example, greater Chicago's population grew by 38 percent between 1950 and 1990, but gobbled up over

124 percent more land in the process. We find similar statistics for many other American cities as well. And this trend is accelerating. Between 1992 and 1997, more than 3 million acres of farmland were lost annually to sprawl. That's up from 1.4 million per year between 1982 and 1992. And clearly we are not making very efficient use of much of that land.

Suburban sprawl in this country destroys green space, increases air and water pollution, divides our neighborhoods, and forces residents to spend too much time sitting in their cars on highways, which resemble giant parking lots more than roads during rush hour. Which brings us to one of the main reasons for suburban sprawl in the first place.

Auto-Hypnosis

It's time to take that long, slow ride through the suburbs I promised at the beginning of the chapter. And it's long and slow mainly because, by its very nature, sprawl is decentralized, inefficient, and wasteful of resources.

Americans have been hypnotized by the automobile ever since the first Model T rolled off the production lines of the Ford Motor Company in 1908. The private automobile offered the prospect of almost unlimited freedom of movement for a nation already hooked on the frontier mentality. Now, instead of riding off into the sunset on your trusty horse to pursue your dream, you could head west (and north, south, and east as well) in your car. And you could bring the family along, too. This was hard to resist, and most Americans didn't.

Paving Paradise

But this new-found freedom came at a price. Our love affair with the automobile doomed a reasonably efficient—and far more environmentally friendly—electric trolley and interurban railway system that connected virtually every major city in the country in the early 1900s. As thousands of miles of electric railway tracks were torn up, many more thousands of miles of paved highways were put down.

The automobile also encouraged the spread of suburban sprawl, especially after World War II, with the start-up of mass-marketed housing subdivisions like Levittown on Long Island. Initially viewed by most people as the embodiment of the American Dream, Levittown and its subsequent look-alike imitations soon developed into suburban sprawl, which isolated its residents and ironically turned them into slaves to the same automobiles that made suburbia possible in the first place.

Driven to Distraction

By the 1990s, tract housing, suburbia, and our wasteful and polluting fossil-fueled automotive transport system were no longer viewed as positive developments. In fact, the American suburban dream had turned into a nightmare for many Americans, populated increasingly by disconnected, dysfunctional families with troubled and neglected children (some with guns in their hands), and causing a general breakdown of community.

And much of this breakdown of community is caused, at least in part, by the physical separation that is encouraged by suburban sprawl planning and zoning. Sprawl has been bad news for the environment in general, and for farmland and open spaces in particular. It has increased dependence on the automobile (contributing to global warming) and is becoming increasingly expensive to support with tax dollars from hard-pressed working families. There has to be a better way. We'll explore some of these ways in Part 5, "A Sustainable Future."

I don't know about you, but I've had enough of suburbia. Let's take a drive out into the country for some fresh air.

Planetary Perils

Suburban sprawl destroys green space, increases air and water pollution, divides neighborhoods, and forces us to use automobiles for every chore. Sprawl is a national and international problem of enormous proportions that will only get worse with a continually growing population.

Down on the Farm

We'll conclude our tour of the land we live on by getting our hands dirty. Just squat down and grab a nice handful of dirt from the field. But you might want to put your protective gloves back on first, because the wonders of modern chemistry have arrived on the farm, too. There's no escape, not even out here in the country.

Traditionally, the soil that we grew our crops in was a living part of the global ecosystem that contained microbes and other living organisms that were all part of the Web of Life. On many farms in this country and elsewhere around the globe, however, that's no longer the case. The heavy use of toxic pesticides and commercial fertilizers has turned the living soil into a biological wasteland. In this new, "improved" system, the soil merely acts as the physical support for the roots of plants that now depend on water, sunlight—and chemicals—for survival.

The Chemical Question

If you only listened to the promotional advertising by the chemical companies, you'd think these agricultural products were the salvation of the planet. But the facts down on the farm tell a very different story.

In the last 40 years, pesticide use has increased ten fold, yet crop loss has almost doubled, according to the EPA. Clearly something is wrong here. Many observant farmers and ranchers, in fact, have come to question the highly touted benefit of pesticides and chemical fertilizers and have started practicing alternative, sustainable farming methods in recent years.

But the majority of farmers who continue to use massive amounts of chemicals endanger not only themselves but also the surrounding environment and our food supply with some chemicals that have been linked to serious health problems by the National Academy of Sciences. Although the individual chemical products are supposed to be safe when properly applied, accidents do happen.

Even more troubling is the fact that a huge amount of the pesticides used in agriculture—around 85 to 90 percent—never reach their intended targets. Instead, they end up blowing away or in the soil or in our water. And the cumulative effects of the thousands of products in use, and their interactions with each other in the environment, have never been properly studied.

Is It a Farm—or a Factory?

Many other farmers have taken the modern corporate approach to farming, and have built huge commercial agricultural enterprises that look more like factories than farms. That's because they essentially *are* factories. Although these operations may be efficient moneymakers, generally speaking they are also environmental and health disasters.

Planetary Perils

Many factory farms pose serious threats to the health and well-being of animals housed in them and to the surrounding environment as well. According to the Environmental Protection Agency, hog, chicken, and cattle waste has polluted 35,000 miles of rivers in 22 states and contaminated groundwater in 17 states.

The inhumane, crowded conditions for the animals—chickens, hogs, calves, etc.—in most of these factories are breeding grounds for contagious diseases, and consequently require the heavy use of antibiotics to keep the animals alive. In addition, to squeeze the maximum amount of profit from the venture, many of the animals are fed large amounts of growth hormones as well.

The wastes from all of these unfortunate creatures end up in huge, stinking manure pits or lagoons that have figured in some spectacular pollution incidents when the holding facilities have ruptured or otherwise failed. Even under the best of circumstances, the disposal of these vast amounts of wastes can be a problem.

And when something goes wrong with the systems in these operations due to power outages, heat waves, or flooding, all the animals can suffer horrible deaths, causing even more environmental hazards. Yes, these factory farms produce huge quantities of relatively cheap food products. But are they really worth the environmental and health risks? We'll take another look at factory farms and their alternatives in Chapter 9, "Food for Thought."

The Web of Life

As you can see, the environmental challenges to the land we live on are substantial. And most of these problems have either direct or indirect connections to most of the other environmental issues we've discussed in previous chapters. The Web of Life again.

The good news is that we have covered most of the major problems and looked at their probable consequences. Now it's time to start talking about solutions, and we're going to do that in the next chapter. But before we move on, a few quick comments.

I hope you have gained an appreciation for the need to change our ways of thinking about our environment. Because, without a healthy environment, all the other advances of our modern society and economy will eventually crumble. And that would be bad news for our children and grandchildren. At the very least, we need to stop treating our planet like dirt, if not for our own sakes, then for theirs.

The Least You Need to Know

➤ We need to reduce the amount of garbage we dispose of.

➤ We need to develop better alternatives to nuclear power.

➤ Many current logging practices are very destructive.

➤ We need to stop the spread of sprawl.

➤ Our love affair with the fossil-fueled automobile has caused many problems.

➤ We need to encourage nondestructive farming practices.

Chapter 6

So, What Can You Do About It?

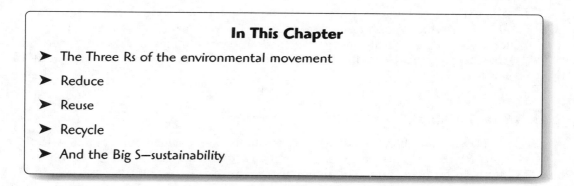
Okay, the planet's a mess. And we're mostly to blame. And by now you're probably wishing there was *something* you could do to help fix things. Happily there is. Actually, there are literally hundreds of things. And I'm going to spend the remaining four sections of the book telling you all about them. But before we leave Part 1, "The Environment and You," I want to explain how we're going to proceed.

The things you can do to help generally fall into four broad categories: reduction, reuse, recycling, and sustainability. While each of these categories will get separate treatment in its own section, I need to point out that there is a good deal of overlap. As you have already learned, the environmental problems that got us to this point are all interconnected. So are the solutions. The Web of Life again.

We'll begin with the basics. I'll start off this chapter by introducing you to the Three Rs of the environmental movement: reduce, reuse and recycle. Then, we'll go through each one of them, and I'll explain why they are so important for the environment—and for you. Finally, I'll give you a quick introduction to the concept of sustainability—the Big S of the environmental movement—and why it's so important for our future.

Don't Just Sit There—Do Something!

I know it's easy to feel overwhelmed by all the terrible environmental problems we've looked at. I've felt that way, too, plenty of times. It's also easy to just want to go hide in a corner and suck your thumb and hope it all simply goes away. It won't. But since we're mostly to blame for getting into this mess, we're also largely responsible for getting ourselves out of it. That means we need to get up out of the corner and do something constructive. Like getting involved in any number of activities, both large and small, that will help make things better.

And that doesn't necessarily mean you have to go out and join an environmental organization (although that's a great idea if you enjoy working with groups like that). As you'll soon see, getting involved can be as simple as heating up less water for your morning cup of tea. That simple act of getting involved at any level magically transforms you from being part of the problem to being part of the solution.

And since you've gotten this far in the book, you're someone who obviously cares about our future. That's good. Now there are at least two of us. Actually, there are a lot more people who are getting involved. And our numbers are growing every day. Together we *can* make a difference. But before we go racing off to save the planet, a few basics.

The Three Rs

Peoplewho have been active in the environmental movement are familiar with the *Three Rs:* reduce, reuse, recycle. These three activities represent the key traditional strategies for being an environmentally responsible citizen. Of the three, recycling has probably gotten the most attention over the years. That's ironic, because recycling is the third, and least effective, of the Rs. The correct emphasis, in descending order of importance, is reduce, reuse, recycle.

Eco-Explanations

The **Three Rs** of the environmental movement are reduce, reuse, and recycle.

The first R—reducing—is the quickest path to a cleaner, greener planet. It's also the hardest to implement, which is why recycling has had so much more visibility over the years. The second R—reusing—is the next most effective strategy for waste management. It conserves more energy and natural resources than recycling. The third R—recycling—as I just noted, is the least effective strategy. Yet, it turns materials that would otherwise become waste into valuable resources.

Combined, the Three Rs could go a long way toward solving many of our most pressing environmental problems—especially if they were adopted by the majority of the world's inhabitants. But how is this possible? you ask. How does cutting back on waste solve global warming? Or groundwater pollution? I'll explain.

Reduce Your Use

On the surface, reducing—or *source reduction* as it is often called—is the simplest and quickest way to cut back on our huge consumption of natural resources, thus helping to resolve many of our environmental crises. Put simply, source reduction means consuming and throwing away less stuff. That simple description covers an awful lot of territory.

Simple source reduction strategies can include purchasing more durable, longer-lasting goods, or looking for products and packaging that are as free of toxic materials as possible. A more complex approach might be to look for those products whose design and manufacture use fewer raw materials, have a longer useful life, and are reusable after their original purpose has been served.

Unfortunately, reducing is also the hardest R to implement because this strategy cuts right to the heart of our problem—our long-standing habits of over-consumption in their many forms that I mentioned earlier in the book. These habits are not only unhealthy for the planet in general; they're also unhealthy for us individually (we'll explore these issues in greater detail in the chapters that follow).

Eco-Explanations

Source reduction refers to reducing the quantity of waste, which in turn lessens the amount of material that enters the waste stream in the first place. This strategy works as well in the home as it does at work or in government and major industries.

What is going to be needed, in order to make source reduction the truly effective strategy it should be, is a major shift in attitudes by consumers around the world. But especially in this country, where just 4.5 percent of the global population consumes a third of the planet's material resources. Obviously, any reductions in our consumption will have an enormous impact on the rest of the world.

Why Reduce?

But why is source reduction so effective—and important? One of the main reasons is that it tackles the problem of waste at the front end—before it occurs—rather than at the back end after it has already happened, the way recycling does. Because source reduction actually prevents the generation of waste in the first place, it is the preferable method of waste management, and is one of the best ways of helping the environment.

Considering the vast amounts of materials that we consume every year, we have almost limitless opportunities to make substantial reductions. For example, in this country, container and packaging waste accounts for about 30 percent of waste that is buried in landfills. Unfortunately, this terrible waste of resources is not all that unusual these days. In fact, most of the materials that move through our modern economies are only used once, and then thrown away. No wonder the world's forests and other natural resources are disappearing at such an awful pace.

Planetary Perils

Most of the materials that move through our modern economies are only used once, and then thrown away. This is a terrible waste of resources that is unsustainable. A plastic foam coffee cup is a good example of this sort of pattern. Not only is it used just once, to make matters worse, after it's thrown away it doesn't degrade in a landfill.

Save Resources

By reducing our overall consumption, we can save huge quantities of natural resources. Put another way, for every pound of trash that we toss in the garbage truck, another 20 to 25 (depending on whose figures you use) pounds of industrial byproducts, fertilizer runoff, and so on ends up in the environment. You don't have to be a mathematician to figure out that the "leverage effect" of waste reduction can be huge. For every ton of trash kept out of the waste stream, we avoid 20 to 25 tons of other waste, along with its related environmental impacts and the high cost of producing it.

The good news is that saving resources doesn't have to be as painful a process as you might think. We are *so* wasteful as a society that cutting back on our consumption would not seriously affect our standard of living. Even modest changes in our lifestyle, such as driving smaller cars and building smaller houses, would still enable us to live in relative luxury, while being more compatible with a sustainable future.

Many people in this country have caught on to this fact and are already living simpler but far more satisfying lives. And they're not only saving resources. They're saving money for better things at the same time (more on that in Chapter 11, "Help, I Wanna Get Off!").

Save Energy

And, of course, all this mining, transport, processing, refining, and manufacturing of new products uses lots of energy. And since our main energy sources are still based on fossil fuels, reductions in energy use help reduce the emission of greenhouse gases, primarily carbon dioxide. And since this country uses one quarter of the world's energy supplies, reductions of any amount will have a significant effect on the global environment.

Reduce Pollution

Source reduction also means fewer environmental repercussions, such as the contamination of groundwater from leaking landfills and air pollution from garbage incinerators. In addition, by reducing our consumption we can cut back on the need to mine for minerals and drill for oil, activities that have polluted thousands of miles of rivers and shorelines in this country, to say nothing of the rest of the world.

Source reduction also removes some of the pressure to log our forests in the unsustainable manner that has been so destructive of both human and wildlife habitat here and abroad. Lowering consumption also reduces the need for manufacturing as many new products from raw materials. Air and water pollution from a wide range of manufacturing plants have caused enormous environmental damage and have sickened millions of people worldwide.

Save Landfill Space

Obviously, if source reduction cuts down on waste, there will be that much less municipal solid waste (MSW) needing to be landfilled. This means that existing landfills will last longer, reducing the need for constructing new ones. And since most newer landfills are located in rural areas, far from the sources of the MSW that goes into them, significant amounts of fossil-based fuels are needed to transport the huge numbers of 2,000-pound bales of garbage involved.

Earth Education

In 1996, the 36 billion aluminum cans that were landfilled had a scrap value of more than $600 million, according to the Container Recycling Institute. This represents an enormous waste of a valuable resource that requires huge amounts of energy to produce. Talk about throwing money into a hole in the ground.

Save Money

If cities and other municipalities in this country aren't shipping their garbage to landfills halfway across the country, they should be able to save some of that money for other things. And if you are putting less garbage out on the curb, your trash bills should be reduced as well, especially if you pay by the bag or container. But the savings associated with source reduction go far beyond that. If you are buying less stuff, obviously you're spending less money. And so is everybody else, including government and industry. Source reduction can be as economical as it is ecological.

What to Reduce

Okay, the benefits of source reduction for most of us are pretty obvious. But just what, exactly, should we be cutting back on? Generally speaking, the best way to reduce waste flow is to reduce our consumption at all levels. This strategy touches on almost every aspect of our lives, from the number and size of the vehicles we drive to the houses we live in, the food we eat, the products we buy in the grocery store and everywhere else, and so on. And the same general strategies that work for consumers also work for government and business. The savings can be enormous. We'll be looking at these issues throughout the rest of the book. But I'll mention just a few obvious areas to get you thinking right now.

Packaging

This is one area where we've made some progress over the years. Especially in Europe. But there's still room for a lot of improvement in this country. Theoretically, most manufacturers could produce products that are surrounded by less packaging. Unfortunately, most traditional marketing techniques have followed the "bigger is better" school of thinking. This provides more room for advertising and catching the buyer's eye. It also means an enormous waste of materials, where the packaging is often twice the size—or more—of the product it covers. We can give manufacturers a lot of incentive to cut back on unnecessary packaging by refusing to buy overpackaged products.

Green Tips

One of the most effective ways you can convince manufacturers to reduce unnecessary packaging is to refuse to buy their products until they respond to your concerns. If you decide not to buy something because of overpackaging, contact the manufacturer and tell them why you made your decision. It doesn't take too many customer complaints before most companies take action.

Materials

In addition to cutting back on the amount of packaging, another important way of reducing waste is to persuade manufacturers to redesign products to use fewer materials. Sometimes they don't even need to be prompted. Aluminum cans are a good example of this. When aluminum cans first appeared on the market, a pound of aluminum was needed to produce 10 cans. Over the years, the number of cans made from that pound of aluminum has more than tripled as the cans have become thinner and thinner.

There are other strategies to reducing materials consumption as well. But the main point is that no product or package should use more resources than is absolutely necessary to get the job done. We'll look at many more ways of reducing materials consumption in the next few chapters.

Reuse Something

Now we come to the second most effective of the Three Rs—reuse. Although there are countless ideas and strategies for reuse, the concept is really quite simple. Reuse minimizes waste and maximizes our use of resources. And just like reducing, reuse helps us to get more for our money and is just as valuable a strategy for individuals as it is for business and government.

Reuse is often confused with recycling, but they really are very different strategies. There are two types of reuse: primary and secondary. Primary reuse implies using an item again for the original purpose, like retreading a tire. With secondary reuse, an item like a used tire is put to some other purpose—say, in a playground.

But the definition of reuse expands well beyond retreading tires. It also includes repairing things instead of throwing them out, borrowing or renting things, selling them if you no longer need them, or even donating them to charity.

Why Reuse?

Considering how many resources it takes to manufacture a product in the first place and how much waste results from the process, it's clear that products should be made to last as long as possible. And reusing things for their full lifespan is far more effective than collecting, sorting, shipping, crushing, melting, purifying, and refabricating recycled materials.

If you just double the lifespan of a product, you cut the energy and materials consumption, as well as waste and pollution, in half. Best yet, you are also probably going to save money at the same time. It's a win-win strategy. I'll tell you much more about reuse later in the book.

Recycle Something

The third environmental R is recycling. As I've already noted, recycling is the least effective of the Three Rs, but it still plays an important role in the environmental picture. Despite the fact that it is at the bottom of the list, recycling is one of the best environmental success stories of the last few decades.

Recycling, including composting, diverted 57 million tons away from landfills and incinerators in 1996. That's up from 34 million tons in 1990, representing a 67 percent increase in just six years. Today, roughly 9,000 recycling programs serve about half of the U.S. population. These programs, along with drop-off and buy-back centers, resulted in a diversion of 31.5 percent of the country's solid waste in 1999.

But just what is recycling? That depends on how broadly or narrowly you want to define it. For our purposes, we'll call it any process in which waste materials are collected, manufactured into new material, and used or sold again in the form of new products or raw materials.

Chart showing the percentages of municipal solid waste (MSW) for recycling, incineration, and landfilling in 1999.

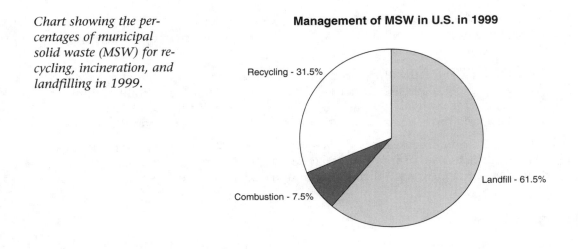

Management of MSW in U.S. in 1999

Recycling - 31.5%

Landfill - 61.5%

Combustion - 7.5%

Why Recycle?

Most of the same benefits of reduction also apply to recycling. By recycling, we conserve precious resources, save energy, reduce pollution, reduce the need for new landfills and incinerators, and save money.

But in addition to those benefits, recycling offers some additional advantages. Recycling supplies valuable raw materials to industry that would otherwise have to be obtained from virgin sources. Recycling also creates jobs. Since recycled materials must be collected, sorted, and processed, it's a fairly labor-intensive activity. While that can be viewed as a problem, it does represent additional employment opportunities.

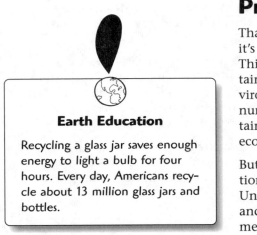

Earth Education

Recycling a glass jar saves enough energy to light a bulb for four hours. Every day, Americans recycle about 13 million glass jars and bottles.

Promote Sustainability

That takes care of the Three Rs for the present. Now it's time to introduce you to the Big S—sustainability. This is not a new idea. For almost two decades "sustainability" has been the main philosophy of most environmental and conservation groups. It comes in a number of variations: sustainable development, sustainable use, sustainable communities, sustainable economies, and so on.

But just what is sustainability? One of the best definitions of the term was put forward in 1987 by the United Nations World Commission on Environment and Development, which said that sustainability means "meeting the needs of the present without compromising the ability of future generations to meet their own needs." That sounds sensible enough. But putting this seemingly simple idea into practice has been anything but simple. The devil is in the details, as the saying goes.

And, of course, reducing, reusing, and recycling are all specific strategies generally aimed at helping us to live more sustainably. But sustainability goes beyond the Three Rs to include a vast range of challenging—and exciting—fields such as renewable energy, transportation, living patterns, population issues, green plans, and much more. We'll look at all of these issues in the chapters contained in Part 5, "A Sustainable Future."

But for the moment, the main thing to remember is that promoting and supporting the wide range of sustainable projects, programs, initiatives, and ideas being proposed and implemented, both here and abroad, is one of the best ways you can help save the environment.

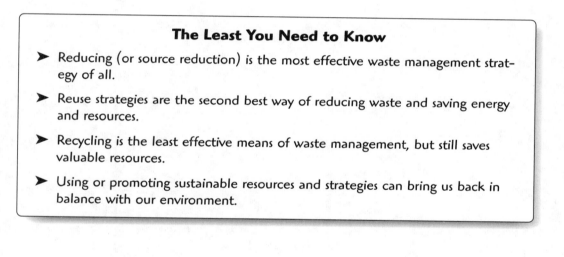

The Least You Need to Know

➤ Reducing (or source reduction) is the most effective waste management strategy of all.

➤ Reuse strategies are the second best way of reducing waste and saving energy and resources.

➤ Recycling is the least effective means of waste management, but still saves valuable resources.

➤ Using or promoting sustainable resources and strategies can bring us back in balance with our environment.

Part 2

Reduce Your Use

Now that you've got a good idea of the problems we face, it's time to look at some solutions. We'll start with the first of the Three Rs of the environmental movement— reduce. We'll take a closer look at the many forms of reduction that are the most direct path to a greener planet. But I'll also explain why there are so many rocks and potholes in the way.

Since we are surrounded by so many opportunities for reducing waste at home, I'll focus on home-based suggestions that you can start using immediately. And since food is such an important subject, we'll go into the kitchen and take a hard look at what we eat. Then, we'll look at ways of eating better while reducing damage to the environment—and ourselves—at the same time.

Then, I'll take you on a shopping trip and show you how various reduction strategies can help you change your buying habits—for the better. Along the way, we'll look at some things that you should consider before you make a purchase. After that, we'll head back home, unplug the TV, and go have some fun. Finally, we'll look at ways some folks are reducing lots of things and living better at the same time.

Chapter 7

The (Not So) Quick Fix

In This Chapter

➤ Why source reduction is the best way to cut waste

➤ Why source reduction is the hardest strategy to implement

➤ How much we really consume

➤ Why we have the largest ecological footprint on the planet

➤ Source reduction and your home

Benjamin Franklin seemed to have had a useful comment on almost every subject. "An ounce of prevention is worth a pound of cure," was excellent advice in Franklin's time. It's still good advice today. Remarkably, Franklin's eighteenth-century observation sums up the main advantages of twenty-first-century source reduction perfectly.

Now, I'm not going to claim that old Ben was an environmentalist, although he certainly took a dim view of the evils of over-consumption. "Buy what thou hast no need of, and ere long thou shalt sell thy necessities," he said in Poor Richard's Almanac. The main point is that he clearly understood the advantages of dealing with a problem at its source, rather than waiting to clean up a huge mess later on. It's the same thing with waste today. Reducing it in the first place is far more effective—and a lot less expensive—than trying to deal with it after it has occurred.

We'll take Ben's advice to heart in this chapter and explore the idea of preventing or reducing waste in many different ways. I'll explain why source reduction is so important, and why it's not being used as effectively as it should be. Then, I'll briefly tell you about some key reduction targets—packaging and hazardous wastes. I'll also explain what an ecological footprint is, and why ours is so big. Finally, we'll bring source reduction home—literally.

Fast Track to a Greener Planet

As I mentioned earlier, source reduction is the best strategy to dramatically reduce our waste stream. This is because it reduces the problem at its source, so there's less mess to clean up afterward. The Environmental Protection Agency, in fact, lists source reduction as the number one initiative to address municipal solid waste issues. Even the National Recycling Coalition agrees, admitting that, "Ton for ton, source reduction is more valuable to society than recycling."

On a personal level, source reduction can be a real money saver, too, if you decide to buy fewer things, or perhaps not to buy certain products at all. It saves money because you didn't spend it in the first place on stuff that you didn't really need anyway. And it saves energy because the stuff you are now happily living without didn't need to be manufactured or transported. And the stuff that wasn't manufactured didn't need the raw materials that cause so much pollution and environmental damage when they are cut, mined, or otherwise extracted. Reducing logging and mining alone would save huge amounts of energy, since these activities consume 75 percent of energy used by industry in some countries. The environmental ripple effect of deciding to consume less is dramatic.

Green Tips

Source reduction can save you money while you save the environment. It's a win–win strategy— if we buy less stuff, we spend less money. At the same time, fewer products need to be manufactured from limited natural resources.

And the benefits of source reduction extend to communities and businesses as well. Reducing waste can help reduce or at least stabilize taxes in your local community. This is because the costs of preventing waste are basically zero, while the costs of recycling and landfilling can be high. This should leave more money for important things like education, fire and police services, and social programs. Source reduction offers a lot of potential benefits for almost everyone.

Easier Said Than Done

As I've also mentioned earlier, reducing is the hardest strategy to implement because it hits so close to home—in fact right in our home—and forces us to confront our long-standing habits of over-consumption as individuals and as a society. We'll begin to examine some of these issues later in this chapter.

But the problem extends well beyond our homes. It expands into almost every aspect of how—and even where—we live. Especially in suburbia. The vast sprawling suburban regions many of us now live in are enormously wasteful of resources. It takes many more miles of water and sewer pipes, electric and telephone lines, paved roads, and so on, to serve a widely dispersed population than it does to serve the same number of people in a relatively compact town or city. And you don't have to be an economist or an ecologist to understand that this is expensive, both financially and environmentally. But suggestions to reverse this trend have met with strong resistance, especially from landowners and developers who stand to profit from a continuation of current sprawl trends.

But that's not the only problem. There has been a lot of resistance to many source reduction strategies and other environmental initiatives from powerful interest groups who feel threatened by them. Landfill owners, who want to encourage the dumping of garbage in their facilities instead of recycling and other conservation strategies, are a prime example. This does not help efforts aimed at waste reduction. Companies whose products or activities are harmful to the environment are another example. And many of these businesses have a lot of money to promote their corporate agendas, and they're not bashful about using it.

It should come as no big surprise that money talks—especially in Washington, D.C.—where well-financed lobbyists have an enormous amount of influence over the folks who are supposed to be representing our interests. It's no wonder that so many environmental initiatives have such an uphill battle to contend with in our nation's capital and elsewhere around the country.

And most of these problems relate to our deeply ingrained "frontier" mentality I mentioned in Chapter 2, "Something Old, Something New," which views resources and the planet's capacity to absorb wastes as almost limitless. And also, unfortunately, this relates to the seemingly limitless capacity for human greed that values short-term profit over long-term consequences.

Earth Education

Americans have doubled the subdivision of farmland, forests, and other open space during the 1990s, according to a report released by the USDA in December 1999. This development has driven up land values, supplying a windfall to farmers and other landowners who live near cities and who choose to sell out. But many critics say that this is hurting the environment and the quality of life in and around these cities.

Old Habits Die Hard

So, even though source reduction makes a lot of sense in theory, in practice it's not so easy to achieve. One of the key things that has to happen before source reduction can reach its true potential is a major shift in thinking, away from the frontier vision of limitless resources to a system that is sustainable in the long run. This would mean a society that makes efficient use of limited resources while minimizing its impact on the environment. And we're still a very long way off from that vision.

Although it's easy to become discouraged by the many glaring examples of wasteful and short-sighted economic, political, and even social thinking that surround us every day, there are some hopeful signs that a few of these old patterns and habits are beginning to change.

Frustrated by a lack of political leadership on these issues at the national level, many Americans are beginning to take matters into their own hands and are starting to integrate environmental concerns into their daily lives. This is just the sort of fundamental shift that is needed to turn any fringe cause into a mainstream movement. I'll show you how to begin to take matters into *your* own hands in a moment.

But source reduction and its associated strategies also make sense for communities and businesses. And many people in these sectors have decided to take matters into their hands, too. It is at this level that some of the most dramatic progress has actually been made in this country and abroad. I'll tell you about these exciting new developments later in the book.

Green Tips

If we shift our thinking away from the idea of limitless resources to an efficient, sustainable use of resources, we can make substantial progress in reducing waste. This includes figuring out ways of doing more with less throughout the economy, from the vehicles we drive to the houses we live in, and from production systems in factories to entire cities and societies.

Eliminate That Waste

Still, reduction is the hardest of the Three Rs to get a handle on. That's because it means not using what we don't need and also using less of what we do need. And because measuring less of something is a lot harder than counting numbers of recycled bottles, or tons of recycled newsprint, for example, it's also initially more difficult to detect the results of our efforts. And the actual rewards in terms of environmental benefits are somewhat elusive as well, because they tend to be somewhat long term. How do you measure a tree that wasn't cut down because you cut back on your excessive use of paper?

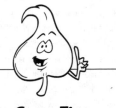

Green Tips

Packaging and hazardous waste are two important areas where individual consumers can make a real difference when they get involved. Refusing to buy overpackaged or hazardous materials, or buying more environmentally friendly substitutes are very powerful strategies for effective source reduction.

Nevertheless, whether or not we can immediately see the results of our efforts, we have to try to eliminate waste in whatever ways we can. While there are many different strategies for source reduction that I'll be talking about, there are two areas where we can have a big impact as individual consumers: packaging and hazardous waste. These are two enormously important issues.

Packaging

Traditionally, most people didn't pay much attention to packaging; they tended to focus mainly on the contents. But because packaging makes up such a significant part of this country's municipal solid waste—roughly 33 percent—it's easy to see why it has received more and more attention in recent years. Considering the huge amount of materials this represents, it's important that we learn how to make informed decisions regarding the use, reuse, and eventual disposal of packaging. We'll revisit packaging later in the book.

Hazardous Waste

You will recall that I described a wide range of hazardous wastes in Chapter 5, "The Land We Live On"—everything from toxic industrial chemicals to nuclear waste. The pollution that results from this kind of waste is an enormous—and growing—problem around the world.

But you might be surprised to learn that the typical American home often contains gallons of hazardous or toxic liquids and other hazardous household products. While that might not sound like much, if you multiply a few gallons by millions of households across the country, it begins to add up to a substantial amount. Especially if it is disposed of improperly.

And traditionally, much of that hazardous waste ended up in landfills. In fact, the Environmental Protection Agency is generally more concerned about the hazardous waste in landfills than with the landfills themselves. Consequently, reducing toxic waste, whether it's located in the home or elsewhere, is a large part of the source reduction picture. We'll look at hazardous waste again.

Do We Really Need to Reduce?

But do we *really* need to reduce our consumption in this country? Yes, I'm afraid there's no escaping that conclusion. Let me explain it to you in a way that brings the issue home. Literally. Imagine for a moment a pile of materials that you—as an average American—normally would use in a day, piled on your kitchen table. A couple of pounds, perhaps, that might fit in a paper grocery bag?

Think again. This pile would contain the wood for your morning newspaper, the chemicals for your bath soap, shampoo, and the synthetic fabrics in your clothing (the grocery bag on the kitchen table just overflowed). Then there's the day's share of plastics and metals in your car, pickup truck, or sport-utility vehicle, and your household appliances. And don't forget your daily share of stone and gravel in the concrete in your office building or place of employment, as well as the streets you drive on. That's followed by the things you don't see, such as the fertilizer used by farmers to grow your food, and the rock and earth that were removed to extract your share of metals and minerals. The list goes on and on.

By now, the kitchen table is probably groaning under its load. In fact, if it isn't very sturdy, the table might have collapsed under the weight, because the total pile comes to over 220 pounds—*a day*. That's over 3 *tons* a month, 37 tons a year, according to the Worldwatch Institute.

That's almost unbelievable. But it's true. And by now, your whole house or apartment building probably would have collapsed into the basement under that load. And that pile of stuff on the table was just your share. Multiply that by the number of people in your household to get your family's total share of resources. What's more, the national total comes to around 10 billion tons of material a year. It's pretty staggering.

Earth Education

Americans consume around 10 billion tons of materials every year. That represents about a third of the total materials used in the global economy. The other industrial nations in Europe, as well as Japan, account for most of the rest of global materials consumption.

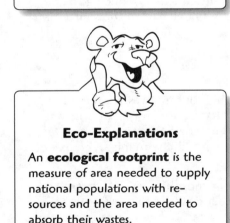

Eco-Explanations

An **ecological footprint** is the measure of area needed to supply national populations with resources and the area needed to absorb their wastes.

Our Trash-Filled Footprint

When viewed from this perspective, it's clear that we need to dig ourselves out from under this mountain of wasted resources before we consume ourselves into an ecological dead end. Which brings up another important concept that will help you to look at this issue from a slightly different angle—our *ecological footprint*.

Let me explain. The footprint measures our impact on nature. In order to live, we consume natural resources. Every one of us has an impact on the planet. This isn't necessarily bad as long as we don't take more from the Earth than it has to offer. The ecological footprint measures our consumption of nature. It shows how much productive land and water we occupy to produce all the resources we consume and to take in all the waste we create.

As you might guess, Americans, with just 4.5 percent of the world's population, have the largest ecological footprint of around 25 acres per person, according to United Nations statistics. And because we consume so many resources and produce so much waste in this country, our ecological footprint is larger than our physical national boundaries. By comparison, the ecological footprint for the Netherlands is 14 acres, Japan is 10 acres, and Mexico, 6. Bangladesh comes in at the bottom of the list at just 1 acre per person.

One of the key findings of the studies that contained these figures is that today the human population as a whole uses over a third more resources and ecological services than what nature can regenerate. What that means, in simple terms, is that we're already taking more than the planet has to offer. We're stealing resources from our children and grandchildren. Sooner or later this problem will come home to haunt us—or what's more likely, our offspring. And speaking of home, that's where we're headed next.

Home, Sweet Home

Okay, I've described source reduction in general terms. Now it's time to bring this idea down to a more personal level. Your home. One of the best ways that you and I (and everybody else) can help save the environment is to take a good hard look at our daily habits at home to see what kind of an impact they have on the environment (it's a lot larger than you might think). Then, based on that knowledge, we can establish new habits that will help make things a little better. Multiply those changes by 275 million Americans and we can have quite an impact here and around the planet. But where to start?

Choosing the Right Home

If you're not quite sure where to start, here's a hint: Let's begin with the biggest issue of all—choosing the right home in the first place. The home has long been a symbol of the American dream. Unfortunately, in recent years it has also become a symbol of the "more is better" corruption of that dream. In the last 50 years, the size of the average American home has roughly doubled, while the average size of the American family has declined from 3.5 to 3.1 members. Somehow, this just doesn't make sense.

The size of our houses is important because home construction represents the second biggest part of our ecological footprint (after transportation) and represents about 25 percent of consumer impact on the environment.

Housing, along with transportation and food, in fact, are three main areas where you and I can make a big difference in source reduction, according to Eric Brown, communications director of the Center for A New American Dream in Takoma Park, MD. "As consumers, we use housing, transportation, and food every day," he says. "And the choices we make have an impact that you can trace."

But the trend toward huge new houses located in suburban sprawl developments in recent years is a matter of special concern for Brown. "The raw materials required to produce a house of 2,000 square feet or more are enormous," he observes. "Then there is the need to heat and cool it, to say nothing of the land required for the building lot. All of these things are magnified by the size of the house."

Earth Education

The median size of a new house built in the United States in 1949 was 1,100 square feet. In 1970, the figure had risen to 1,385 square feet. By 1997, it was up to 1,975 square feet. Now, it's more than 2,000 square feet.

So, even a simple decision on your part not to buy such a large house can have an enormous ripple effect on resources and on the environment. Multiply that decision by millions of our neighbors, and the long-term effects could be profound. This doesn't mean that the home-building sector of the economy would collapse. Not at all. It just means that contractors would be building smaller houses. And we'd be living quite comfortably in them. Now, I said I was going to tell you how to take matters into your own hands. This is as good a place as any to start.

Decisions, Decisions, Decisions

Okay, let's say you're in the market for a new home. When you're trying to make up your mind about that home, there are many things to consider. The Center for A New American Dream (www.newdream.org) has some good suggestions:

➤ Size—Do I really need a 2,000-square-foot home and 2.5 baths and a guest room?

➤ Location—Does this home contribute to sprawl?

➤ Is there a sense of community?

➤ Will I be car-dependent here?

➤ Efficiency—Have I considered what resources will go into building my house and what will be necessary to sustain it throughout its life?

➤ Have I considered all my options, including solar panels, top insulation, and other forms of eco-design?

I think it would also be logical to question whether you need a three- or four-car garage and any number of other symbols of conspicuous consumption—or in this case, conspicuous storage—of all the stuff we seem intent on accumulating these days.

An Older Home

Even if a new home is not in your immediate future, there are a number of questions you can ask yourself about an older home that relate to source reduction:

➤ What steps can I take to retrofit this house that will make it more energy efficient?

➤ Would solar hot water or solar electrical panels make sense?

➤ What can I do to reduce water consumption?

➤ What can I do in terms of landscaping that will make this house cooler in the summer and warmer in the winter?

You can actually do quite a few things to an older home that will bring it more in line with current energy efficiency and conservation standards. We'll look at a lot of them in the next chapter.

Waste Not, Want Not

Okay, I'll admit it: Source reduction is probably the toughest issue to deal with because it affects all of us in so many ways. And we'll be looking at many of them in the next four chapters. Looking honestly at these issues encourages us to begin thinking about them. And once we start to think about them, we may be moved to take them to heart and begin to act. And that can lead us to start making hard, sometimes uncomfortable choices. But making uncomfortable choices now is far better than being forced into making impossible choices later because we failed to act soon enough.

I hasten to add that there is no one "right" way to approach these subjects. Just the way that works for you. Every honest attempt toward source reduction, however large or small, is both worthwhile and worth the effort. In the end, whatever approach you take, I guess it all boils down to the old saying, "Waste not, want not." And I think that's something that old Ben Franklin would agree with.

The Least You Need to Know

➤ Reducing our consumption is the best way to cut waste and pollution.

➤ It's hard to break old consumption habits.

➤ We are currently using more ecological resources than nature can regenerate.

➤ We can begin to reduce our excessive consumption with our choice of a home.

Chapter 8

A Houseful of Savings

In This Chapter

➤ Reducing waste starts at home

➤ How to save energy

➤ Ways to save water

➤ How to stop heat loss

➤ Reducing or eliminating hazardous waste

You've heard the old saying, "There's no place like home." When it comes to reducing waste, there really is no place like home, because this is where we use the most energy, water, and products as individual consumers. And most of this consumption contributes to the many environmental problems I've told you about in the first part of this book. That's the bad news.

Now the good news. Because we tend to be so wasteful, we have numerous opportunities to save a lot of resources by reducing our levels of consumption—while saving money at the same time. The planet wins, and so does your household checking account when it comes time to pay your monthly bills. That's a great combination that's hard to beat.

In this chapter, I'm going to offer lots of suggestions for saving energy right in your own home, and share some of my own experiences with you as well. We'll look at the benefits of energy-efficient appliances and compact fluorescent light bulbs. Then I'll tell you about a variety of water conservation strategies and the advantages of an energy audit. Finally, we'll look under the kitchen sink and find some interesting ways to reduce hazardous waste.

Start Saving at Home

Enough talk. Now it's time for some action. In the last chapter I mentioned how you can make a major source reduction decision about the size of your house. That's fine if you are about to buy a new home, but if you're already happily settled down you'll want to know how you can help in other ways. And it really doesn't matter if you own your home, or rent a condo or an apartment—many of the strategies we'll be looking at can be used in almost any setting.

Energy Conservation

Let's start with energy conservation. As long as our major utilities continue to burn fossil fuels for electrical generation, one of the best ways to reduce global warming—and your utility bills at the same time—is to cut back on your energy use. It's a lot easier than you might imagine. In many cases it's simply a matter of consciously thinking about how you use your energy resources every day, and then taking appropriate action.

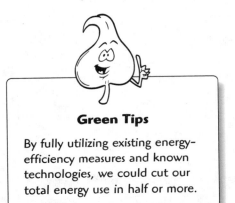

Green Tips

By fully utilizing existing energy-efficiency measures and known technologies, we could cut our total energy use in half or more.

We all make choices about when to use energy and when not to. Every time you fail to turn off the light when you leave a room, or fill the kettle to the top to boil water for a single cup of coffee or tea, you are making an environmental choice. Where you set your thermostat for heating in the winter or for cooling in the summer, and how you use windows, shades, and fans can all make a difference—for better or worse—on your consumption of energy. But you can save on energy in lots of other ways as well. Let's start by taking a look at the many appliances in our homes.

Energy Efficient Appliances

Replacing older, less energy-efficient appliances as they wear out with newer, more efficient models can result in big long-term savings. The most important thing to remember when you buy an appliance is that, in addition to the initial cost, you must also pay for its operating expenses for as long as you own it. If it's an energy hog, those costs can quickly add up to far more than the original price of the appliance.

The ENERGY STAR program, a collaboration between the U.S. Department of Energy, the Environmental Protection Agency, and many manufacturers, is designed to prevent pollution by helping consumers buy products that use less energy. Check out the ENERGY STAR site (www.energystar.gov) for lots of information on this program.

But there are also some simple, common sense things that you can do to get the most out of your appliances regardless of their age. Let's take a tour of your home and see what we can do to maximize the efficiency of your appliances.

Cool Stuff

We'll start in the kitchen. If your home is anything like mine, the refrigerator is probably the most frequently visited appliance (to say nothing of its utility as a bulletin board). The energy efficiency of refrigerators has improved dramatically over the past 20 years. A typical new refrigerator with automatic defrost and a top-mounted freezer uses less than 650 *kilowatt hours* (kWh) per year (the typical model sold in the early 1970s used nearly 2,000 kWh per year). But even a new energy-efficient model can run you about $100 a year in electric charges, so efficiency is obviously an important consideration.

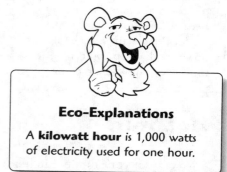

Eco-Explanations

A **kilowatt hour** is 1,000 watts of electricity used for one hour.

Here are some tips to get the most out of your refrigerator, whether it's brand new or an old veteran:

➤ Try to locate the refrigerator away from any source of heat, especially away from the stove or a home-heating vent, and out of direct sunlight.

➤ Make sure that the grille or vents for the compressor are clean and not blocked. Clean the vents and grilles once a year to increase efficiency and lifespan.

➤ Excess humidity makes the compressor work harder—and uses more energy. Always keep liquids and food covered or wrapped, and wipe excess moisture from containers. This reduces humidity.

➤ Be sure the door gasket makes a tight seal. Check it by closing the door on a dollar bill. If you can pull the bill out with no resistance, it's time to replace the seal.

➤ If your refrigerator has a power-saving or summer-winter switch, use it to save electricity.

➤ If your refrigerator has a freezer, it operates more efficiently when it's at least two-thirds full. If it's not, try refilling plastic milk or juice containers with water and use them to temporarily fill the space.

➤ If you have an older model freezer, don't let frost build up.

➤ Automatic ice trays can be a power drain. Old-fashioned ice trays are generally a more energy-efficient way of making ice.

Green Tips

Let hot dishes cool before you put them in the refrigerator or freezer. There's no point in paying for the electricity to cool down foods when you can do it for free on the kitchen counter.

➤ Think about what you need from the refrigerator or freezer *before* you open the door.

Refrigerators with freezers mounted on the top or bottom typically use about 12 percent less energy than side-by-side door designs. Bottom-mounted freezers (which are harder to find in stores) are the most efficient design. Also, in the case of separate freezers, chest models are more efficient than uprights.

If you are in the market for a new refrigerator or freezer, check with your local utility to see if they offer rebates or other incentives for the purchase of energy-efficient models. You might be able to save some cool cash while saving the environment.

Hot Stuff

Appliances that use heat to perform their work are generally the heaviest users of energy in your home. Kitchen ranges, clothes dryers, hot water heaters, and baseboard electric heaters all make your electric meter spin like crazy. Even if you use natural gas for most of these needs, it's still a major part of your energy usage. Let's take a quick look at each of these appliances.

Whether you use an electric or gas stove to cook your food, here are a number of tips that will save you energy and money:

➤ Cover your pots with lids to prevent up to two thirds of potential heat loss.

➤ Use the smallest frying pan (and burner) necessary for the item you are cooking.

➤ Use a pressure cooker when appropriate. Cooking time can be reduced by 50 to 75 percent.

➤ If you are using the oven, consider cooking several dishes at the same time.

➤ Turn off the oven a few minutes before the food is cooked and use the remaining heat to finish the job.

Your clothes dryer is a big energy waster—especially if you use it inefficiently. The best strategy of all, of course, is to hang your clothes outside and use the big, free, solar-powered clothes dryer in the sky. This is admittedly tough in cold, cloudy northern climates—like Vermont—where your clothes would freeze solid in about 30 seconds for a good part of the year. Hanging your clothes up indoors to dry on a folding drying rack is another alternative if you've got the space to do it.

If you *must* use your regular clothes dryer, here are some tips to get the most out of it:

➤ Run full loads, but not too full, because the dryer will not operate efficiently if overfilled.

➤ Try drying two or more loads in a row, so you can take advantage of a preheated machine for subsequent loads.

➤ Don't overdry your clothes. Use your machine's moisture sensor if it has one.

➤ If your machine has a cool-down cycle, use it to take advantage of the remaining heat to finish drying.

➤ Always clean the lint filter before every new load.

Earth Education

Water heating consumes 15 to 30 percent of the energy used in your home, depending on your water-usage habits and the number of people in your family.

A hot water heater is another appliance where you can save on energy and costs, regardless of whether it's heated by electricity, gas, or oil. First of all, the capacity of your hot water heater is important. Your heater should be able to provide enough hot water for the heaviest usage of the day.

The ability of a hot water heater to meet peak demands is called its "first hour rating." If there are only two of you in your family, 30 gallons of hot water an hour might be more than enough capacity. On the other hand, if there are six members in your family, a 70-gallon-per-hour tank might be required. The *actual* size you will need depends on your hot water usage habits. If you are thrifty in your use of hot water, you might be able to get by on a smaller tank. Matching the size of your water heater to your actual needs can save you both money and aggravation.

In addition, here are some things you can do to reduce your water heater's energy consumption:

➤ Turn down the temperature. A thermostat setting over 140°F is wasteful and can even be dangerous in a shower. Somewhere between 115 and 120°F is adequate for most purposes.

➤ Insulate the hot water tank and pipes. Inexpensive easy-to-install insulating jackets and pipe wraps are available at most hardware stores.

➤ If you are going to be away for more than a few days, use your heater's vacation setting if there is one, or just turn it off.

➤ If you need a new water heater, consider a newer tankless model that typically saves 15 percent in standby energy loss, and never rusts out because there's no tank.

Many utilities offer free or low-cost water heater jackets and pipe insulation supplies or services. Check with your utility to see what is available in your area. You may find a real hot deal on these supplies, just like I did. They were free.

Round and Round

One of the most exciting developments in clothes washers is the reemergence of horizontal-axis (front-loading) units in this country. These models use substantially less water and also get clothes much cleaner than top-loaders. And since the spin cycles of these front-loaders generally are faster, they remove more moisture from your clothes, reducing the amount of energy needed to dry them. Front-loaders tend to be more expensive than top-loaders, but the long-term benefits are substantial. If your old washer has finally died, check out a front-loader.

Regardless of the type of clothes washer you have, here are some helpful energy-saving hints:

➤ Low-temperature washing saves both energy and money. Avoid the hot water cycle whenever possible, and always use the cold water rinse.

➤ Try to wash full loads, or, if possible, adjust the setting to use less water for smaller loads.

➤ Try to locate your washer as close to the hot water heater as possible and insulate the hot water pipe between the two.

➤ If you have a stubborn stain, try a pre-rinse or laundry stain remover rather than the hot water setting on your washer.

Many utilities are offering rebates and other incentives to encourage the purchase of front-loading washers. Check them out. You may be able to wring out some additional savings.

Green Tips

Just switching your water setting from hot to warm can cut your energy use for your clothes washer in half. Switching from warm to cold saves even more.

Earth Education

Old-fashioned incandescent light bulbs are highly inefficient; they convert 90 percent of the electricity they use into heat and only 10 percent into visible light. The typical household spends about $110 per year on electricity for incandescent bulbs.

A Bright Idea

While our government dithers over complying with tougher international treaties designed to reduce global warming, you and I can just go ahead and take direct personal action. Since lighting accounts for about 15 percent of electricity used in our homes, anything we can do to make our lighting more efficient can result in savings.

Old-fashioned incandescent light bulbs are highly inefficient. Consequently, installing new compact fluorescent lamps (CFLs), which use one-quarter to one-third as much electricity, will save you both energy and money. And they last up to 10 times as long as incandescent bulbs.

Now, I admit it, I used to hate fluorescent lighting. I still do, especially the harsh, ugly, flickering sort of fluorescent lights you frequently find in institutional or commercial settings. So I resisted getting CFLs for years. Then, as part of an energy conservation initiative, our local electrical utility offered a free energy audit of our home—and best of all—free CFLs for our most frequently used lighting fixtures.

Being the cheapskate that I am, it was too good a deal to pass up. So, we gave it a try. The utility representative carefully matched the size and style of bulb for the particular lighting fixture and its intended purpose. Now I'm a believer. Frankly, I never even noticed the difference in the light—because there really wasn't any. But I did notice that our electric bill went down in the months that followed. Even if you have to pay for your bulbs, the "return" on your investment is between 25 and 40 percent a year. Don't wonder about this strategy. Just do it.

Beat Heat Loss

Another great way of saving money and the environment is to cut your heat loss from your home with a variety of different strategies. This is especially important in northern climates where winter temperatures are low and heating bills are high. But many of these strategies can be helpful almost anywhere.

In most areas, your local utility or energy office will offer a free energy audit of your home. Or, you can perform your own. Try typing "energy audit" into your favorite Web browser, and you'll have numerous possibilities to choose from. Energy audits will help you find many different ways to save energy and money. We've already discussed some of these strategies earlier in this chapter. Here are more, specifically related to heat loss.

Green Tips

Contact your local utility to see if they offer in-home energy audits. Some will do it for free (or at very low cost), and what they find can save you big money in your energy bills.

It's Great to Insulate

Adding insulation to parts of your home that need it is one of the best ways to cut down on energy loss. Properly installed insulation can save you up to 40 percent on your total energy use and can pay for itself in reduced costs in just a few years.

Although insulation by itself does not heat or cool, it does keep heat from escaping from your home. Ceiling insulation in your attic area is one of the most effective ways of keeping your heating dollars from going through the roof. Other places to insulate include exterior walls, walls between heated and unheated spaces, as well as floors over unheated or outside spaces.

Plug Those Leaks

Hidden air leaks are among the largest source of heat loss in older homes. You should consider weatherproofing your home by caulking and sealing cracks in walls or in holes around pipes and wiring. You'll also want to add weather stripping around exterior doors and windows, especially if they are old and drafty. This keeps excess air from passing in or out of your home. These steps can reduce your energy bills by as much as 15 percent, and at the very least will make your home more comfortable. If you need a quick fix for a drafty door or window, you can use an old bath towel rolled up to temporarily block the air until you can install proper weather stripping.

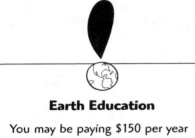

Earth Education

You may be paying $150 per year to heat and cool the outdoors if your windows aren't energy efficient. Spending your hard-earned money on indoor temperature control makes a lot more sense.

Draw the Drapes

Installing insulated window shades or quilts is another great way of cutting down on heat loss, especially if your windows are old and not very energy efficient. Shades and drapes are also useful for screening out the hot summer sun to help keep your home cooler. As useful as these strategies are, there is an even more effective way of achieving the same benefits with less daily labor on your part—high-performance windows.

High-Performance Windows

Choosing the right windows for your home and climate is important because they can have such a huge effect on your home's comfort and energy use. Windows account for around 25 percent of the heating and cooling bills in a typical home due to heat loss in the winter and heat gain in the summer.

The huge availability of high-performance windows these days can cut your energy bills and reduce pollution at its source. These windows feature double or triple glazing, special coatings, insulating gas between panes, and better-insulated frames.

If you are building a new home or are adding to your existing home, these windows are a must, right from the start. But if your old windows are in need of replacement, new high-tech windows can help cut your utility bills, too.

Water Conservation

As a society, we tend to waste huge amounts of water. We can reduce much of this waste by simply becoming more aware of how we consume water in and around the house, and then cut back on excessive use.

Okay, it's pop quiz time. Question: What's the biggest water consumer in your home? Answer: It may be your toilet. On average, a single person in this country contaminates over 7,500 gallons of fresh water every year to dispose of 160 gallons of sewage. New low-flow toilets are now available in many styles and colors that use 60 percent less water than a traditional model. Some ultra-low flow models use 80 percent less water.

Whether your toilet is new or old, you should also check it for leaks. It's estimated that as many as 40 percent of toilets leak. And many of them are easy to fix by adjusting or replacing the float control at the top or the flapper valve at the bottom of the tank. You can check your toilet to see if it leaks by putting a little food coloring in the tank. If the coloring shows up in the bowl within about 15 minutes (before you flush), you've got a leak.

Also, check your faucets throughout your home. If they leak, fix them. It's usually just a matter of replacing a worn washer or an o-ring. Leaky faucets and toilets can waste hundreds of gallons of water.

Here are some additional tips to save both water and money around the house:

Earth Education

Leaky faucets account for about 5 percent of all indoor water use in the home. It may be more in your home. Communities that have encouraged residents to repair their leaky plumbing have saved huge amounts of water in recent years.

➤ Put a plastic bottle with an inch or two of sand or pebbles, filled with water, in the bottom of your toilet tank (away from the operating mechanism). Over time, this should save hundreds of gallons of water.

➤ Take a shower instead of a bath. A shower generally uses one third the amount of water a bath does.

➤ Take shorter showers. Long, hot showers can waste 5 to 10 gallons of water for every extra minute.

➤ Install water-saving showerheads or flow restrictors.

➤ Fill a glass to rinse your mouth and then turn off the water after you wet your toothbrush. You can easily save a gallon or 2 of water every time you brush.

➤ Don't leave the hot water running while you shave. Either fill the sink with several inches of hot water first, or turn the water on just long enough to rinse your shaver.

Green Tips

Keep a bottle of drinking water from your tap in the refrigerator and use it when you're thirsty. This eliminates the wasteful practice of running tap water to cool it off in the summer.

➤ If you wash dishes by hand, don't leave the water running constantly for rinsing.

The more you think about these strategies, the more ideas you will come up with. I realized that I was wasting a lot of water just standing around waiting for the water to get hot in our upstairs bathroom (it turned out to be a gallon every time). Now I save that water in a plastic one-gallon bucket and use it to refill our humidifier or water houseplants. I'll bet you can think of even better ideas.

But some of the worst examples of wasted water aren't in the home—they're just outside the home in our yards and driveways. And you don't have to look very far for glaring examples.

Here are some ideas for saving water outside the home:

➤ Use a broom to sweep your driveway, sidewalk, and steps, instead of hosing it down. This can save hundreds of gallons.

➤ Don't run the hose while washing your car. Use a pail of soapy water, then turn on the hose just long enough to rinse.

➤ Only water your lawn when it really needs it. Infrequent watering encourages deeper root growth, making your lawn more drought resistant.

➤ You can reduce evaporation by deep soaking your lawn early in the morning before the sun is hot. Early morning is also better because it helps prevent the growth of fungus.

➤ Adding a layer of mulch around trees and plants will slow evaporation of moisture.

➤ Consider planting drought-resistant trees and plants.

And remember, when you save water in or around the home you are generally saving money in two ways—with lower water bills, and with lower energy costs from not heating excess water. Win-win, again.

Hazardous Waste

Finally, we're going to take a peek under your kitchen sink. If it's anything like ours, it's a real catch-all of home cleaning products—many of which aren't so earth-friendly. The furniture polish, floor wax, window cleaner, tile disinfectant, and so on that you use each week contribute to the hazardous waste problem in this country.

Enormous quantities of these products are manufactured every year from toxic chemicals like sulfuric acid, hydrochloric acid, and benzene. Pollution from these chemicals continues to be a problem both in our air and our waters. And when you dispose of the empty—or almost empty—containers, most of them end up in landfills, where the toxins can eventually leach into the groundwater.

One of the best ways of reducing this problem is to stop using these products. Remarkably, most of your general housecleaning needs can be met with a simple homemade recipe:

Planetary Perils

When making your own home cleaning products, never mix ammonia and bleach, which produces an extremely toxic gas.

> 1 gallon hot water
>
> ¹/₄ cup sudsy ammonia
>
> ¹/₄ cup vinegar
>
> 1 tablespoon baking soda

This mixture is safe for virtually any surface, and is easily rinsed with water. If you need a wax stripper, double all ingredients except the water.

Here are a few other nontoxic household cleaning ideas:

➤ A strong solution of vinegar will remove most lime scale from your toilet bowl or bathtub without polluting the water.

➤ Presoak especially soiled clothes in cool water before you put them in the washer to avoid the need for chlorine bleach.

➤ To unclog a drain, try ¹/₄ cup baking soda, followed by ¹/₂ cup vinegar. Close the drain until it stops fizzing, then flush with boiling water.

➤ You can reduce or eliminate many household odors with baking soda rather than commercial air fresheners. Try an open box in your refrigerator; sprinkle a little in your garbage can, or in the diaper pail.

If you don't want to mix your own cleaning products, you may be able to get nontoxic substitutes from your grocery store. If not, try your local natural foods store or co-op. Some companies specialize in manufacturing these products, such as Seventh Generation (www.seventhgen.com) here in Vermont. You can order their safe home-cleaning products and much more online from Green Marketplace (www.greenmarketplace.com). Bio Pac of Nevada (www.bio-pac.com) is another cleaning products manufacturer you might want to check out.

We can reduce waste so many different ways. And I admit that I've really only scratched the surface. I didn't mention replacing paper products such as paper towels and napkins with reusable cloth versions (more on that in Chapter 14, "At Home").

Or strategies for better use of dishwashers. And on and on. I'm sure you can think of many more.

But it's probably obvious by now that each of us can really make a difference in lots of small ways, which, taken together, can add up to big savings—both for us, and for the planet. Remember, "There's no place like home." And the Earth is our only home.

The Least You Need to Know

➤ Reducing waste saves you money while you save the environment.

➤ Energy-efficient appliances pay for themselves in lower operating costs.

➤ Compact fluorescent light bulbs are a great long-term investment, and they reduce electricity use.

➤ You can reduce your use of water in many ways.

➤ An energy audit of your home can help to save you a lot of money on your energy bills.

➤ You can replace virtually all toxic home cleaning products with nontoxic alternatives.

Chapter 9

Food for Thought

In This Chapter

➤ Why we need to change our eating habits

➤ Why much of our commercial food chain doesn't make environmental sense

➤ What's in our food

➤ Why we need to shift our food-buying patterns

➤ The many benefits of food co-ops, community-supported agriculture, and farmers' markets

---

"You are what you eat," the TV commercials tell us. If you believed the seductive images you see, then we'd all be slim, trim, twenty-something, and fashion-model gorgeous. Recent medical studies paint a very different picture, however. One in five adults and one in four children in this country are obese. And while we may be what we eat, what we're eating is killing us in record numbers.

What we are doing to ourselves with our overeating is bad enough, but what we are doing to our environment is even worse. Our chemical-intensive factory-farming approach to food production in this country is ruining our soils, poisoning our water supplies, breeding pesticide-resistant weeds and insects, and fouling the air with the massive fossil-fueled transport system necessary to haul agricultural products from one end of the country to the other.

In the last chapter, we looked at ways to cut waste by reducing consumption around the house. In this chapter, we'll continue that strategy by taking a look at the food we eat. First, we're going to look at waste reduction and waist reduction as related issues.

I'm also going to tell you about where your food comes from, and why you should care. Then we'll look at some healthy food choices, and I'll explain the many benefits of co-ops, Community Supported Agriculture (CSA) programs, and farmers' markets.

The Overfed American

The effects of over-consumption in this country are not just limited to our environment. Our wasteful habits are reflected in our expanding waistlines as well. We're eating too much of the wrong kinds of foods, grown in the wrong places, with the wrong chemicals, pesticides, and fertilizers for the wrong markets. These are two separate but related issues: wasteful over-consumption of food, and wasteful food-production practices.

Part of the solution, of course, is to simply cut back on the amount of food we eat to bring it in line with our actual physical needs. That would help solve the bulging waist problem. But the other part involves a shift away from the food-growing and buying patterns we have become accustomed to. As you'll soon see, this shift will benefit both the environment and us in many ways.

Fat City

Obesity is an epidemic in this country. Although this has been a problem for many years, obesity has soared in the past decade, and now affects nearly one in five adults, according to a group of studies published in the *Journal of the American Medical Association* in late 1999. Even worse, obesity is linked to the deaths of some 300,000 Americans annually.

Eco-Explanations

Obesity, or excessive body fat, generally occurs when the food energy you eat exceeds the food energy you use.

The number of Americans considered obese—defined as more than 30 percent over their ideal body weight—increased from around one in eight in 1991 to nearly one in five in 1998. And the trend is pretty much across the board, with a steady increase in both sexes, all races, all educational levels, and has occurred regardless of smoking status, according to one of the studies.

But the trend toward obesity in school-age children is even more alarming. The surgeon general has said that one in four children are now obese, and describes the situation as an epidemic. I'm afraid he's right. All you have to do is look at kids these days to realize we've got a problem.

Calories to Burn

The continuing growth in the heavy marketing of fast food and junk food, coupled with a lack of exercise, are the key reasons why people in this country are consuming more calories than they burn. Children, in particular, watch more television, sit in front of computers longer, participate in less physical education at school, and tend more often to be driven around in automobiles by their parents instead of walking or riding bicycles, than ever before. Our sprawling suburban living patterns are partially responsible for the automobile piece of this issue (more on that in Chapter 24, "Living Patterns"), but for now I want to focus on food.

Regardless of the reasons, this escalating trend toward over-consumption of food and lack of exercise is extremely unhealthy and needs to be reversed. Remarkably, we find the same general health problems associated with overfed and overweight people as we find with underfed and underweight people. Both of these examples of malnutrition result in the same health effects—increased susceptibility to illness, and reduced life expectancy. And while we're busily eating ourselves to death, millions of other people around the world are starving to death.

Ironically, the healthiest people in the world are not those who consume the most food, but rather, those in the middle who consume less food in general, and less fat-rich livestock products in particular. The life expectancy of the average Italian, for example, is higher than the average American, while eating half the quantity of grain and a lot less red meat than we do. Our unhealthy eating habits are literally killing us.

Planetary Perils

In this country, obesity is the second-leading cause of preventable deaths after smoking, despite the fact that weight-loss products and services are a $33 billion-a-year industry.

Time for Action

Happily, we don't have to wait for the government or anybody else to "do something" about this problem. We can take immediate action ourselves today. Or maybe tomorrow. Or whenever you go food shopping the next time.

Now, don't get me wrong, I'm not advocating a national crash diet. Crash diets don't work for individuals in the long run and they wouldn't work for the country either. What I am suggesting is a gradual, thoughtful shift in both the amount of food we eat, the kind of food we eat, and where it is produced. This will benefit both the environment and us. In order to do this in an informed way, you need to understand where our food comes from.

The Well-Traveled Meal

When you buy your food, do you give much thought to where it comes from? You should. Because where your food was grown has an impact on the environment. Let me explain. The average mouthful of food you eat at the kitchen or dining room table has traveled 1,300 miles before it lands on your plate, according to one estimate. And almost every state in the nation buys 85 to 90 percent of its food from someplace else. This is an absurd situation from both an environmental and local economic standpoint.

Green Tips

Increased local food production for local consumption could add millions of dollars to many states' economies, according to recent studies. Why send your money out of state or overseas when you can help your neighbors?

The out-of-season strawberries and other fruits and vegetables that we eat here in Northern New England probably have come from California, Florida, or any number of foreign countries. Although it's nice to have all these choices in the grocery store, the mass movement of all this food from one part of the globe to another represents an enormous amount of fossil-fueled transportation, which results in a good deal of global warming.

Think Global—Buy Local

I don't know about you, but I've gotten tired of buying food—produce in particular—that looks good in the bins at the supermarket, but tastes about as exciting as card-board. This is due mainly to the fact that a lot of agribusiness produce is designed to look good and to maintain its appearance while it's being shipped from coast to coast, and later, while it's sitting on the shelf. But how this stuff actually tastes is another matter. A few stores actually color some of their fruit to make it look ripe—even if it isn't.

There's a simple solution to this problem: Buy local produce. In Vermont, there has been a statewide campaign to buy local products for many years. I suspect your state probably has a similar program. This strategy makes a lot of sense. Why should you send your hard-earned dollars out of state or even out of country, when you can keep them circulating in your local economy? When you buy locally, you generally support smaller, local businesses, help employ local workers, and reduce the need for shipping products over long distances.

This is a particularly sound strategy for food products—especially farm products. From an environmental standpoint it makes far more sense to produce as much food as possible for local consumption, eliminating the need to waste resources on long-distance shipping. Admittedly, some foods simply can't be grown in certain areas, but it makes no sense for me to buy an ear of sweet corn shipped all the way from the West Coast when there are local farmers right here in Addison County who can supply my needs.

And, yes, that means that I need to eat most of these foods in season, rather than whenever the mood strikes me. But, for me at least, returning to a more natural yearly progression of fresh foods is part of what makes each season special—and delicious. And if that helps the environment and the local economy at the same time, all the better.

Do You Really Want to Eat That?

But the advantages of buying locally produced foods extend well beyond freshness and transportation issues. Increasingly, huge agribusiness companies grow much of the food produced in this country. Like it or not, large farms dominate agricultural production in the United States. Out of two million farms, the largest 8 percent (with sales of more than $250,000 a year) account for 72 percent of output on only 35 percent of the land.

While these corporate entities are obviously very efficient at what they do, their farming practices come at a huge cost to the environment, and raise a number of other troubling questions. Because these farming operations are so huge, they have to rely on heavy mechanization, and even heavier use of chemical fertilizers, pesticides, and herbicides for their crops. And a lot of these chemicals never reach their intended targets, but end up instead on adjacent land or in our water supply.

Planetary Perils

Industrial agricultural practices in this country, which rely heavily on chemical pesticides and fertilizers, damage the soil, deplete the groundwater, pollute the rivers, and encourage topsoil erosion.

Virtually all of these chemicals come from nonrenewable petroleum-based resources. And, as I've mentioned previously, the extraction, transport, and refining of petroleum has its own environmental hazards. Large scale, chemical-dependent agriculture also contributes to serious soil erosion. Millions of tons of prime topsoil have been washed into the Gulf of Mexico and elsewhere as a result.

But there's another problem. The crops these corporations grow have to be able to withstand a lot of mechanical processing. Although some crops are hand picked (often by migrant workers who are sometimes exposed to dangerous herbicides), others are not. In either case, the produce goes through a lot of sorting, treating, and packaging, before being shipped to distant markets. It should come as no great surprise that fruits and vegetables that don't withstand mechanized processing never get planted in the first place, while produce that does is preferred. So what about freshness and good taste—probably the two most important things most people look for in their foods? Good question.

Then there are the troubling—and highly controversial—issues of various types of growth hormones, genetically engineered animals and crops, and other strategies that are popular with many of the huge agribusiness companies and their related chemical and biotech industries. Entire books are written on these subjects. And the debate is just getting started. I'm only going to say that, at the very least, many people view these developments as a move in the wrong direction toward even more chemical-intensive, factory-farm-produced foods.

How Do You Pronounce This?

Now we come to the question of food additives. Because a lot of the food you buy at the supermarket takes a long time to get from producer to consumer, and sometimes sits around in warehouses and distribution centers for a while, it frequently contains any number of additives designed to "maintain product consistency or palatability," "improve or maintain nutritional value," "enhance flavor or impart desired color," and so on. What most of this really means is "longer shelf life."

This longer life is assisted by a number of food additives. It's not unusual to read the ingredients listed on a food label and find such unpronounceable items as: mono- and diglycerides, methyl cellulose, sodium aluminosilicate, propionic acid, butylated hydroxyanisole (BHA), butylated hydroxytoluene (BHT), benzoates, sulfites, sodium nitrite, erythorbates, and fumaric acid. And don't forget the artificial food colors like FD&C Red No. 40, FD&C Yellow No. 6, FD&C Yellow No. 5, and so on.

Earth Education

The Federal Food, Drug, and Cosmetic (FD&C) Act of 1938 gives the Food and Drug Administration (FDA) authority over food and food ingredients. The Food Additives Amendment to the FD&C Act, passed in 1958, requires FDA approval for the use of any additive prior to its inclusion in food.

For many years, there's been a good deal of speculation about what the effects of ingesting this stuff over time might be. Some of the speculation has proven to be unfounded, or at least hard to document. But the fact remains that at least some people are allergic to FD&C Yellow No. 5 (or tartrazine), which may cause hives.

Even more disturbing, however, is the fact that a small segment of the population has been found to develop shortness of breath or fatal shock shortly after exposure to sulfites. Sulfites are capable of producing severe asthma attacks in sulfite-sensitive asthmatics. For that reason, in 1986 the FDA banned the use of sulfites on fresh fruits and vegetables intended to be sold or served raw to consumers. Sulfites, however, are still added to some prepared or packaged foods.

Frankly, I don't care whether the FDA says this stuff is safe or not. I don't want to eat it at all. You have to decide for yourself, but one of the best ways to avoid these food additives is to buy fresh, local food as much as possible.

A Gradual Shift

Because the chemical and pesticide-intensive agribusiness style of farming in this country is such bad news for our environment and is simply not sustainable over the long haul, we need to gradually shift to a style that is. Anything that you can do to encourage this shift will help. Supporting smaller family farms in your area with your food dollars is one way to do this.

This is not to say that every family farm in this country is a model of environmental sensitivity. Many are not. But the small family (or community) farm offers the best potential for the development of local, more natural food production models that could help us improve the quality of our food, while improving the environment at the same time. But this is only part of the picture.

Bye Bye Burger?

Another way of improving the efficiency of our use of natural resources, while improving our health, would be to reduce our consumption of fat-rich livestock products. It takes 7 pounds of grain to add 1 pound of weight on cattle in feedlots. By comparison, it takes about 4 pounds of grain to add that same pound of gain on pork. For poultry it's just over 2 pounds, and for a fish farm operation it's less than 2 pounds, according to the Worldwatch Institute.

It takes 10 times as much land to provide a pound of beef as it does to provide a pound of wheat. Since it takes a lot of water to produce grain, and since beef cattle require so much of both, there are clearly better alternatives to beef. And because the heavy consumption of red meats has been shown to be unhealthy, we also need to look at ways to reduce our intake of red meats—especially beef. This strategy will also help slow the growth of our waistlines and the national trend toward obesity I mentioned earlier.

Now, don't get me wrong. I'm not a wild-eyed vegetarian with carrots sticking out of my ears. I like a hot hamburger or a nice juicy steak like most Americans. And I'm not suggesting we stop eating beef completely. But I've gradually come to enjoy these things as tasty but limited parts of a much more varied and healthy diet that is less centered on red meats. You can, too. This shift away from red meats has actually been taking place in this country for quite some time, so this is not a new idea by any means.

Green Tips

We could save a lot of grain and water by decreasing our consumption of beef and pork and increasing our consumption of chicken and fish. Or, we could eat grain-based foods instead of meat in the first place. Any of these strategies would be a healthy change in our eating habits.

I also hasten to add that I have nothing personally against cattle ranchers. They're hard working, honest folks who are generally following long family traditions. But the shift away from red meat is an idea whose time has clearly come in this country. And ranchers—like everyone else these days—are going to have to learn to adapt to changing times, as painful as that may be. A shift to premium-quality, organically raised beef is one possible alternative for some smaller beef farms. Which brings us to a very exciting trend—organic foods.

Hello, Organic

One of the most obvious signs of changing times has been the phenomenal growth in demand for *organic foods*. In addition to a variety of personal health concerns, the growing public awareness of the damage that pesticides, fertilizers, and herbicides do to our environment has led many Americans to start buying natural, organically grown foods in recent years. As a result, organic foods, which were already the fastest-growing segment of the U.S. food industry, have now entered the mainstream market in a big way.

Sales of organic produce, in fact, grew from $1 billion per year in 1992 to $6 billion in 1999, according to the Organic Trade Association. And in response to growing consumer demand, more than 50 percent of all grocery stores nationwide now carry at least some organic produce. This is remarkable growth indeed for an industry that barely showed up on the radar screen 20 years ago.

Even the federal government finally took notice of these trends, and after a good deal of prodding, attempted to define a new set of national standards for organic foods several years ago. The first attempt by the USDA, however, was embarrassingly lax, and the labeling rules went back for major revision after the department received more than 280,000 protest letters from irate consumers and organic farmers. The revised rules were finally announced in January 2000 and are expected to go into effect later in the year.

So, why are so many people opting to eat organic foods? Many believe that organics are more nutritious —a view that some scientists dispute. But most people correctly feel that organic foods are healthier in general for themselves and for the environment. In addition, many claim that organics taste better.

In my own personal experience I have found that some organics definitely do taste better. On the other hand, some organic produce definitely does not look as good as the chemically sprayed variety. But if I have to choose between taste and appearance, taste always wins.

Eco-Explanations

Simply stated, **organic foods** are grown without chemicals that can harm the land and water. New USDA rules require organic producers to get their farming practices verified by a state or local agency that oversees the industry.

Co-ops

Okay, a significant shift toward organic, natural foods is taking place in this country. But where can you find this stuff? One great place to look is your local food co-op. Natural foods co-ops generally have their roots back in the 1970s as preorder buying clubs that provided members with wholesome, natural food products that were otherwise unavailable in grocery stores at the time. Most foods were ordered in bulk and then repackaged into more manageable quantities and divided up among members.

In more recent years, many of these organizations have added or expanded retail storefronts and now cater to the general public as well as their members. Many co-ops generally try to buy local, organic produce whenever possible. They also generally avoid *irradiated foods,* meat or dairy products from animals that have been treated with hormones or antibiotics, and foods that contain artificial color, flavor, or preservatives. If you have been buying most of your food from a big chain supermarket and have a food co-op in your area, you might want to check it out.

In our community, we are blessed with a well-established (and wonderful) natural foods co-op. The employees are friendly, courteous, and helpful, the atmosphere is pleasant, and the foods—both bulk and packaged—are simply wonderful. During the long winter months when local farm produce is not available, the co-op is our main source. In fact, between the co-op and another small local grocery store, we've been able to switch virtually all of our grocery shopping from the big chain supermarkets. And you know what? Our food expenses haven't gone up at all. But the quality and freshness of our food has.

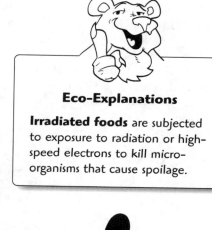

Eco-Explanations

Irradiated foods are subjected to exposure to radiation or high-speed electrons to kill micro-organisms that cause spoilage.

Community-Supported Agriculture

There's nothing quite like tasting fresh, organic vegetables for the first time. Especially if you've been raised on the bland varieties often found in big supermarket chains. But for many busy working people, finding the time or space (especially if they live in an apartment) to actually raise organic vegetables themselves is simply out of the question. But these folks would still like to eat good, fresh, local produce. They can. And so can you.

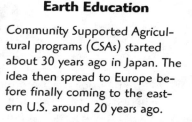

Earth Education

Community Supported Agricultural programs (CSAs) started about 30 years ago in Japan. The idea then spread to Europe before finally coming to the eastern U.S. around 20 years ago.

In response, a relatively new phenomenon has been taking root in this country—Community Supported Agriculture (CSA). Customers of CSA programs essentially become shareholders in small local farms by investing (or pre-buying) a certain amount of produce in advance. Then, as the season progresses, they receive an assortment of wonderful fruits and vegetables as it becomes available. Sometimes the farmer delivers the food, and sometimes it is picked up at the farm. Either way, it's a great opportunity to get fresh, usually organic food, and to establish a direct connection with the people who grow it.

Today, there are over 1,000 of these farms in the United States and Canada. And the number is growing almost as fast as the lettuce, cucumbers, and zucchini. If your family eats a lot of produce, this might be a great strategy to try.

Farmer's Markets

Now, for some small families—like mine—shelling out $400 or $500 in advance for a huge quantity of produce may not make much sense. But happily, there is another option—the farmers' market. Long a tradition in Europe and other parts of the world, these markets had all but disappeared in the United States, especially after World War II with the spread of supermarkets. But in the last 10 years or so, well over 2,000 farmers' markets have sprung up across the country in response to the growing demand for fresh, mainly organic foods.

Farmers' market.

(Photo copyright Greg Pahl)

Buying your fresh produce in season at a local farmers' market offers a number of benefits. First of all, the produce is *really* fresh. And because it is generally picked the same day it's sold, it's also riper and at its peak for flavor and nutrition. Foods from a farmers' market simply taste better than supermarket fare. No question about it. And

I'm speaking from direct personal experience. I'm a devoted and enthusiastic customer of our local farmers' market.

But that's not all. When you buy from a farmers' market that features organic produce you are also helping the environment by reducing the demand for the chemicals, pesticides, and fertilizers, which are the mainstay of large commercial farming operations. In addition, by purchasing locally grown food, you eliminate the need to ship it long distances, thereby reducing global warming. And all of this helps encourage the development of more sustainable agricultural practices, which is the ultimate goal of virtually everything I've discussed in this chapter. And more sustainable agriculture will help encourage a more sustainable global economy, which is the main point of this book.

But there are even more benefits. In all likelihood you are also helping to support local family farmers, and perhaps are slowing the spread of suburban sprawl by keeping agricultural lands in production. Then there's the social aspect. Going to your local farmers' market gives you a great chance to visit with your neighbors as well as local farmers. It's a real community-building opportunity that's almost beyond value. No matter how you look at them, local farmers' markets are a great idea.

As you can see, there are many, many ways you can reduce your waistline while reducing the waste of natural resources, improving the environment, and eating fresher, better-tasting foods all at the same time. That's a win-win-win-win strategy. And one of the most effective ways of doing this is by supporting local producers with your food-shopping dollars. Talk about putting your money where your mouth is.

The Least You Need to Know

➤ Reducing the amount of food we eat to match what we actually need is a good idea.

➤ What we choose to eat can have a positive impact on the environment.

➤ Organically grown and natural foods are a healthy choice for you and your family.

➤ Shopping at a local farmers' market or food co-op is a good strategy for many reasons.

Chapter 10

More Ways to Reduce

Years ago, when I worked in a large discount department store, I watched two women who had been busily pawing their way through dozens of bins full of clothing. My main interest was due to the fact that I was the one who was going to have to refold the trail of disordered garments these two had left in their wake. "Let's go; I don't see anything," one of them finally said. "Wait," the other replied with a hint of desperation in her voice, "Let's keep looking—maybe we'll find something we need."

I've never forgotten that little scene, or the irony of the reply. If they had truly known what they needed, they wouldn't have spent the previous half hour idly turning my department into what looked like the aftermath of a tornado touchdown. Sadly, this little melodrama is repeated countless times every day all across this country as millions of us wander through shopping centers, malls, and big box stores in the hopes of "finding something we need." This zombie-like behavior, encouraged by a relentless barrage of media advertising, is incredibly unhealthy both for us and for the planet.

But what can we do about it? Quite a lot, actually. And it relates to becoming more conscious consumers, reducing waste at its source. I'm going to begin this chapter with some ideas on reduction strategies that can make you a more savvy shopper, help the environment—and save you money all at the same time. Then, I'll tell you about something productive you can do with your TV. After that, we'll look at ways to have more fun with less stuff. Finally, we're going to take a brief, well-deserved vacation.

Become a Savvy Shopper

In this part of the book we've been focusing on reduction strategies and how they can cut waste at the source, rather than dealing with it after it has occurred. And becoming a savvy—and environmentally conscious—shopper is one of the most effective ways you can cut waste, by exerting pressure on businesses with your shopping dollars. We've already looked at food issues in the previous chapter. Now we're going to look at a host of other consumer issues. Ready? Let's start by going shopping.

Eliminate Impulse Buying

Wow, look at all this stuff! There are those new high definition TVs we've heard so much about. And here are the latest styles and colors you saw in a fashion magazine last week. And what about those great-looking watches—they're 50 percent off! And there's that mini food chopper that was advertised on TV ....

Green Tips

Cutting back on impulse buying is one of the best things you can do for your checking account and for the environment. Most impulse buying has almost nothing to do with actual need, which is why it is such an unhealthy pattern to follow. Avoid impulse buying, and save money while saving on the resources used to produce these products.

Okay, enough. The point I'm trying to make is that shopping can be a highly addictive activity. Although you may have come to the store to buy one thing, you may end up going home with something else altogether. Or several somethings. And plenty of businesses in this country would like to get you hooked on impulse buying. And keep you hooked, regardless of the harm this behavior can do to you, to your bank account, to our society, and to the planet.

The fact that we have racked up a record $1.38 trillion in personal debt (1999), while at the same time sinking to an all-time low in personal savings in this country, is a sad commentary on the effectiveness of advertising campaigns aimed at encouraging excessive consumerism.

Reducing impulse buying is an important first step toward more responsible shopping. And it's also a great way of reducing waste. Plan your next shopping trip in advance and make a list of the things you need. And stick to it.

Is It Sustainable?

But I freely admit that we can't stop consuming completely. That's not even desirable. So the next best strategy is to buy products consciously—weighing the environmental consequences carefully before making a decision. But how do you do that?

One of the main things to keep in mind is the concept of sustainability. As I explained earlier, the natural world is a series of interconnected, self-regulating systems. These systems involve a balance between give and take. And as long as this balance is maintained, the process can continue indefinitely—or sustainably (much more on sustainability in Part 5, "A Sustainable Future").

This is actually a useful concept to keep in mind when you're shopping—especially if you're trying to decide between several products that are making conflicting claims of their environmental benefits. The recent upsurge of consumer interest in environmental issues has been reflected in a huge increase in manufacturers trying to cash in on that interest. Sometimes it can get pretty confusing.

You need to ask yourself: Which product is most likely to fit in with the natural cycle of giving and taking that we see in nature? The answer to that question may not be immediately apparent, but just asking the question may open your eyes to a whole range of issues you might not have thought about before.

Green Tips

The most important question to ask yourself before you buy something is "Do I really need this?" If the honest answer is "no," save your money—and the environment. This is the most effective method of source reduction.

The following questions should help you find the most sustainable choice. As an environmentally conscious shopper, before you buy something, ask yourself the following:

➤ Do I really need this—can I get by without it?

➤ Is it safe (nontoxic) to use?

➤ Is it practical, durable, and well made?

➤ Is it made from renewable or nonrenewable resources?

➤ Is it made of recycled materials, and is it recyclable?

➤ Can it be maintained and repaired?

➤ How far has it been shipped to reach this store?

➤ Is it over-packaged?

➤ How long will it last, and how will I dispose of it?

You might also ask yourself whether you could buy this item secondhand, or if you can borrow or rent it (more on these strategies in a moment). In addition, ask yourself whether this product is worth the time you worked to pay for it, and the cost to the environment. As you can see, there are any number of reasons why you might actually decide not to buy something. I suppose you could consider these questions your unshopping list.

Helpful Hints

Some of these strategies may be a little hard to get a handle on right off, so here are some quick hints to help you become a more savvy shopper and help the environment.

The following are things you should consider buying:

➤ A reusable shopping bag (saves on paper or plastic bags)

➤ Rechargeable batteries (save on waste and pollution from disposables)

➤ Concentrated products, like detergents (more product, smaller package)

➤ Compact fluorescent light bulbs

➤ Cloth napkins and diapers instead of paper

➤ A water filter rather than bottled water

The water filter suggestion is important because the production, packaging, and transportation of bottled water uses a lot of resources for something that you already have right in your own home. But be sure to compare water filters carefully before you buy one.

And here's a short list of things to avoid whenever possible:

➤ Plastic foam cups

➤ Paper towels, especially those that use chlorine bleach in their manufacture

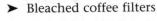

➤ Bleached coffee filters

➤ Teak and mahogany wood products from rain forests

➤ Plastic bags and wrap

Earth Education

Each year Americans use enough polystyrene foam cups to circle the Earth 436 times. That's a lot of cups.

The potential list of things to buy or to avoid is huge. And sometimes the choices aren't so clear. But once you begin to think about the issues behind your choices, the right way to proceed begins to become more obvious. If you just view this as an ongoing educational process that's going to last the rest of your life, you can relax and just take it one day at a time.

Avoid Excessive Packaging

As you may recall, packaging accounts for about a third of all municipal solid waste in this country. Consequently, anything you can do to help reduce packaging helps cut a lot of waste. Ideally, try to find products that have little or no packaging in the first place. Some things can be bought in bulk, eliminating packaging completely (you may have to bring a container to fill). But if packaging is unavoidable, choose the product with the least amount of packaging. And check to see if the packaging is recyclable and if it is made from recycled materials.

Packaging issues can get fairly complicated. And depending on whom you listen to, almost any packaging can be represented as environmentally friendly. The plastics industry has recently made a big deal about how their thin, flexible packaging is superior to other, bulkier packaging materials like cardboard or glass. But plastics don't measure up very well when viewed from the standpoint of sustainability because they come from nonrenewable crude oil and are not indefinitely recyclable the way glass is. Still, sometimes it's a tough call.

And remember, a sustainable package does not guarantee a sustainable product. Read the "green" claims on the packaging carefully. Do they refer to just the packaging or the product—or both? And are the claims backed up by any additional data? An unsubstantiated claim of "environmentally friendly" may simply be misleading hype. I recall a plastic cup manufacturer that claimed their cups "saved trees."

Products that display the Green Seal have met rigorous independent environmental standards.

(Green Seal, Inc.)

Another good way to sort through all the environmental claims you'll see on many products is to look for the Green Seal logo—a blue planet with a green check mark—indicating the product has met rigorous independent environmental standards.

Green Seal is an independent, nonprofit organization in this country that is dedicated to protecting the environment by promoting the manufacture and sale of environmentally responsible consumer products. It sets environmental standards and awards a "Green Seal of Approval" to products that cause less harm to the environment than other similar products. Visit its Web site at www.greenseal.org for more information.

Another prominent certification organization is Scientific Certification Systems (SCS). Among its many activities, the company's environmental division certifies a wide variety of claims related to environmental achievement in the product-manufacturing sector. Check out its Web site at www.scs1.com for additional information.

Eliminate Single-Use Products

One of the most damaging trends for the environment has been the development and proliferation of single-use products: from expanded plastic foam cups and plates to paper towels, and from disposable diapers to throwaway cameras, to name just a few. These products, promoted mainly for their convenience, unfortunately reinforce our frontier attitudes about limitless natural resources at a time when we should be conserving them. Even worse, throwaways run totally counter to the idea of sustainability. Whenever possible, single-use products should be avoided because they are so utterly wasteful of resources.

Disposable Razors

There are lots of things I could mention, but disposable plastic razors are as good (or bad) an example as any. We throw away somewhere around two billion disposable razors and blades every year in this country. Despite their undeniable convenience, disposable plastic shavers are clearly a terrible idea from an environmental standpoint. Because they are primarily made of plastic, they consume energy and chemicals in their manufacture. And, because of their design, they are virtually impossible to recycle. So, they end up in landfills, or create noxious air pollution if they are incinerated.

What are the alternatives? The choices admittedly involve some tradeoffs. You could buy a more durable shaver with long-lasting disposable blades, an old-fashioned straight razor, or perhaps an electric shaver.

The durable shaver lasts indefinitely, but the disposable blades are still a problem. The old-fashioned straight razor is probably the longest-lasting product, but is not the best choice for those with unsteady hands (that's the voice of experience talking). The average electric shaver, unfortunately, doesn't generally last more than about five years and also consumes electricity. On the plus side, the electricity used to power an electric shaver is minimal compared to the energy needed to manufacture and eventually dispose of the throwaway plastic variety. You decide.

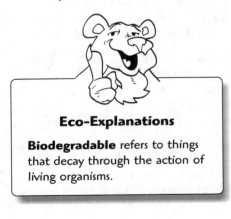

Eco-Explanations

Biodegradable refers to things that decay through the action of living organisms.

The Diaper Debate

Then there are disposable diapers. The Great Diaper Debate has been raging for years over whether you should use disposables or the traditional cloth version. Some disposables now claim to be *biodegradable*. Perhaps they are. But the fact remains that billions of disposables are landfilled each year, wasting somewhere around 100,000 tons of plastic and 800,000 tons of paper pulp. That's not surprising, as just one child can run through well over 8,000 diapers before becoming toilet trained.

Regardless of whether the disposables are biodegradable or not, the 800 million pounds of paper used annually in their manufacture are not recyclable. Worse yet, somewhere around 85 million pounds of raw fecal matter end up in landfills, creating public health hazards as well as potential for groundwater contamination. Landfills simply were not designed to be sewage treatment plants.

From an environmental standpoint, cloth diapers are clearly the preferred choice, even though they require water, detergents, and bleach to clean them. But here's another advantage: You can save money, too. It has been estimated that you can save over $1,000 by using cloth diapers if you do the washing yourself. Even if you use a diaper cleaning service, you should still come out ahead by $300 to $600 per child.

Yes, I know, some of these throwaway products make life easier (if you ignore the environmental consequences). And I admit that eliminating the use of disposables can be a challenge (I've used disposable shavers for years, so I'm just as guilty as anyone). In many cases, shifting your habits requires some tradeoffs. But because single-use products have become such a pervasive part of our throwaway society, weaning ourselves from them can have a major positive impact on the environment. Think about it the next time you're about to buy another package of throwaways—and I promise I will, too.

What About Seldom-Used Products?

Sometimes you might be tempted to buy something that would be really handy to have once in a while, but realistically, it would probable spend most of its time in the back of a closet or in the basement. Resist the temptation.

As a former building contractor, I was a hopeless tool junkie—years after I had become a journalist and writer. I just couldn't let go of all those wonderful tools that "might come in handy some day." But what I should have remembered from my contracting days was that even our construction company didn't try to stock every conceivable tool we might require. When we needed a special-purpose item we didn't have, we rented it. And you can do the same thing.

Rental of seldom-used items is a great strategy for source reduction because it eliminates the need for you to buy something that would just sit around gathering dust most of the time. Almost anything can be rented these days, so if you need something just once in a while, rental may be the best way to go.

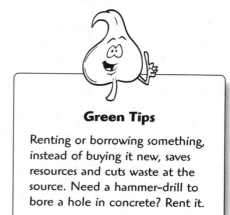

Green Tips

Renting or borrowing something, instead of buying it new, saves resources and cuts waste at the source. Need a hammer-drill to bore a hole in concrete? Rent it.

Another good strategy is to share an item that is only used occasionally. This can work within your extended family if they live nearby, or perhaps with your friends and neighbors. Someone in your family may have just what you need sitting around; it doesn't hurt to ask.

For example, every once in a while I need a post-hole digger. I don't own one. But my uncle does. And he's perfectly happy to let me borrow it. This strategy works for me. Maybe it can work for you, too.

Obviously, if you are sharing an item on a regular basis with others it's a good idea to have a basic agreement about who is responsible for maintenance or repairs, especially if the item is some sort of machinery like a lawn mower or garden tiller (more in this in Chapter 13, "Reuse Strategies").

Is Cheaper Better?

Some people who consider themselves savvy shoppers make it a point to spend as little as possible on the things they buy. Although it doesn't make sense to spend more than you need to, cheaper is not always better—particularly from an environmental standpoint. Here's why.

Let's just use shoes as an example. Although you might be able to save money on an inexpensive pair of shoes at a discount store, chances are they were made with less-than-top-quality materials and workmanship. If they wear out more quickly than a premium-quality pair of shoes, they end up costing you—and the environment—more due to their shorter lifespan. And if the cheaper shoes aren't very comfortable either, it's a real lose-lose situation. The old expression, "penny wise and pound foolish" definitely applies here.

Planetary Perils

Buying cheap products may end up costing you more in the long run and can waste valuable natural resources because cheap items generally don't last as long as better-made products. Ultimately, you may end up spending more money to replace the cheap item and using more resources at the same time.

But there's another often overlooked element to this issue. Though you can save some money buying, say, a winter coat from a discount house, if it wears out halfway through your second winter, chances are you are just out in the cold. But if you had spent more on your initial purchase from a high-quality manufacturer such as L.L. Bean or others that offer an unconditional guarantee, if anything ever goes wrong with your coat, just follow the procedure to send it back to the manufacturer, and it will fix it for free. If you can make your $200 coat last 15 years instead of two or three years for a $50 coat, it's clear that the "more expensive" coat is the real bargain. And it saves a lot of resources, too.

TV or not TV?

Now it's time for a commercial break. I'm going to share a little secret with you. I've actually found something productive you can do with your TV that also helps the environment. Unplug it.

Of all the negative influences on our society—and especially on our children—TV is arguably the worst offender. Take a look at these statistics complied by TV-Free America (www.tvfa.org):

➤ The average American watches three hours and 46 minutes of TV each day (more than 52 days of nonstop TV-watching per year).

➤ By age 65, the average American will have spent nearly nine *years* glued to the tube.

➤ TV is on in an average U.S. home for seven hours, 12 minutes per day.

➤ Number of videos rented daily in the U.S.: six million.

➤ Number of public library items checked out daily: three million.

This is bad enough. But I think the statistics related to our children are even worse:

➤ Number of minutes per week that the average American child aged 2 to 11 watches television: 1,197.

➤ Number of minutes per week that parents spend in meaningful conversation with their children: 38.5.

➤ Average number of hours per week that American youth aged 12 to 17 watch television: 20 hours, 20 minutes.

➤ Hours of TV watching per week shown to negatively affect academic achievement: 10 or more.

➤ Number of medical studies since 1985 linking excessive television watching to increasing rates of obesity: 12.

➤ Number of ads aired for "junk food" during four hours of Saturday morning cartoons: 202.

➤ Percentage of toy-advertising dollars spent on television commercials in 1997: 92.

➤ Estimated number of TV commercials seen by American children before graduating high school: 360,000.

Green Tips

Unplugging your TV is one of the best things you can do for yourself, for your kids, and for the environment. Try reading a good book or spending quality time with your family or friends instead.

I could go on and on. But what's all this got to do with the environment, you ask? Quite a lot, actually. Recent studies have shown that there is a definite relationship between TV watching and consumer-spending patterns. It works out to something like $4 worth of advertising-induced spending for every hour of TV viewing on average, nationwide.

Now, if this spending were for basic necessities, that would be one thing. But unfortunately, most of the products advertised on TV don't qualify. Not even close. The whole point of most of this advertising is to try to convince you that you want these products—even if you don't really need them (of course, they try to convince you that you need them as well). And this artificially created demand for all these things is essentially at the root of our over-consumptive habits that cause so much waste in our society—and around the globe.

So, what can you do? For starters, you can just cut back on your TV viewing yourself, and limit your kids' time in front of the tube as well. Or you can get involved in a larger initiative. For the past six years an organized campaign has been encouraging people to turn off the tube. TV-Turnoff Week has motivated millions of Americans and others around the globe to shut off their TVs every April. The surgeon general, 31 governors, and 61 organizations have endorsed this event. Now, if this strategy could just be extended to the other 11 months of the year ....

Planetary Perils

Emissions from power plants needed to supply the electricity for idle TVs and VCRs in this country every year equals the pollution caused by two million cars.

But turning off the tube isn't enough. You need to literally pull the plug because idle plugged-in appliances account for 5 percent of total U.S. energy consumption, cost us more than $3 billion every year, and spew 18 million tons of carbon into the atmosphere. Idle TVs and VCRs alone cost us more than $1 billion annually, or about $10 per household. Unfortunately, even when it's turned off, your TV contributes to global warming. So pull the plug. And the longer it stays unplugged the better.

If all 274 million of us reduced our TV watching by just one hour per week, as a nation we'd have over 14 billion hours to spend on more worthwhile activities like connecting with our families and friends, strengthening our communities, enjoying nature, or just plain having fun.

More Fun, Less Stuff

And, speaking of having fun, I think it's high time I pointed out that being environmentally conscious offers plenty of opportunities for having fun, too. It's not all gloom and doom by any means. In fact, when you become more conscious about your consumption and start to cut back on unhealthy and wasteful habits, you will find that you have more time and money for things that are more important and fun than accumulating more stuff.

Here are a few ideas:

➤ Give a gift of a special event or "happening," like an outing, trip to a museum, or other quality time together to a child or friend, instead of a toy or physical gift.

➤ Pack a lunch and go for a picnic at your favorite nature spot with your family, a friend, or even by yourself.

➤ Build a bird feeder with your kids.

➤ Go swimming.

➤ Go camping.

➤ Go biking.

➤ Go hiking.

➤ Spend a day at the beach.

➤ Play ball with the kids outdoors.

➤ Plant a butterfly garden.

➤ Invite friends over for a potluck dinner.

➤ Go to the library, check out a bunch of books—and enjoy.

➤ Play some music with friends.

I'm sure you can think of lots more ways to have fun with less stuff. The main point is to substitute quality time with friends, family, or even yourself, for the wasteful and largely useless products that clutter our lives and ultimately damage our environment. So, unplug the TV, avoid the mall, and go have some fun!

It's Vacation Time!

While we're on the subject of having fun, let's take a mini-vacation that can be good for us and good for the environment at the same time. Tourism is big business worldwide. It accounts for over 10 percent of the planet's gross national (or international) product and generates over $3.5 trillion annually. And the fastest growing segment of the tourist industry is "green" tourism, also known as *ecotourism*.

Eco-Explanations

Ecotourism is travel to places to learn about the culture and natural history of that location while not damaging its environment. It also usually involves trying to help the local economy and the local population.

More and more people are abandoning traditional beach or resort hotel vacations in favor of ecotourism to more exotic, remote areas where they hope to experience something of the local culture and to learn new things while causing the smallest negative impact to the environment. They also hope to leave money behind in the hands of the local population, rather than in the bank accounts of large foreign resort and hotel chains.

Although the rapid rise in green tourism has actually harmed the environments of some remote areas because it has been so popular, generally speaking it's still a sound strategy that you can follow both abroad and at home. Many communities and even cities in this country are beginning to develop green tourist programs. Some of these may be almost literally in your own back yard. How we decide to spend our money on vacation is just as important for the environment as how we spend our money at home in the supermarket.

Regardless of where you decide to go for a vacation, here are some things you can do to become a greener tourist:

➤ Walk, bike, inline skate, or use public transportation or an alternatively fueled vehicle.

➤ Reduce, reuse, recycle, and never litter.

➤ Support local economies and communities.

➤ Learn something about the local heritage, cultural diversity, and natural environment.

Though you may not necessarily spend less money on a green vacation (extremely exotic locations can be even more expensive than a traditional vacation), at least you will generally be supporting local businesses or communities rather than enriching some huge corporation. A good place to start looking for more information on ecotourism is the Eco-Source Network (www.ecosourcenetwork.com). And have fun.

As you can see, being a conscious consumer has huge implications for the environment. So the next time you find yourself out shopping for "something you need," vote carefully for a better environment with your shopping dollars. And remember, a sustainable future is something we all need.

The Least You Need to Know

➤ Considering the environmental consequences of your purchases can help cut waste dramatically.

➤ Renting or sharing seldom-used products is a useful strategy.

➤ Unplugging your TV could be one of the best things you ever do to improve your quality of life—and the environment.

➤ You don't have to spend a lot of money or buy a lot of stuff to have fun.

➤ Ecotourism can be fun for you and good for the environment.

Chapter 11

Help, I Wanna Get Off!

In This Chapter

➤ The American Dream

➤ What is Affluenza?

➤ A hard look at ourselves

➤ Downshifting and voluntary simplicity explained

How do you feel when you leave work at the end of the day? Has it been another harried, stressful, unpleasant blur of activity that leaves you wanting to just go home and lie down on the couch and fall asleep? Or hide in a corner? Is earning a living ruining the rest of your life? Do you even have a life outside of your job?

A lot of Americans have been asking themselves these same questions lately, and frequently their answers have not been very flattering for their jobs—or their lifestyles. Many of them have come to the conclusion that the price they are paying to pursue the American Dream is simply too high. Perhaps you have come to the same conclusion.

In this chapter we're going to get right to the heart of our consumption problems by taking a good hard look at the American Dream and how it—and we—have gone astray. Then we'll see what some people are doing to reinvent that dream by reshaping their lives. I'll explain the increasingly popular trends of downshifting and voluntary simplicity and how they relate to source reduction. Finally, I'll share some ideas on how to reinvent your own lifestyle.

Waking Up from the American Dream

By now, I'm sure you realize we have a little problem in this country with over-consumption. Actually, it's a big problem. As I've previously mentioned, with just 4.5 percent of the world's population we consume roughly 33 percent of the world's materials and have the largest ecological footprint on the planet. And if the rest of the present population of the world were to successfully pursue the American Dream—something they are already trying to do—we would need the resources of three planets to meet their desires.

Earth Education

The American Dream has been based largely on the assumption of limitless possibilities for individual achievement and limitless resources. This has led to a situation in which "success" is usually measured by how much we take, rather than on how much we contribute to society. But in a world of limited resources, the idea of limitlessness is impossible. It's time we learned to live within those limits and redefine our notion of success.

Obviously, this is an unsustainable situation. Clearly, something has to change, or we are going to be in big trouble. Yet, as a nation, we continue to pursue the old American Dream in a futile attempt to buy happiness with more stuff than we know what to do with. Unfortunately, this trend has only accelerated in the past decade of unprecedented economic growth. And things that were once viewed as unattainable luxuries are now routinely accepted as necessities, and the more we accumulate, the more we want.

This all-consuming passion is eroding not only our ecological foundations, but our social and personal well-being, too. We may be rich in things, but we're often poor in happiness and spirit. What's more, this over-consumption has also weakened our economy, according to leading economic observers like Lester Thurow of M.I.T., Charles Schultze of the Brookings Institute, and Alfred E. Kahn of Cornell University. All three say that the nation's economic health depends on consuming less and saving more, which isn't what you'll hear from most corporations with consumer products to sell.

Ironically, while much of the rest of the world is busily trying to copy the American economic model, a small but increasing number of Americans are deciding that the American Dream has become a nightmare. And because we are the ones responsible in the first place for creating this terrible monster that is devouring the planet, it is only fitting that we be the ones to bring it under control. We need to do whatever we can to help undo the damage we have done, to ourselves and to the rest of the planet, before it's too late.

Affluenza

Our heedless pursuit of materialism that has resulted in such terrible waste has also resulted in a good deal of spiritual unease in this country, especially in the past decade. This situation was spotlighted in a program titled "Affluenza," produced by KCTS in Seattle. The program, shown a number of times on Public Television stations in recent years, helped to bring these issues to a much wider audience. Affluenza was described in the program as ...

1. The bloated, sluggish, and unfulfilled feeling that results from efforts to keep up with the Joneses.

2. An epidemic of stress, overwork, waste, and indebtedness caused by dogged pursuit of the American Dream.

3. An unsustainable addiction to economic growth.

In addition to these problems, if you add the erosion of family and community, unprecedented levels of bankruptcy filings, and the continually growing gap between rich and poor, it's no wonder that more and more people are viewing the American Dream as a nightmare. The thousands of homeless people who live on the streets and back alleys of almost every major U.S. city are graphic proof of the dark side of the American Dream.

This is not a pretty picture. And it stands in stark contrast to the glowing reports we have been hearing for years on the evening news about how wonderful the economy is. Business has unquestionably been good. In fact, it simply doesn't get much better than it has been in the past decade. Yet, despite this, more and more Americans are feeling bad. Something is very wrong here.

Green Tips

It doesn't cost anything to escape from Affluenza except changing your attitudes about money and consumption habits. One of the keys to this transformation is the careful use of your money as a conscientious and educated consumer.

For one thing, a disproportionate share of the financial gains has been benefiting a small number of people at the very top of the economic heap who need it the least. Meanwhile, the majority of the people in the middle have actually seen their financial position slip as more and more Americans suffer the consequences of continual corporate downsizing and the flight of jobs to foreign countries. And too many people, regardless of their financial standing, are working too many hours to buy too much stuff—resulting in too little true happiness.

So, what's the cure for Affluenza? In theory, at least, it's pretty simple. And I've been talking about it for the past five chapters: source reduction. And this doesn't have to be painful. In fact, if you decide to take the cure for Affluenza, you could end up saving money while making your life better at the same time. Too good to be true? Not really.

Here are a few suggestions from the Affluenza Web site (www.pbs.org/kcts/affluenza) for ways to reduce the effects of Affluenza:

➤ Before you buy something, ask yourself: Do I need it at all? Do I want to dust (dry-clean or otherwise maintain) it?

➤ Is there anything I already own that I could substitute for it?

➤ Avoid the mall. Go hiking or play with the kids instead.

➤ Figure out what public transportation can save you (time, money for gas and parking, peace of mind).

➤ Become an advertising critic. Don't be sucked in by efforts to make you feel inadequate so you'll buy more stuff you don't need.

➤ Volunteer for a school or community group.

➤ Pretend the Joneses are the thriftiest, least wasteful people on the block. Then try to keep up with them.

Green Tips

Consciously treat yourself to a few small luxuries now and then. You will really appreciate them more than if they happen all the time. And you don't have to spend a lot of money, either. A nice bottle of your favorite wine, for example, might be just the right touch for a dinner with friends.

As you can see, a lot of these suggestions relate to reducing your consumption or to opportunities for consumption, and also to substituting better alternatives. And most of them are right in line with what I've been talking about in previous chapters.

But figuring out exactly what to reduce and how much to reduce—or whether you even really want to reduce—can be a challenge for many people. At the very least, you need to take a look at your lifestyle and your consumption habits to see if they really are in line with the values that are important to you.

Mirror, Mirror on the Wall

So, take a long, honest look at yourself and try to figure out what's really important in your life. Is your lifestyle in line with your beliefs? It may be comforting to know that you're not alone in this exercise. As I mentioned earlier, millions of other Americans have been taking a good, hard look at themselves—and our society—and many of them don't like what they are seeing.

Okay, it's pop quiz time again. This may help you in your self-appraisal. Question: What are the top four things that people in this country say are most important to them? Money? A new car? A big house? Or maybe a big boat? Nope. Answer: Americans consistently report they care most about their children, their families, their communities, and their personal development.

That's what we say. Yet this is often at odds with what we do, which is to pursue happiness and the American Dream with the consumption of more and more stuff regardless of the consequences for our children, families, communities, and the planet. We have clearly been led astray by consumptive habits that may not be in line with our core values. How did we get into this mess?

Although consumerism in this country has its roots in the 1880s and 1890s, the consumer society that we live in today began to develop after World War I. Consumerism really took off after World War II, and accelerated even more in the 1980s and 1990s. Currently in this country, it can only be described as out of control.

But deep down, most of us realize we are in trouble. A 1995 study prepared for the Merck Family Fund, "Yearning for Balance," offers some keen insights into how we feel about ourselves—and our consumptive habits. These four key findings emerged from the study:

> **Earth Education**
>
> In the 1930s the government and business made a concerted effort to stimulate the economy by promoting heavy consumerism. The main message to Americans in the press and on the radio was to buy "new," "modern," or "convenient" products to replace their "old-fashioned" counterparts.

- ➤ As Americans, we believe our priorities are out of whack.
- ➤ We are alarmed about the future.
- ➤ We see the environment as connected to these concerns—in general terms.
- ➤ We have conflicting thoughts on what to do about it.

Fully 95 percent of the people who participated in the survey felt that "most" of their fellow citizens are "very materialistic." And 82 percent of them agreed that most of us buy and consume far more than we need.

Almost everyone surveyed was concerned that our skewed values are destructive to family life and are having an especially negative effect on our children. In addition, they felt that if this trend continues unchecked, it would lead to even more serious problems when our children grow up.

Those surveyed also believed that our current materialistic ethic is unsustainable in both human and environmental terms. But the understanding of the links between consumption and the environment, unfortunately, were somewhat fuzzy. This is clearly demonstrated by the fact that only 51 percent agreed that their *own* buying habits have a negative effect on the environment.

Nevertheless, 86 percent of those surveyed said they were concerned about the quality of the environment. And a whopping 91 percent agreed that an underlying cause of environmental problems is that "we focus too much on getting what we want now and not enough on future generations." And the vast majority of those surveyed, 88 percent, agreed that "protecting the environment will require most of us to make changes in the way we live."

Planetary Perils

The inability to come to a consensus on what to do about our personal levels of over-consumption has led to a troubling continuation of our wasteful habits. The lack of national (or even regional) agreement on how to proceed has resulted in virtually no major, coordinated initiatives to tackle over-consumption.

But when it came to trying to figure out what to do, those surveyed had conflicting thoughts about how to proceed. Part of the problem has to do with our love of the good things that come with material wealth. We like our current standard of living. Another tough issue is our belief in the freedom to choose in this country. Most of the survey participants were reluctant to suggest how others should live. This ambivalence in our attitude seems to have led to national paralysis, where we know what we should be doing collectively, but just can't seem to do it.

Clearly, we broadly agree that we have a problem and need to do something about it. Unfortunately, in the five years since the survey was published, the orgy of consumption in this country has surged to new and almost unbelievable heights, raising grave doubts about whether we are actually willing to take any serious collective action on our concerns. Most of us seem to be waiting for somebody else to do something first.

Happily, the picture isn't entirely bleak. Some folks have decided not to wait around for everybody else. They're taking matters into their own hands and are creating their own New American Dream. And, lacking any clear national consensus, perhaps this is the way it's going to happen—a grass roots movement of people who are willing to actually live their beliefs and ideals and lead by example.

New Lifestyle Strategies

These new lifestyle pioneers have generally adopted one of two separate but related strategies: downshifting or voluntary simplicity. And both of these approaches contain varying degrees of reduction strategies.

But these new lifestyle approaches go well beyond the kind of small-scale (but important) changes I've suggested in previous chapters, such as conserving electricity or water, or cutting back on your use of paper towels. What's involved here is a fundamental shift in lifestyle to bring it in line with new priorities. Let's take a look at each strategy.

Downshifting

The growing unhappiness of many Americans with their overworked and overstressed lives has sparked an increase in the number of people who are voluntarily cutting back on their workloads, hours, or simply deciding to get out of the corporate rat race completely. This is generally called voluntary *downshifting* and involves a reduction of consumption due to lower income. It also includes a conscious effort to focus on a different set of priorities.

This movement, which was essentially invisible 10 years ago, is becoming increasingly popular, especially among two-income couples employed as managers, professionals, and technology workers. In fact, about one half of women and about 20 percent of men in that grouping would like to work part time, according to a recent Cornell University study.

Downshifters have a wide range of motivations for making their lifestyle change. About 68 percent want a more balanced life, 66 percent want more time, and 63 percent want a less stressful life, according to the Merck study. And roughly half (53 percent) want to spend more time caring for their children.

Eco-Explanations

Downshifting is a voluntary decision to cut back on your work hours, or to take a new, lower-paying job in exchange for more time to spend with family or other parts of your life that are more important.

Nevertheless, this desire to cut back is seemingly at odds with all the good economic news of the past decade or so. But there is another reason why downshifting is becoming so popular, according to Juliet Schor, author of *The Overspent American*. "The story of the '80s and '90s is that millions of Americans ended the period having more but feeling poorer. Nearly all of the pundits missed this dynamic, recognizing only the income trends of the spending increases," she says in her book.

Between 1990 and 1996, about 19 percent of all adult Americans made a voluntary lifestyle change that involved earning less money, according to Schor. And 85 percent of them reported being happy about the change. Of course, not everyone who wants to downshift actually does. Many fear that their employers or co-workers will view them unfavorably if they try to cut back on their work schedules.

Nevertheless, downshifting enables those who pursue it to bring their lifestyle back into alignment with their core values. For most downshifters, the problems that come with lower incomes seem to be offset by the advantages offered by more personal time, less stress, and a more balanced life. Many downshifters, in fact, say they don't miss the excess consumption that was a part of their previous lifestyle.

If you really would like to spend more quality time at home (or anywhere), you might want to think about downshifting—as long as you're willing to accept the tradeoffs. It's certainly an effective way to achieve lower consumption in any case. Help yourself have a better, more satisfying life, and help the environment at the same time.

For more information on downshifting, check out the Center for a New American Dream (www.newdream.org).

Voluntary Simplicity

The other lifestyle option that has become increasingly popular is *voluntary simplicity*, or "simple living," as it is also known. Duane Elgin popularized the term in his 1981 book (revised in 1993), *Voluntary Simplicity: Toward a Way of Life That Is Outwardly Simple, Inwardly Rich*. If you've never read the book, I highly recommend it.

Eco-Explanations

Voluntary simplicity is a lifestyle movement that generally stresses very low consumption, careful spending, and a deep concern for a variety of ethical, moral, environmental, and spiritual issues.

Voluntary simplicity basically begins where downshifting leaves off. And it takes the concept of source reduction much further—about as far as it can realistically go. The downshifter would like to have more money but is willing to live on less in exchange for a better quality of life. But "simple-livers," as they are sometimes called, move past this view and eventually settle at a low level of income where additional spending and consumption are no longer viewed as positive.

Simple-livers tend to be motivated by a number of ethical, moral, and spiritual concerns that extend far beyond money issues. Nevertheless, they put a lot of emphasis on careful, conscious spending, and tend to buy products that are durable, easy to repair, energy efficient, functional, and nonpolluting in their manufacture and use. They also tend to boycott goods and services of companies whose actions or policies they believe to be unethical or environmentally unsound.

It's hard to generalize about simple-livers, but most of them tend to live in modest housing, drive older cars (if they drive at all), shop in thrift shops or secondhand markets, and tend to wear what they find there. They normally avoid expensive entertainment such as first-run movies, theater performances, and restaurants, preferring instead home-cooked meals, potluck gatherings, and other low-cost but high-quality-of-life activities that focus on family, community, and personal friendships.

It's important to note that simple living is as much a spiritual transformation as a lifestyle change. And becoming a simple-liver doesn't usually happen overnight. For most folks it's normally a gradual process of altering habits and thinking about small, everyday things that eventually add up to more substantial changes in lifestyle later on.

And this is really an individual choice. If you decide to follow this path, you begin wherever you happen to be at the present time and grow into the process as you learn more about yourself, your habits, and your environment. Simple living, like life itself, is more like a journey than a destination. And each journey is unique.

In any case, simple-livers are proving that it is possible to reduce consumption dramatically, while maintaining a reasonably comfortable lifestyle that offers many other, nonmaterial benefits along the way.

There's one final point I want to make about voluntary simplicity and its related strategies. One of the main advantages of these strategies at the moment is that they're still voluntary. But if we continue to waste precious time in making the necessary cuts in our consumption until Mother Nature starts making choices for us, "voluntary" will no longer be an option. And nature can be very cruel.

If you'd like to learn more about voluntary simplicity, I suggest you check out the recently published *The Complete Idiot's Guide to Simple Living*, by Georgene Lockwood. It's filled with lots of current, helpful information. Another excellent resource is the Simple Living Network (www.simpleliving.net).

Earth Education

Seattle, Washington, has one of the largest and most active simple-living communities in the nation. It's also credited as being the source of the voluntary simplicity movement. In addition, Seattle is the home of gurus of the movement, such as Vicki Robin and Joe Dominguez, authors of *Your Money or Your Life*. And more pamphlets, newsletters, and guides about the joys of simple living seem to come from Seattle than anywhere else.

It's Not So Simple

Okay, I admit these strategies aren't as simple as they might sound. You have to be willing or able to get by on less income. And maybe you're just not ready to downshift or become a simple-liver right now. That's okay. I'm not suggesting you should follow any particular path. Just your path, whatever it may be. But I want you to be aware of your options.

One slight word of caution: If you are excited about making a major lifestyle change such as downshifting or voluntary simplicity but your partner or your adolescent children are not, it probably won't work. At least not on a family level. The constant friction caused by one half of a family heading in one direction while the other half is moving in the opposite direction may cause real problems. But if everyone is onboard, go for it.

On the other hand, if you are the only one in your family who wants to practice a simpler lifestyle, you don't have to wait for everyone else. Just get started, quietly following your own path. You may find that other family members will become more supportive over time as long as you aren't trying to drag them along. You have your life to live. They have theirs.

Green Tips

If you are thinking about making a major lifestyle change such as downshifting or voluntary simplicity for your family, be sure the rest of your household is in basic agreement; otherwise, these strategies probably won't work. And while there is no single "correct" way to approach these changes, it's probably best to take the process slowly, and gradually develop your new lifestyle one area at a time.

Actually, before we move on, there are a number of other alternative approaches to dealing with job stress that may be easier to try. Here are a few of the most popular:

➤ **Flex time** Maybe you can rearrange your work schedule to accommodate childcare or other activities. Many companies are willing to consider this strategy—especially in a tight job market.

➤ **Telecommuting** If you've got a computer, a modem, and a fax capability, you can stay in touch with the office from home and avoid the commute, cutting down on global warming.

➤ **Job sharing** Some companies allow two people to share one job. This new twist to part-time work is increasingly popular with some companies.

Or, perhaps you can come up with a mix of different parts of these strategies we've looked at in this chapter. You may be able to create a unique variation that works for you.

Live Better on Less

Living better on less is possible. Millions of Americans have already clearly demonstrated that it's not only possible, but also preferable. If they can do it, so can you. But one of the first things we need to do is to redefine success so that we measure wealth in terms of quality of life, rather than material possessions. That's a big leap for some people, but an important one.

So, if your job and your lifestyle are getting you down, and you want to help the planet at the same time, reinvent your lifestyle. And don't wait around for everybody else.

The Least You Need to Know

➤ The old American Dream is unsustainable.

➤ Affluenza has infected our entire nation.

➤ Most Americans believe that our priorities are out of whack.

➤ Downshifting can give you more time for more important things in your life.

➤ Voluntary simplicity is increasingly popular in this country.

➤ You definitely can live better on less—some Americans already are.

Part 3
Reuse It

It's time to turn our attention to the second of the Three Rs of the environmental movement—reuse. We'll start with a quick look at the history of reuse. Then, I'll introduce you to the many types of reuse that not only help to save the environment, but can help you to save money, too.

After that, I'll explain reuse strategies in more detail and show you how some can even give you a tax deduction. I'll also offer numerous home-based suggestions that apply to almost every room in your house. Then, we'll look at reuse strategies for the office and other locations in the workplace.

Finally, we're going to take a new look at some old traditions such as auctions, secondhand stores, flea markets, and tag sales and find out why they are so hot these days.

Chapter 12

Choose to Reuse

In This Chapter

➤ Reuse in the past

➤ Why you should reuse

➤ Primary and secondary reuse

➤ Reuse basics

➤ When not to reuse

Do you remember refillable bottles? I do. It wasn't all that long ago when many drinks, from Coca-Cola to milk, came in sturdy glass bottles. When they were empty, you returned the bottles to the store or the milkman picked them up, and after they were washed, they were refilled. These bottles often lasted for years. Unfortunately, this perfectly sensible reuse strategy was almost totally blown away by the introduction of plastic and aluminum cans and the throwaway lifestyle that came with them.

The refillable bottle was one of the last vestiges of a massive reuse system that had been operating in this country for hundreds of years. That system, in fact, had roots that went back to the Pilgrims and beyond. It's ironic, in fact, that one of the oldest strategies on the planet is now viewed by many as a wonderful new solution to some of our current environmental problems.

A collection of refillable bottles.

(Photo copyright Greg Pahl)

We'll start this chapter by taking a quick look at the long history of reuse, and then I'll tell you about its many benefits. I'll follow that up by explaining the two main types of reuse. Then we'll go through all the basics. Finally, I'll caution you about a few situations where reuse isn't such a good idea.

A Very Old Strategy

Reuse is nothing new. Actually, it's about as old as the hills. Or at least the pyramids. The Great Pyramid at Giza, in fact, lost its original white outer casing to somewhat over-enthusiastic reuse by builders from the Middle Ages who found the supply of fine dressed limestone hard to resist for their projects in Cairo.

More recently, in this country reuse has had its ups and downs depending on the state of the economy and how society viewed thrift. In our early history, reuse of common materials was a necessity. Leftover food was fed to farm animals. Old clothes were salvaged for children's clothing, patchwork quilts, and rag rugs. Bones were used for knife handles, hair ornaments, buttons, and even for dice and dominoes.

Broken or worn-out items were often repaired and reused. Things beyond repair were dismantled and their parts were reused or sold. In fact, almost anything and everything that could possibly be reused or recycled was.

What wasn't reused at home was reused elsewhere. A large number of street scavengers and peddlers assisted this strategy by traveling around cities or the countryside on foot or in wagons, buying the waste from households and then selling it to waste dealers, who in turn sold it back to manufacturers. This closed loop for waste was more or less self-sustaining.

These frugal national habits continued as the country grew. In fact, reuse was actively encouraged throughout most of the nineteenth century. In the home, things such as flour sacks were often reused as dish towels and even remade into articles of clothing. Many durable items were put to some other useful purpose after their original function had ended.

The Decline of Reuse

In the late 1800s and early 1900s, the system began to change with the rise in large-scale manufacturing of consumer products for the national market. The old-fashioned habits of thrift, reuse, and recycling didn't disappear overnight, but the trend toward a mass consumer society was already well underway.

What's more, people increasingly associated scavenging and reuse with activities for poor people who couldn't afford all the wonderful new consumer products. The old door-to-door peddler trade, and the system that had supported it, began to disappear.

In the first half of the twentieth century manufacturers deliberately encouraged Americans to throw away perfectly good, functional products rather than reuse them simply because they were out-of-date. Fashion, style, cleanliness, and convenience were in. Frugality, reuse, and recycling were out.

The strategy worked. Our throwaway society was now established, although it was temporarily interrupted by the depression as well as by World War II. Reuse, except in the poorest families and communities, was essentially dead.

The Rebirth of Reuse

Then, in the 1960s and 1970s, with the arrival of the Hippie counterculture and its environmental concerns, reuse suddenly became hip. Remade bell-bottomed jeans and "vintage" clothing fashions were all the rage. Garage sales, yard sales, and secondhand stores became popular places for environmentally conscious shoppers—who were also looking for a good deal.

Earth Education

In the nineteenth century, glass bottles were generally refilled and were usually discarded only after they broke. A variety of empty candy jars, pickle bottles, jelly glasses, and other containers were frequently reused for storing canned, preserved, or dried fruits and vegetables.

Earth Education

By 1981 it is estimated that Americans held more than six million garage sales annually, generating $1 billion in sales. It's hard to go anywhere on a weekend these days without seeing garage sales, yard sales, or swap meets of some kind in most parts of the country.

Although bell-bottoms and tie-dyed shirts fell out of favor (they've recently made a comeback), reuse has continually increased in popularity to the point where it's actually spawned a recent wave of upscale franchises (more on that in Chapter 16, "The Used Marketplace"). While we're not generally making buttons out of bones anymore, reuse is a strategy whose time has clearly come—again.

Why Should You Reuse?

There are many reasons why reuse is such a great conservation strategy. In many ways, the advantages of reuse—saving money and resources while cutting pollution and waste—are the same as those offered by the other Rs, reduction and recycling. So, if some of this begins to sound a little familiar, you're right; these similarities are a reminder of just how interrelated these issues are.

But reuse has some distinctive features of its own—creating jobs and offering potential tax benefits—which I'll describe in greater detail when we get to them. Okay, let's look at the advantages one at a time.

Save Money

One of the primary advantages of reuse is that it normally helps you to save money. That's something almost everybody can get excited about. And reuse is just as effective a money-saving strategy for businesses, institutions, and governments, as it is for individuals.

Green Tips

Reuse strategies can save you money while you help save the environment. In addition to saving the cost of materials you don't have to buy, you might also save in garbage-disposal fees. This is an especially effective strategy for businesses and governments that frequently have large quantities of waste to dispose of.

One way you can save money with reuse is by cutting your original purchase costs. As I mentioned earlier in the book, you can save money using cloth diapers instead of disposables. And diapers are a good example of the interrelationships between environmental issues. Using cloth diapers instead of disposables is a great reuse strategy for the cloth diaper. But it's also a super source-reduction strategy for the trees you save at the same time—it's a win-win situation.

Save Resources

Reuse also saves resources because when items are reused you cut down on the number of new products that have to be manufactured, as well as the need for the raw materials to produce them. In addition, reuse saves energy that would otherwise be needed for manufacturing or recycling.

Saving energy, in fact, is a key advantage of re-use strategies. And *embodied energy* is a useful term that will help you to understand the potential energy savings involved with reuse. The embodied energy in items such as aluminum and plastic are extremely high, while embodied energy for concrete is relatively low (more on building materials in Chapter 14, "At Home"). The average homeowner is not likely to be reusing many concrete items, but plenty of products contain aluminum and plastic, so reuse of them—and of almost any other product as well—makes a good deal of sense. Reuse, unlike recycling, saves much of this embodied energy, and this is a key difference between these two strategies.

Eco-Explanations

Embodied energy refers to the amount of energy needed to produce any product initially. This includes the energy of all of the processes associated with the production of an item, from the acquisition of natural resources to product delivery, including mining, manufacturing, and transport.

Cut Pollution

Reuse cuts down on air and water pollution caused by dumping and incinerating waste. Reuse also causes less pollution than either producing a new item or recycling. But reuse can help to reduce pollution to soil and groundwater from potentially hazardous wastes as well. Collecting and reusing latex paint, for example, is one strategy that has been used successfully in recent years. Using reclaimed motor oil and antifreeze is another. We'll look at these and many more strategies to cut pollution later.

Cut Waste

Another significant benefit of reuse is that it reduces the quantity of goods and materials that enter the waste stream. This means less groundwater contamination from leaching landfills and less air pollution from trash-burning facilities, as well as lower solid waste management costs.

Numerous reuse strategies cut waste. Excellent examples are the numerous local businesses and organizations that collect, recondition, and resell all types of household appliances.

Create Jobs

Unlike the source-reduction strategies we looked at in the previous chapters, reuse has enormous potential to create new jobs and spur economic activity. The growing interest in keeping things running longer creates significant employment opportunities in the repair sector, which has been hit hard by the proliferation of throwaway products.

Earth Education

Reuse can create new local jobs and spur domestic economic activity. Businesses that repair and rebuild products such as household appliances, auto parts, computers, and office machines provide jobs for local skilled workers. Most laser toner cartridge recharging companies, in fact, are local American businesses, whereas new toner cartridges are manufactured overseas, primarily in Asia.

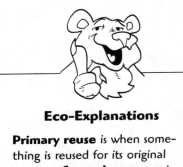

Eco-Explanations

Primary reuse is when something is reused for its original purpose. **Secondary reuse** is when it's used for some other purpose.

Tax Benefits

Reuse also offers a unique advantage—possible tax benefits. While there are some limitations, items that are donated to public schools, parks, veteran's groups, churches, and many other nonprofit organizations can normally be taken as tax-deductible contributions. The amount of the deduction is based on the fair market value of the item(s) at the time of donation. This can mean big tax savings for the donor.

Participation

Finally, like the other environmental Rs, reuse offers everyone an equal opportunity to participate in making personal choices on a daily basis that can have a profound impact on the environment. This is something that can't be emphasized too much. If everyone would take advantage of these many opportunities, we'd be well on our way to making serious progress toward a sustainable future.

Types of Reuse

As I mentioned earlier in the book, there are two types of reuse: primary and secondary. *Primary reuse* is the reuse of a product for its original purpose. A retread tire is a good example. *Secondary reuse* is using an item for some purpose other than what it was originally designed for. Using a tire as some sort of fixture in a playground, or perhaps as a bumper on a loading dock, are examples of secondary reuse.

At this point I want to pause just long enough to be sure that you understand that reuse is not the same thing as recycling. The two terms are frequently confused, but reuse and recycling are very different activities. I think the tire example will be the best way to illustrate the difference.

Putting a new tread on an old tire is reusing. But, if you take that old tire and grind it up for use in highway pavement you have recycled it. So, when you reprocess something into a raw material for use in a new product, that's technically recycling, not reusing.

But the definition of reuse includes strategies that extend well beyond retreading tires. Let's take a look at them.

Reuse Basics

Okay, reuse obviously has a lot of financial and environmental advantages. But just exactly what kinds of strategies come under the reuse umbrella? Reuse actually includes a whole range of interrelated strategies that, taken together, can get a lot more mileage out of almost any item.

Starting with well-designed, long-lasting products is the very foundation of effective reuse strategies. Based on that firm foundation, reuse includes maintaining, repairing, or remanufacturing those durable items instead of throwing them out. It also involves borrowing or renting things that you use infrequently, selling or exchanging them if they are no longer needed, or perhaps donating them to charity. Let's take a quick look at each of these strategies (a more in-depth examination of reuse strategies will follow in the next chapter).

Buy Durable Goods

One of the primary reuse strategies is to buy dur–able goods in the first place. This may seem like an obvious strategy, but it's not used as frequently as it should be.

Green Tips

Buying well-made, well-designed durable goods is a sound long-term reuse strategy. A sturdy, well-made tool, for example, could be handed down to your children long after a cheaper version breaks and ends up in a landfill.

Though saving money initially on cheaper products may seem like a good idea, often a more expensive alternative makes much more sense, both from a financial and an environmental standpoint. This is especially true for products that are designed for frequent or heavy use. One sturdy, well-made item—preferably with a solid manufacturer's warranty—can easily outlast three or four cheaper alternatives (more on the importance of design in the next chapter).

Long-lasting goods also are easier on the environment because they stay out of the waste stream far longer than their cheaper alternatives. And well-made products have a much better long-term prospect of being repeatedly reused, even after the first owner has finished with them.

Maintenance

Another important part of the reuse strategy is to make maximum use of a product's embodied energy. The longer a product lasts, the greater the use of the energy that was required for its initial production. If you properly maintain something, chances are it will last a lot longer. And just like a well-made product, well-maintained items stand a better likelihood of being reused by another owner later on.

Repair

If you throw something away rather than repairing it when it breaks or stops working, much of the embodied energy is wasted along with the item. Consequently, repair is another important piece of the reuse picture. Unfortunately, there are a whole series of reasons why repair is an increasingly difficult strategy to use these days. I'll explain why in Chapter 13, "Reuse Strategies."

Green Tips

Need a solid old desk? Try a used furniture store. Looking for a classic style dress or suit? A thrift store might have just what you need. Having trouble finding a nice old clock? Check out a local estate auction.

Buy and Sell Used Stuff

Buying and selling used products is another key part of reuse. Time-honored strategies such as flea markets, swap meets, thrift stores, and auctions can save you a lot of money when you are looking for a used product, and they can earn you some additional cash when you want to get rid of an item you no longer need.

Used markets have been around as long as there have been markets. And these have always had a small but devoted following. These markets can be a lot of fun, too. But used markets have become even more popular in recent years. I'll tell you more about the exciting developments in the used marketplace in Chapter 16.

Borrow It

Borrowing things that you don't use very often is one of those sort of fuzzy categories that tend to straddle the line between reuse and source reduction. Nevertheless, borrowing is a valid reuse strategy. And hey, why buy something brand new—or even used—and just have it sit around most of the time gathering dust? Someone you know may already have it and might be willing to lend it to you.

Rent It

Rental is another fuzzy category that straddles reuse and source reduction. In any case, it makes far more sense to rent a tool or another rarely used item than to buy it outright. And talk about using up all the embodied energy; rental equipment generally wrings out every last kilowatt and gallon conceivable.

Remanufacture It

Remanufacture is not a strategy for the average consumer. But it's a valid approach for getting more life out of a product by replacing worn or outdated parts in, say, a computer or copier, and then selling or leasing it as a remanufactured item. This has been a very successful strategy for some companies.

Exchange It

Another reuse strategy that has been especially useful for industry in recent years is the so-called "waste exchange." These regional and national Internet-based services match businesses that have potentially reusable byproducts with other businesses that can use them. The success of these exchanges is mirrored in their phenomenal growth. I'll tell you more about waste exchanges in Chapter 16.

Donate It

Donation is a reuse strategy that should not be overlooked. As I mentioned earlier, donations to nonprofit organizations offer definite tax advantages. It also gives the donor the satisfaction of knowing that things that might otherwise have gone to waste in a landfill will, instead, be put to productive reuse by organizations that probably could not have afforded them in the first place.

When Not to Reuse

Although reuse is a valuable strategy, occasionally certain things should not be reused for a variety of reasons. Let's look at some of them.

Appliances with damaged electrical cords or broken electrical elements obviously should not be reused until the damage has been repaired. It's also a tough call on what to do with inefficient older major electrical appliances such as refrigerators, freezers, and dishwashers. On the one hand, it's a good idea to get as much use as possible out of an old appliance. On the other hand, if it's an energy hog it might be best to replace it with a newer, more efficient model.

Older-model automobiles offer a similar dilemma. If your car still runs well and hasn't rusted out, there is a huge temptation to continue to drive it

Planetary Perils

Never reuse any containers that have held toxic products in them. They should be properly disposed of instead, preferably at a household hazardous waste collection center. Contact your local recycling contractor or co-ordinator for more information on proper disposal.

until it finally expires. But if it's a real gas-guzzler and is beginning to emit substantial amounts of pollutants it might be better to trade it in on a more efficient, recent model. Sometimes it's a difficult decision with no clear-cut answer.

Used children's furniture is another problematic area. Some older baby equipment may not meet current safety standards. At the very least, you should carefully inspect these items for missing hardware, broken pieces, sharp edges, tears, or holes that might be a potential hazard for your little one. The U.S. Consumer Product Safety Commission (www.cpsc.gov) offers tips and guidelines for many items.

A little care and common sense will generally avoid most problems associated with reuse. Overall, reuse is a great way to save money and the environment at the same time. And we'll look at many ways to do both, right at home, in the next chapter.

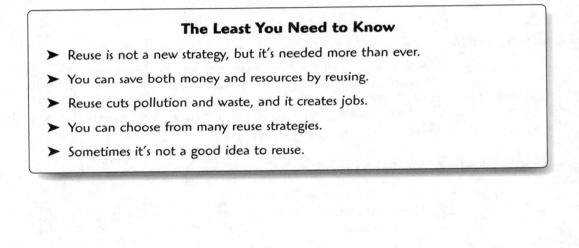

The Least You Need to Know

➤ Reuse is not a new strategy, but it's needed more than ever.

➤ You can save both money and resources by reusing.

➤ Reuse cuts pollution and waste, and it creates jobs.

➤ You can choose from many reuse strategies.

➤ Sometimes it's not a good idea to reuse.

Chapter 13

Reuse Strategies

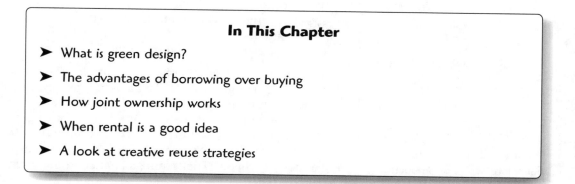

In This Chapter

➤ What is green design?

➤ The advantages of borrowing over buying

➤ How joint ownership works

➤ When rental is a good idea

➤ A look at creative reuse strategies

You've probably heard the old saying, "Neither a borrower nor a lender be." You may—or may not—be aware that it's part of a longer quote from William Shakespeare's famous play, *Hamlet*. Old Will goes on to say that loans often go astray, damaging friendships in the process (he says it better, but then, he always did have a way with words).

On the one hand, he's right. Failing to return borrowed stuff (or money) to a friend doesn't improve the relationship very much. But, at the risk of upsetting millions of Shakespeare fans around the world, I beg to differ with his apparent disapproval of borrowing and lending, both of which are excellent reuse strategies from an environmental standpoint. And they're particularly noteworthy because they represent a co-operative approach.

In this chapter, we're going to take a closer look at these reuse strategies—and many others. I'll begin with green design and how it relates to maintenance and repair.

Then we'll move on to borrowing, joint ownership, and rental. We'll also take a look at remanufacture, regeneration, and donation. Finally, I'll tell you about some places where you may find some reusable stuff for free.

Green Design

In the last chapter, I mentioned that an important part of reuse strategies are products that are well-designed and long-lasting. Unfortunately, many products on the market today are neither. This makes reuse extremely difficult, if not impossible, for those items. *Planned obsolescence* has become so widespread in our economy that reversing that trend is going to be a challenge. Difficult, but not impossible.

In fact, a variety of governmental agencies, nonprofit organizations, and companies are currently rethinking the fundamentals of product design to include considerations such as durability, ease of maintenance, repair, and remanufacture, among other things. And because products that incorporate such improvements will last longer, the environment will benefit from a reduced waste stream and its related costs. This design revolution is generally referred to as "green design."

The U.S. Congressional Office of Technology Assessment describes green design as "a design process in which environmental attributes of a product are treated as design objectives rather than as constraints." In other words, such things as waste prevention and better materials management become part of the initial design scheme. That's quite a change from current thinking.

Programs to encourage this kind of design have been set up in various countries around the world. In the U.S., the Green Seal program I mentioned in Chapter 10, "More Ways to Reduce," is actively promoting new environmental design standards, product certification, and education. North of the border, the Canadian Environmental Choice Program has a similar mission, and its EcoLogo appears on products and services that meet their standards.

Eco-Explanations

Planned obsolescence is the deliberate design of products to wear out or break down in a fairly short period of time. As early as the 1930s, an engineer working for General Electric suggested increasing sales of flashlight bulbs by shortening their lifespan. By the 1950s, planned obsolescence had become routine for many consumer products.

Although progress so far has been relatively slow, reuse considerations are beginning to show up more often in product design in this country. This trend will accelerate in the years to come as more and more companies realize the long-term advantages of reuse for the environment—and the bottom line.

Some companies, in fact, have already recognized the potential of the "green consumer" sector of the marketplace. Research has consistently shown that anywhere from 2 to 30 percent of all consumers prefer low-waste alternatives and are willing to pay more for better-designed, longer-lasting products. Patagonia®, the successful California-based clothing retailer with its strong environmental business philosophy, is a prime example.

The Canadian EcoLogo.

(Environmental Choice Program)

Maintenance

Obviously, products that are designed to be easy to maintain will have a longer lifespan than those that are not. Easy disassembly, availability of spare replacement parts, and easy-to-follow repair manuals are all important maintenance considerations. As an individual consumer you don't have any direct control over design, but you can extend the life of almost any product by maintaining it properly.

As important as design is, if we ignore basic maintenance of our appliances, automobiles, and other products, they simply aren't going to last as long as they should. And that's expensive for us as well as for the environment. The average American home contains thousands of dollars' worth of appliances. You can protect your investment by following the manufacturer's maintenance guidelines in the owner's manual. In the long run, you'll save a lot of money if you do.

Green Tips

If you've lost the owner's manual to a major appliance (or if you never had it in the first place) you can usually get one from the manufacturer or appliance dealer. By following the maintenance procedures in the manual, you can often add years of productive life to many products.

Repair

Green design also emphasizes easy repair. But this is an area where there is currently a lot of room for improvement. While some items can still be repaired, many consumer products today are deliberately designed and manufactured to be throwaways. That makes repair almost impossible, and has also led to the demise of much of the repair industry in this country—and higher labor rates for those that remain in business.

One way out of this dilemma is to refuse to buy this cheap junk, and, instead, demand well-designed, long-lasting, repairable products. Eventually, manufacturers will be forced to respond to market demand. And we'll be helping to cut a lot of waste at the same time. Want to help? Vote with your shopping dollars.

Timely repairs can extend the life of most products. But, unfortunately, many poorly designed, hard-to-fix appliances are frequently thrown away when they break down. Also, the high cost of labor unfortunately tends to discourage repair, even if the appliance is reasonably easy to fix. In fact, in a 1998 *Consumer Reports* survey, half of those people who threw out appliances blamed the high cost of repair, and a third cited the low cost of replacement, as the main reasons why they decided to throw the items away.

Nevertheless, there are still plenty of times when repair makes sense, especially if the problem is relatively minor. We'll look at a number of appliance-repair situations in the next chapter to try to help you decide when it makes sense to repair.

Green Tips

One of the best ways to help you remember to return something that you borrowed is to make sure it is marked with the owner's identity. It also may be helpful to have a verbal, or even written, agreement about when you will return the item. And if you return the item in even better condition than it was when you received it—cleaned, lubricated, sharpened, and so on—chances are your future requests will be welcomed.

Something Borrowed

Borrowing things that you only need once—or once in a while—is another great reuse strategy. Borrowing something temporarily and then returning it when you are finished with it is nothing new. In fact, our entire public library system is based on this idea.

And while we're on the subject, have you been to your local library lately? If not, you may be surprised to find that in addition to books, magazines, and newspapers, many libraries now offer movies and music. Some even lend tools. So, check out your local public reuse center, and while you're there, check out some great stuff.

But the concept of borrowing extends well beyond libraries. Family members, friends, and neighbors frequently borrow or lend things like clothing or tools. It's a great strategy.

Joint Ownership

Joint ownership is a somewhat more formal variation of the cooperative strategy. But it still makes a lot of sense, especially for large, expensive tools or equipment such as a garden tiller that you would only use occasionally.

Depending on how many joint owners are involved, it's usually a good idea to have a written agreement about such things as repair, maintenance, and use. You might also want to include provisions on what to do when one of the owners moves out of town, or about requests for use by non-owners. Joint ownership can be tricky, but a little advanced planning can avoid many potential problems with this otherwise excellent approach.

Rental

Although you've probably rented videotapes and perhaps an automobile, it's probable that, like the majority of Americans, you may not have considered renting much else. That's too bad, because rental is a great reuse strategy.

Renting things that you only need on rare occasions makes a lot of sense both from a financial and an environmental standpoint. And it's amazing what you can rent these days: from hammer drills to tents, and backhoes to wedding gowns. The staff at most rental outlets will be happy to help you find the right tool or item for your particular needs. And they'll show you how to use it properly and safely. So, if it's an expensive item (or even if it's not so expensive), and you only need it for a few hours or days, rent it.

For more information on rental, check out the American Rental Association Web site (www.ararental.org), which contains information on the organization and its members, a local rental company finder, and some handy household tips as well.

Earth Education

The rental industry has grown dramatically in recent years. Currently more than 12,000 retail outlets of rental agencies are in the United States and Canada. Long-dominated by Mom-and-Pop operations, the industry now includes everything from small family businesses to multi-store chains and franchises, according to the American Rental Association, a trade group with around 7,200 members.

Remanufacture

Even a well-designed, sturdy product that has been carefully maintained and repaired eventually wears out. But, instead of being recycled, some items can be remanufactured, which is a better alternative.

While remanufacture is not something that the average consumer can tackle, it's a sound and profitable strategy for many businesses. In fact, in 1996 the remanufacturing sector in this country employed 10 times as many workers as metals mining, and earned $53 billion—a sum greater than the sales of the entire consumer durable goods industry, according to the Worldwatch Institute.

Unlike reconditioning or refurbishing, in which only broken or worn out parts are replaced, remanufacture involves the complete disassembly of an item. Then, it is thoroughly cleaned, inspected, and reassembled with new or upgraded parts where appropriate. The result is a product that is normally as good as new.

Remanufacture saves a good deal of the embodied energy of the original product, and typically reduces production costs by 40 to 60 percent. Consumer items that are often remanufactured include auto parts, copying machines, toner cartridges, and computers. If you're in the market for one of these items, don't overlook remanufacture. Most remanufacturers offer a warranty that meets or beats new product guarantees.

Regeneration

As I mentioned earlier, the demise of much of the traditional repair sector in this country due to cheap, throwaway products has led to high labor charges by those individuals who remain. And many parts of this country have virtually no repair options at all for many products. I now have to drive 70 miles round trip to have a pair of shoes repaired. That's absurd. To say nothing about the pollution involved with the trip.

Eco-Explanations

A **regeneration center** is a central location where various skilled repair technicians are encouraged to go into business to provide a wide range of repair capabilities for the community.

But a new movement is developing that might change this bleak picture. It involves setting up what are generally called *regeneration centers*. The main idea is to encourage a group of businesses that specialize in the repair of appliances and other products to set up shop in a mall-type setting where people can bring things that need to be fixed.

Not only does this strategy help to solve the repair dilemma, but it also stimulates the creation of new local jobs and it cuts down on the waste stream. And this idea works for businesses as well as for the average consumer. Obviously, this won't work if the products being brought in are junk to begin with, so this strategy needs to accompany a major move toward green product design.

Donation

Have you got some old stuff sitting around in the basement or the attic that is still serviceable, but you just don't use or need it anymore? Though you might consider selling it, another excellent reuse option is to donate it to a worthy cause. And passing unused goods on to others who can use them is much better than throwing those items away.

Donation has a number of advantages:

➤ It keeps things out of landfills.

➤ It gives used items a chance for a second life.

➤ It helps other people.

➤ It may have tax benefits for you.

➤ Best of all, it makes you feel good.

A wide range of standard household goods such as furniture, appliances, electronics, toys, baby gear, tools, and so on are prime candidates for donation as long as they are in usable condition.

It's Free!

Almost everyone likes a free offer. Especially if it involves free stuff. What if you could get your hands on free items for reuse—and help save the environment at the same time? It's possible.

You can do this in a number of ways. First is the time-honored tradition of dump picking. Then there's the more recent practice of dumpster diving. And finally, an increasing number of imaginative "reuse events" are popping up all across the country.

Sound good? It is. But, of course, there are some problems associated with some of these strategies. Let's take a look at the strategies—and the problems.

Dump Picking

It wasn't that long ago when spending a portion of your Saturday morning exploring the local dump for perfectly good, reusable stuff was a regular part of life in many parts of this country. The problem, of course, was that you might end up coming back home with more stuff in your pickup than you started out with in the first place. All of that has ended in most locations with the closure of old-style dumps and their replacement by highly mechanized sanitary landfills. But the old practice of dump picking has been revived in some places—in a slightly different form.

Green Tips

If you decide to donate used goods to a qualified nonprofit group or organization, you not only help the group, but you may be entitled to a tax deduction at the end of the year as well. See IRS publications No. 526, *Charitable Contributions*, and No. 561, *Determining the Value of Donated Property*, both of which appear on the IRS Web site (www.irs.ustreas.gov) under Forms and Pubs.

Earth Education

Hundreds of tons of reusable materials are often disposed of at recycling or waste transfer stations without cost to the community when local residents pick up things they can reuse. This strategy has been highly successful in some towns. Many reusable items reportedly barely have time to hit the ground before an enthusiastic new owner scoops them up.

In many communities that have recycling or waste transfer stations, certain areas are now set aside for the temporary storage of reusable items. These areas are sometimes referred to as "reuse yards" (more on this in Chapter 16, "The Used Marketplace"). And local residents are encouraged to drop off things they don't need anymore and to pick up other items that they do need.

And, in some locations, the old social aspects of dump picking have been revived as well. The Recycling and Disposal Facility in Wellesley, Massachusetts, reportedly hosts frequent informal, friendly gatherings—even picnics—in addition to offering free compost, firewood, a book exchange, and drop-off spots for a number of local charities. If it works for them, it can work for your community, too.

Dumpster Diving

I admit that dumpster diving isn't for everyone. But salvaging free reusable treasures from those big steel garbage containers can be rewarding. Some even claim that it's fun. These folks happily haul their finds home, and, after cleaning them up or making minor repairs, they normally sell them at flea markets or to secondhand shops.

For those concerned about the legal aspects of dumpster diving, I'm not aware of any federal laws specifically prohibiting it. However, state laws or local ordinances might place restrictions on the practice, so you need to check them out before you proceed.

Planetary Perils

Dumpster diving can be dangerous, and it may be illegal in some areas. Special precautions need to be taken before you engage in this activity. Be aware of the potential dangers of broken glass, sharp edges, and the possibility of toxic or other dangerous materials. At the very least, wear heavy work gloves.

Assuming that there are no local prohibitions, you are generally allowed to salvage other people's discards as long as you observe two basic commonsense rules:

1. Don't trespass.
2. Don't steal.

So, first thing, get permission before you start to poke through a private dumpster. Also, it's not safe to actually climb into a dumpster, so it might be better to use a long pole with a hook on the end while you stand outside.

Dumpsters located at or near colleges and universities can offer particularly good pickings after the end of semesters or graduation. Theater dumpsters also are another potential treasure trove after a production ends.

I don't personally recommend dumpster diving because of the potential hazards involved, but if you're the adventurous sort and want to try it, that's up to you. Be sure it's legal in your area first. Then be careful.

Special Reuse Events

In addition to the strategies above, a growing number of special events across the country encourage folks to reuse things—cutting down on municipal solid waste and the consumption of new products at the same time.

For quite a few years folks in the Upper Connecticut River Valley area of Vermont and New Hampshire have been getting together annually for "UP-for-Grabs: The Reusable Goods Festival." Co-sponsored by a number of environmental groups, the festival encourages people to bring still-usable items for free exchange to a central location. Anyone is allowed to participate, whether they bring anything or not. Food and live music add to the festive atmosphere. At the end of the day, dealers are allowed to pick through whatever is left, and the remainder is donated to charities, recycled, or hauled off as trash.

In other parts of the country, many towns organize a special "Spring Cleaning" drive that allows residents to place unwanted but functional or repairable goods at the curb. Then, a reasonable amount of time is given to everyone to pick through the stuff before the remainder is hauled away.

Many other initiatives both public and private, large and small, follow similar themes. And they're all aimed at encouraging less waste. But that's what reuse strategies are about. They're good for you, for your pocketbook, and for the planet. And I think that's something that even William Shakespeare would approve of.

The Least You Need to Know

➤ Green design is good for the environment as well as the bottom line for many companies.

➤ Borrowing things can be a great strategy to save money and the environment—as long as you remember to return them.

➤ Joint ownership can be a valuable reuse strategy if it's carefully set up.

➤ Renting things that you only need briefly is a great reuse idea.

➤ Imaginative reuse strategies can be fun as well as good for the environment.

At Home

In This Chapter

➤ Ways to make your appliances last longer

➤ Reuse hints in the kitchen

➤ Reuse opportunities in your medicine cabinet

➤ Reuse strategies for the bedroom

➤ The best reuse ideas for your living room

When you were growing up, did your mother warn you against "bad habits" like chewing gum or slouching at the dinner table? Or maybe even wasting things—like uneaten broccoli? But while you were being lectured, was she busily mopping up a kitchen spill with a handful of paper towels? Or covering leftover food with plastic wrap or tinfoil? Chances are, she was.

Though Mom's advice may have been well-intended, the bad household habits she was practicing herself were even worse than the behavior she was warning you about. The overuse of disposable paper, plastic, and other products in this country has far more serious environmental consequences than poor table posture ever will.

Now, I'm not really picking on Mom. It could have been almost anyone in your family—or mine for that matter. But recognizing our bad environmental habits, and then doing something to improve them, is a key part of the reuse picture.

And because the routine choices we make at home play such a key role in this, we're going to focus entirely on home-based reuse ideas in this chapter (in addition to the home-based source-reduction suggestions we looked at in Chapter 8, "A Houseful of

Earth Education

It has been estimated that if we could extend the life of our major household appliances by one third with proper maintenance and repair, we could cut the number of appliances entering the waste stream by 12 million every year. To add a little extra incentive, a growing number of states have banned many major appliances from their landfills, making reuse a far more attractive alternative.

Green Tips

If you repair your own appliances, you can save about two thirds of what it would cost to have someone else do it for you. The general rule of thumb for appliance repair is that if the cost of repair is 50 percent or less than the cost of a new item, it's probably worth it to make the repair.

Savings"). I'm going to tell you about a whole array of reuse strategies that you can employ throughout your home, from the kitchen to the bathroom, and from the bedroom to just about everywhere else. And best of all, we'll be saving money and resources as we go.

Reuse at Home

We are literally surrounded with countless opportunities to help improve the environment every day in our homes (or apartment, or condo). But just exactly what are they, and how do we take advantage of them?

Because so many possibilities abound, I'm going to have to limit the number of strategies somewhat. I'll describe some in detail, mention others briefly, and leave it up to your creative impulses to come up with even more ideas. You're limited only by your imagination.

Appliances

Let's start with appliances. The longer your household appliances remain in operating condition, the longer they stay out of the waste stream. That saves money on waste disposal costs and conserves the resources needed to replace them. And probably one of the most important reuse strategies you can follow with your appliances is to keep them maintained and in good repair.

Simply keeping your appliances clean and following the basic maintenance instructions in the owner's manual can often add years of additional service. And when a part fails in a major appliance, such as a dishwasher, clothes dryer, or stove, it's usually worth it to have it repaired.

Obviously, this depends on the particular problem, but appliance service technicians have told me that in many cases a small part that only costs a few dollars can keep an otherwise sound appliance going for years. I know, it's the labor costs that are the killer, but even so, if a $150 repair job keeps your $450 dishwasher going for another five years, it's still a good deal for you—and the environment.

But you can extend the life of appliances in other ways. If your stove, for example, works well but looks a little tired, you might want to spruce it up with a new top or perhaps an oven door. Some appliances can be repainted with lead-free epoxy spray paint or professionally re-porcelainized. If you get another five or ten years out of an appliance like this, the costs are definitely worth it.

And when it finally comes time to dispose of your trusty old stove or washing machine, rather than hauling it to the dump or recycling center you might want to see whether someone in your area reconditions dead appliances. Sometimes they pick up for free.

In the Kitchen

Let's move on to the kitchen. In many homes the kitchen is more-or-less the operations center for the entire family. It also offers a large number of opportunities for a variety of reuse strategies.

Coffee Filters

If you need a hot cup of java to help kick-start your day, you have a great opportunity to help the environment while making a better cup of coffee at the same time. Coffee filters made from white, chlorine-bleached paper may contain tiny traces of highly toxic dioxin that can actually end up in your coffee. The same toxic chemical may end up in the environment at the paper mill as well. And then there are the trees that are being chopped down to make the paper. All that for a cup of coffee?

The solution? You have several choices:

➤ Cloth filters

➤ Metal filters

➤ Press-type coffeemakers

➤ Old-fashioned percolators

Metal filters come in stainless steel, chrome, or gold-plated versions and last for years. Unlike paper filters, these metal filters don't impart any taste to the coffee. Many coffee connoisseurs insist that the fine-mesh, gold-plated filters make the best-tasting brew. You decide. Cleanup is a snap. A simple rinse under hot water does the trick.

Green Tips

Cloth filters made of unbleached cotton muslin may be reused for up to two years. Simply rinse after use in plain hot water. Don't use soapy water or you will end up brewing off-flavored coffee. Occasionally soak the cloth filter in a solution of 2 cups of boiling water and 1 tablespoon of baking soda to freshen the filter and remove stains. Rinse thoroughly before reuse.

There are also a number of nondrip coffeemakers with permanent washable screens that filter the grounds from the java. These include stovetop espresso pots, European press types, and old-fashioned percolators.

Food Storage Containers

Foods come in so many miscellaneous reusable containers these days that you really don't need to buy extras, (with the possible exception of a basic set of plastic storage containers with airtight lids).

Yogurt, cottage cheese, and deli containers, as well as glass jars with screw tops can all be reused for other foods once they have been emptied of their original contents and thoroughly cleaned and sanitized. So many containers are available, in fact, that the main challenge is trying to figure out what to do with them all. (Reminder: Never reuse containers that have held cleaning products or other possibly toxic substances.)

Reusing food containers is not only a great strategy because you are extending their useful life, but at the same time you are hopefully not using as much disposable plastic wrap and aluminum foil. Another way to cut your use of wrap and foil is to buy a set of washable vinyl bowl covers, which resemble shower caps. You can leave the leftover food right in the bowl and pop on a cover.

Planetary Perils

Plastic bags that have held meat, poultry, fish, or cheese should not be reused for other foods because of the danger of bacteria transfer. If the bag has printed advertising on the outside, make sure the printing stays on the outside, away from the food, because the print may contain trace amounts of toxic metals. Of course, always keep plastic bags away from babies to avoid the dangers of suffocation.

Plastic Food Bags

So many foods and other products come in plastic bags these days that they're hard to avoid. But if you can't avoid them, at least reuse them. You've already paid for these bags anyway, so you might as well get your money's worth. Depending on what they contained, you may want to wash them out first. You can even buy a small wooden drying rack, specifically designed for this purpose, from environmentally oriented stores, by mail order, or online (www.realgoods.com).

You have lots of reuse possibilities. Produce bags make great lunch or sandwich bags. You can also bring them back to the store and use them again as produce bags. They're also handy for carrying wet bathing suits or soiled diapers while you're traveling.

Grocery Bags

You might be tempted to think that paper grocery bags aren't a big deal. Maybe one bag isn't. But the 40 billion disposable bags we use in the U.S. every year is a big deal for the environment and for the trees cut down to manufacture them. It has been estimated that if every household in this country used just one less grocery bag per week, we'd save the energy and trees needed to make more than five billion bags a year.

One way to save bags is to bring back the paper sack from last week's shopping and reuse it. Most supermarkets offer a few cents' credit for reused bags. Better yet, use a sturdy, inexpensive canvas bag. String or net bags are another alternative that have the added convenience of being handy to store in your pocket or purse.

Whatever approach you decide to use, it's a good idea to keep a few bags in your car or someplace handy at home where you'll remember to bring them with you when you go shopping. It's a small habit change that can have big repercussions.

Kitchen Towels

As I mentioned earlier, using paper towels for routine cleaning chores is a bad habit. I know, I know: They're so handy for mopping up messy, greasy spills. And for drying your hands. And for use as table napkins. And on and on. Unfortunately, when you multiply this times 365 days a year and 275 million Americans, it really begins to add up. In fact, it's estimated that we have a 27-million-trees-a-year paper towel habit in this country.

But there is a simple solution: Use cotton kitchen towels as often as possible instead of paper. And while you're at it, replace your paper table napkins with washable cloth napkins, too. And if you just can't let go of paper towels completely yet, at least buy a brand that contains recycled post-consumer waste paper and does not use any chlorine bleach in its production (read the fine print on the package). That's a step in the right direction.

Green Tips

If a family of four uses cloth napkins at every meal for a year instead of paper, they will keep 4,380 paper napkins out of the waste stream. If you buy your cotton kitchen towels by the dozen, the individual cost can be just a few dollars. And not only will you save trees, you'll also save money. A $2 towel can easily outlast $25 or $30 worth of paper towels.

The Bathroom

Let's move on to the bathroom. You probably have a number of reuse possibilities that are hiding in your medicine cabinet.

Cosmetics

Most cosmetics, from shampoo to moisturizer, and makeup to hand cream, come in containers that are rarely reused. But a few companies have responded to this wasteful

Planetary Perils

Regardless of their packaging, almost all cosmetics can cause allergic reactions in certain individuals. The first sign of a reaction is often a mild redness and irritation. Discontinue use of any cosmetic that causes an allergic reaction.

Green Tips

Reglazing an old cast-iron bathtub generally costs 25 percent or less than the cost of a new tub. This strategy also works on porcelain or enamel sinks and appliances. Or you can have the tub relined with a molded acrylic or PVC plastic liner. Tub renewals generally only take a day or two to accomplish.

situation by offering refills of their products. The Body Shop (www.the-body-shop.com), an international chain with 1,500 outlets around the world, encourages reuse by offering discounts when you bring back your empties for refilling its personal care products.

Bio Pac, Inc. (www.bio-pac.com) is another company that offers its castile soap, shampoo, and hair conditioner (and a wide range of household cleaning products) in bulk so that you can refill your reusable containers at most natural food stores. Other cosmetic manufacturers are beginning to offer refills as well. Look for them at your local drugstore or supermarket.

Deodorants

Most deodorants stink when it comes to their throw-away packaging and containers. But there are a few exceptions. Tom's of Maine, a manufacturer of natural personal care products, offers a refillable roll-on deodorant (see "Retailers" in Appendix D for contact information). A few other environmentally enlightened manufacturers are beginning to follow Tom's good example. Another alternative is a crystal deodorant stone made from natural mineral salts. One of these can last up to a year. You may be able to find these in your local natural foods co-op or by mail order.

Bathtubs

This one's too big to fit in your medicine cabinet. But if you have an old cast-iron bathtub that is still usable but a little battered, you might want to consider a number of possible money-saving reuse strategies. You can repair small chips, cracks, or scratches with a porcelain repair kit yourself for just a few dollars.

The Bedroom

The bedroom offers a number of reuse opportunities. In the nineteenth century it was common for women to make some of the family bedding out of old clothing and fabric scraps. Most patchwork quilts today are generally made from kits.

These days, the biggest reuse opportunity for bedding is not in making it, but in making better use of it when you no longer need it. It's not unusual for a large quantity of used sheets, pillowcases, blankets, pillows, and bedspreads to end up in storage when you've changed bed sizes or decorating schemes. If you're not using these items, consider donating them to a local charitable organization.

Mattresses

The best reuse strategy for mattresses is to make them last as long as possible. Most manufacturers recommend that you rotate your mattress periodically by turning it over and also flipping it end to end occasionally.

Because mattresses take up so much space in landfills, it's better to donate an old mattress to a thrift shop or similar organization if it's still usable (many states require used mattresses to be sanitized before resale to the public).

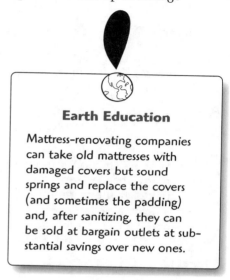

Earth Education

Mattress-renovating companies can take old mattresses with damaged covers but sound springs and replace the covers (and sometimes the padding) and, after sanitizing, they can be sold at bargain outlets at substantial savings over new ones.

Clothing

Remember the "vintage" clothing craze of the 1960s I mentioned earlier? Well, what goes around comes around, as the saying goes. Clothing reuse has become trendy again. Not only that, but Americans are buying fewer items and wearing what they do buy longer. Regardless of whether you buy new or reused clothing, how you take care of it affects how long it will last.

Here are a few basic tips to help you get the most out of your wardrobe:

➤ Avoid the planned obsolescence of trendy fashion statements by purchasing well-made, classic basics that will last longer and look great the whole time.

➤ Gentle laundering extends the life of most garments—go easy on the bleach, use cold water whenever possible, and hang your clothes on a line to dry outside if you can (turn them inside out to avoid sun-fading).

➤ Repair small rips or unraveling seams before they get larger (or have someone do it for you).

➤ Remove all stains promptly.

The same basic strategies work for children's clothing as well. But children's wear has substantial additional reuse opportunities because kids—and especially infants—grow out of it so quickly. If you have a big family, you can pass the clothing on to the next child that comes along. If not, giving it to a neighbor's or friend's child is a good alternative. Or you can sell it to a growing number of resale shops that special-ize in children's clothing and furniture (more on them in Chapter 16, "The Used Marketplace").

Shoes

You can get a lot of mileage out of a good pair of shoes. Sturdy, well-made, classic-design shoes will last long after their trendy or "bargain" competitors have dropped out of the race—and into the waste stream.

Some basic maintenance goes a long way toward keep shoes looking good, and it helps them to last longer, too. A little shoe polish now and then, or, in the case of hiking boots, waterproofing, can extend the life of footwear substantially.

Shoe repair shops can give a whole new life to an old pair of well-made shoes. But many cheaper—especially imported—models are constructed in a way that makes re-pair difficult or impossible. Keep this in mind the next time you are in the market for a new pair of shoes. You may end up paying more money in the short run, but will end up saving a lot more in the long run. And you'll be helping the environment, too.

The Living Room

Your home hardly has a place where there aren't some reuse possibilities, and the liv-ing room is no exception. Although furniture is found throughout the house, the largest concentration is normally in the living room.

Green Tips

Especially if you have children, removable, washable slipcovers for your armchairs and sofa can substantially extend the life of your living room furniture. A fab-ric protector sprayed on your up-holstered furniture will make cleanup easier. Most furniture dealers offer this as an option.

Furniture

Living room furniture, especially stuffed and uphol-stered chairs, sofas, and recliners, are prime candidates for careful reuse strategies because they take up so much space in landfills and cost so much to replace.

Keeping your furniture clean and in good repair is one of your best reuse strategies. This can admittedly be a challenge in combination with lively young children. But quick cleanup of accidental spills and regular vac-uuming is always a good idea.

Regardless of whether or not you have children, an old sofa or armchair that has become hopelessly dirty or threadbare can be restored to like-new appearance by reupholstering. But be forewarned, it's not cheap if you have it done professionally. Well-made furniture with hardwood frames, glued joints, and reinforcing blocks at the corners is worth reupholstering. Furniture with cheap plywood or stapled softwood frames is generally not worth the expense. Many adult education programs include reupholstering in their class offerings; learn a new skill, and save money at the same time.

Carpets, Rugs, and Draperies

Regular maintenance of your carpets is the best way to get the longest life out of them. Vacuum carpets weekly to keep ground-in dirt particles from damaging the fibers when they're walked on. Clean up spills promptly. Consider deep-cleaning your carpets every year or two.

And if something awful happens to a carpet, such as a cigarette burn or a stain that resists your best efforts to remove, don't give up. Professional carpet repairs can often save a carpet from the landfill with a variety of techniques.

Have you gotten tired of those old drapes in the living room? If it's time to redecorate, go ahead, but don't toss those drapes if they're still in reasonably good shape. Your trash may be someone else's treasure. Consider donating them to a charity such as the Goodwill, the Salvation Army, or a similar organization.

Green Tips

Local theater groups often can use old drapes in their productions, so don't overlook that reuse possibility. Depending on the material, you might also be able to transform drapes into any number of creations, such as laundry bags, a washable cover for your pet's bed, or a small cushion or pillow. At the very least, your old drapes can probably serve as rags for house cleaning and painting projects as their final curtain call.

Throughout the Home

Everywhere in your home are so many reuse possibilities that it's hard to decide which ones to mention. Here are a few more ideas to get your little gray cells working:

➤ Disposable baby wipes are expensive and wasteful; you can use dampened cotton washcloths instead, and wash them with the diapers.

➤ If you just can't part with the convenience of disposable baby wipes, at least get refill packs for your heavy-duty plastic baby-wipe tub.

➤ Sell the books you are finished with to a secondhand bookstore or donate them to a local library book sale.

➤ The comics' section of your newspaper makes great gift-wrap.

➤ You can double the life of greeting cards by cutting off the message and reusing the front part as a post card or gift tag.

➤ Instead of trashing your magazines, try donating them to hospitals or convalescent homes.

➤ Foam polystyrene packing pellets, or "peanuts," are not biodegradable; you should reuse these as packing material whenever possible.

As you can see, there's no lack of ideas for creative reuse strategies around the home. And, in most cases, it's just a matter of turning bad old habits into good new ones. What's more, you can save money and the environment at the same time. I think Mom would agree: That's a good habit to develop.

The Least You Need to Know

➤ Your home has many reuse opportunities.

➤ Repairing many major appliances makes good financial and environmental sense.

➤ You can save a lot of money and trees by using cloth towels instead of paper towels.

➤ Well-made, classic-design clothes and shoes outlast their "bargain" alternatives many times over.

➤ Reupholstering can give well-built furniture a second life.

Chapter 15

At Work ... and Beyond

> ## In This Chapter
>
> ➤ How you can save resources and money through reuse in the work environment
>
> ➤ When a reused computer makes sense
>
> ➤ What to look for in copying-machine design
>
> ➤ A look at used office furniture
>
> ➤ Ways to reuse shipping supplies

One of the most encouraging developments in the reuse arena has been the fact that many businesses and governmental organizations have discovered that they can save a lot of money while reducing waste and helping the environment at the same time. Some businesses, in fact, have been real pioneers in this field.

The Xerox Corporation, for example, has reduced its purchases of a wide variety of copying-machine parts by reclaiming, refurbishing, and reusing existing parts, while saving several hundred million dollars in purchases annually. Many other companies are following similar strategies. Obviously, not everyone will save that kind of money. But the possibilities for improving the bottom line are substantial in almost any business—even your own.

And that's what we're going to focus on in this chapter. We'll look at a number of money-saving reuse ideas in the office, in the shipping department, and elsewhere in your work environment. And most of these ideas can help whether you work in some large company, in a medium-sized business, or in a small home office.

Earth Education

Each year in this country, around 50 million pulpwood trees are cut down to supply offices with business forms. Office paper is one of the fastest growing parts of the waste stream and currently represents about 12 million tons annually, up from 8 million tons in 1988.

Earth Education

It should come as no great surprise that about 40 percent of all new computers bought today are replacing older ones. Every year businesses in this country dispose of around 10 million computers for newer models, according to a Carnegie-Mellon University study. If current trends continue, around 150 million computers will have been buried in landfills by the year 2005.

In the Office

You don't have to look very far in many offices for good examples of bad habits that waste a lot of money and resources. Wastebaskets filled with polystyrene coffee cups, old file folders, envelopes, old ballpoint pens, batteries, and so on are, unfortunately, a common sight.

Then there's office furniture. It's not unusual for slightly battered but otherwise perfectly functional office furniture to be hauled off and get replaced with brand new items in many companies and organizations. While that may be good for company image—and office equipment manufacturers—it's not so good for the environment. And this strategy generally doesn't make much financial sense either.

I could go on, but I think you get the idea—there's lots of room for improvement in the workplace. Let's take a look at some of the main problem areas, and see what can be done about them.

Computers

Some of the basic reuse strategies I mentioned in Chapter 13, "Reuse Strategies," such as rental (or leasing), buying used equipment, and finding a new home for old equipment, make a lot of sense in the office. But there are plenty of other strategies to choose from. Let's start with what has become an indispensable piece of office equipment—the computer.

While the computer has unquestionably increased worker productivity, this has come at a fairly high environmental cost. Talk about engineered obsolescence! The breathtaking speed of technological advancements in the computer field leaves brand new models practically obsolete the moment you take them out of the box.

The good news is that many older models can be refurbished and sold to new users who don't need all the latest bells and whistles. Many small businesses find that last year's model (or even older) is just fine for word processing or spreadsheets. Chances are, a computer that has successfully made it through its first few years still has a lot of number-crunching life left in it, since a computer basically either works or it doesn't.

Remarkably, the computer resale business, which barely existed 10 years ago, now exceeds $5 billion a year, according to some industry experts. While much of this figure represents business-to-business purchases, it still highlights the dramatic growth in this important segment of the resale market.

And used machines can be a real bargain. Around 60 percent of the 2.4 million used computers bought in this country in 1995 were priced under $500. If anything, that price has gone down even further since then, while computing power has gone up. Used computers are widely available at computer dealers who take trade-ins, or from companies that repair, recondition, and sell them—often known as refurbishers—from computer exchanges, and from individuals (more on the used marketplace in Chapter 16, "The Used Marketplace").

Here are a few hints to help you get the most out of a used computer:

➤ Look for a warranty from a computer refurbisher—most offer 30-day guarantees, but some will give a 90-day warranty.

➤ Check on the availability of spare parts for the unit you are buying—most refurbishers stock used parts.

➤ Find out how upgradable the computer is—the more expansion slots and room for memory upgrades the better.

And, whether your computer is used or new, always plug it and its components into a surge protector to guard them from electrical spikes.

Keeping your computer clean is a simple but effective way to extend its life substantially. Dust sucked inside the case by the cooling fan can coat the interior and cause some components to overheat and burn out prematurely. Regular vacuuming around the air intakes of your computer's case will help reduce the amount of dust that gets inside.

Cleaning the inside of a computer can be a tricky business because of the danger of damaging components with a static electrical charge. And opening the cover can void some warranties. But if your warranty has run out, or if you are fairly experienced in computer maintenance, careful dust removal is good preventive maintenance. And if you don't want to tackle this yourself, many computer repair shops can do it for you for under $50.

One final computer tip: Many companies (and individuals) are finding computer leasing to be an increasingly attractive option, especially considering the speed with which computers become obsolete. Compare the numbers and decide if it makes sense for you.

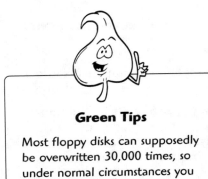

Computer Supplies

But what about the care and feeding of your computers? Every year computers and printers devour a billion floppy disks, 60 million laser toner cartridges, 100 million printer ribbons, and countless inkjet cartridges. But a number of reuse strategies available can soften the effects of this excessive consumption.

Even inkjet cartridges can be refilled from two to five times. Many of the same companies that recharge toner cartridges will do this. Also, refill kits are available at most stationery and office-supply outlets, and mail-in refill services are available at many of these stores.

In this country the nylon ribbons used by dot matrix printers are often thrown out when they start to fade. But it is possible to reink them at least 10 times without harm to the ribbon or the printer. Reinking machines are available for about $70. Or, as an alternative, faded ribbons can be given to a cartridge reloader who will install a fresh ribbon for about 40 percent of the cost of a new one.

But what about the 30 million disks that contain outdated retail software every year? In the past, most of them have ended up shredded and landfilled or incinerated to protect the copyright. But in recent years a number of environmentally aware companies have begun to rescue these reusable diskettes by magnetically erasing them, relabeling and repackaging them for sale. These renewed disks are generally sold for 10 to 50 percent off the price of new ones.

Copying Machines

Almost every office—large or small—has a copying machine. But this is another area where frequent advances in technology and design changes make older models hard to sell, reducing their potential for reuse. One way to avoid this dilemma is to buy a well-designed copier in the first place that contains standardized parts and is easy to repair and upgrade.

Both Kodak and Xerox make copiers that meet these criteria. Their machines include "modular" components that are easy to maintain or replace by the user. And, as I mentioned earlier, Xerox uses a number of refurbished or reclaimed parts that are also interchangeable between some of their different models of copiers.

But Xerox has taken the concept of reuse to new heights by fundamentally reinventing itself as a provider of document services rather than a seller of copying machines. As a consequence, the company now leases most of its copy machines. This has given Xerox a tremendous incentive to maximize the use—and reuse—of its copiers. In recent years, Xerox has increased the number of remanufactured machines to 28 percent, and hopes to eventually boost that figure to 84 percent. This is a striking reuse model that could be—well—copied by many other businesses.

Green Tips

Leasing or renting a copier might make a lot of sense for you or your office as well as for the environment. A leased machine eliminates the dilemma of what to do with an outdated copier and shifts that burden to the leasing company. It also gives that company an incentive to make that machine last as long as possible.

And if you have an older-model copier sitting around that is no longer being used but is still serviceable, you might be able to donate it to a local group or organization that otherwise could not afford one. You'll give the old machine a new life and help some folks out at the same time.

Fax Machines

In the long run, I think fax machines will become as extinct as the dodo. Most computers now have fax sending and receiving capabilities (or can have them added easily) so why bother with a separate machine?

But if you do have a fax machine, you can at least eliminate the cover sheet by using a customized reusable rubber stamp with places for the sender's name, address, phone number, fax number, receiver's name, and number of pages being sent. Just stamp the first sheet and fill in the blanks.

And if you do decide to buy a fax machine, consider one that will print on plain paper. Thermal transfer or inkjet units are generally able to print on the backside of paper already used on the other side. Check with the fax salesperson first to be sure.

Office Supplies

When it comes to miscellaneous office supplies, there are numerous reuse opportunities. And many of them may be right in your desk drawer or filing cabinet.

Green Tips

Paper already printed on one side makes good scrap or notepaper. Use the other side for draft versions or file copies.

As early as 1988 the State of Connecticut passed a law that required state agencies to eliminate nonreusable products whenever possible. Other governmental organizations have followed Connecticut's lead, and programs designed to encourage the use of refillable pens, reinked ribbons for typewriters and printers, and refillable toner cartridges are increasingly common.

But reuse strategies have also become popular with smaller items such as rubber bands, paper clips, brass fasteners, envelopes, and file folders. Although these small items may sound like a waste of time, they really add up in larger organizations. They can add up in yours as well. And nationwide, these combined efforts can save a lot of resources.

Here are some office reuse ideas almost anyone can try:

➤ Reuse file folders by applying a new label over the old one, or by folding the folder in reverse and writing on the back of the tab.

➤ Reuse envelopes that have metal clasps.

➤ Reuse envelopes as scrap or notepaper.

➤ Buy refillable tape dispensers.

➤ Use a rubber stamp instead of return address labels.

➤ Use rechargeable batteries instead of the single-use variety in handheld devices such as calculators, dictation machines, and beepers.

Some larger organizations or companies have set up sophisticated computerized reuse databases and locator systems. But you can use something as low-tech as a bulletin board or special section of a newsletter to list supplies that are available for swapping between departments or even personal items from home.

Furniture

As I mentioned earlier, office furniture is a category that frequently involves a good deal of unnecessary spending. But at the same time, this is an area where reuse has become well-established.

There is an extensive infrastructure of office furniture repairers, refinishers, refurbishers, and remanufacturers who routinely take older desks, chairs, cabinets, shelves, partitions, and carrels and transform them into serviceable items that are often hard to distinguish from new. And it's big business. These companies do about $600 million in sales annually.

This previously owned furniture—often incorrectly referred to as "recycled"—is then sold by a large network of brokers and retailers to buyers who are looking for good furniture at a good price. You may be able to find some good deals, too.

Shipping Supplies

The shipping/receiving department of most companies offers numerous opportunities for creative reuse strategies. Depending on the size of your operation, you may be able to use some or all of these ideas. And whether your shipping department is in a corner of your home office (like mine) or fills an entire warehouse, you can save money with these ideas.

There are two main categories of reusable shipping supplies: corrugated cardboard boxes and polystyrene foam packaging. While other shipping products are available, these two are the most widely used and consequently offer the most opportunities for reuse. Let's start with the boxes.

Green Tips

When you buy refurbished office furniture instead of new, you can save 20 to 50 percent off the price of new items. And virtually every type of furniture that you might buy new can be found from a refurbisher. Check the Yellow Pages for dealers in your area.

Corrugated Boxes

For most people, corrugated boxes are about as exciting as a cement block wall. But don't underestimate their importance. These boxes carry between 90 and 95 percent of all goods that are shipped in this country, and represent about a third of packaging waste. Any time you receive a corrugated box that is the right size for reuse—go for it! If it's a good standard size, but you don't have an immediate need, you can break it down and store it flat until you can use it later on.

Despite their lack of sex appeal, there has been a lot of imaginative thinking about these utilitarian containers. Some companies have redesigned their cartons to be quickly collapsible when empty and easily returnable for reuse. Others shred their incoming boxes and turn them into packing material that replaces polystyrene packing (more on polystyrene in a moment). Still others have replaced their corrugated boxes altogether with specially designed shipping containers that can be reused many times. The possibilities seem endless.

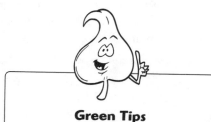

Green Tips

If you are worried that your customers might get a bad impression of your business because you are using slightly battered cardboard boxes—fear not. You can turn your reused cartons into positive advertising. Just add a stamped message on the box or a printed statement on your shipping label that explains your conservation strategy. A number of label manufacturers now offer them.

Polystyrene Foam Packaging

Polystyrene foam pellets—usually referred to as peanuts— are an environmental nightmare because they are not biodegradable. They're also extremely unsightly—and annoying—as they blow around the landscape. Have you ever tried to pick the blasted things up outside in a high wind?

The good news is that peanuts are highly reusable, and many individuals and businesses regularly save and reuse them. A number of biodegradable alternatives exist, but these frequently get mixed in with the polystyrene variety, so you might as well reuse all of them regardless of which kind they are.

Earth Education

Most pack-and-ship stores such as The Packaging Store; Mail Boxes, Etc; Pak-Mail, and others accept clean, used plastic peanuts. Many small manufacturers and other local businesses also gladly take peanuts for reuse in their shipping departments. The Plastic Loose-Fill Producers' Council has a hot-line (1-800-828-2214) that you can call to help locate a business in your area that will take your extra peanuts. On average, about 15,000 people return packing peanuts for reuse every week in this country.

But you might want to hang on to them for your own use. I keep a large bag full of peanuts (and other shapes) that I've received in incoming packages and reuse them for outgoing shipments (especially around Christmas). This peanut supply seems to remain more or less in balance most of the time and I've never actually had to buy any. I wish I could say the same for my supply of honey peanuts in the kitchen.

Pallets

Now, pallets—or skids, as they are sometimes called—are right down there with cardboard boxes when it comes to consumer excitement. Maybe even lower, because most people are barely aware of them. Yet hardwood pallets, which are used to ship most types of commercial freight, have an enormous—and destructive—effect on the environment. And that's why I've decided to mention them.

The numbers are mind-boggling. Around 1.9 billion pallets are used in this country on an annual basis. And the approximately 500 million pallets manufactured every year in the U.S. consume a staggering 40 to 45 percent of our total hardwood production. Considering that many pallets traditionally were used once and then thrown away, that's an unbelievable waste of trees. It has been estimated that between two to four million tons of pallet wood ends up in landfills every year.

There are some hopeful signs of change, however. One increasingly popular reuse strategy for pallets is repair. Quite a few companies now repair damaged pallets.

Another increasingly popular strategy is rental. This has been successful in quite a few foreign countries for years, and it's beginning to catch on here as well. Many companies have switched from buying to renting their pallets, saving substantially on both purchase and disposal costs. What's more, rental pallets are designed and built to last much longer than their throwaway alternatives, reducing the demand for new ones.

Green Tips

Reusing pallets 20 to 30 times could reduce associated lumber needs by almost 60 percent. People in the northern part of the country often use them as a base for their woodpile. They're also handy for keeping things off damp garage or basement floors. A number of small companies have used the salvaged hardwood to make such things as soap dishes, flooring, and furniture.

Other Reuse Ideas

Actually, so many possible reuse strategies abound for so many things at work, at home, and elsewhere that I can only begin to scratch the surface. Here are a few more quick ideas for you:

➤ Bring a reusable coffee mug with you to work and use it instead of throwaway plastic cups.

➤ Shred or crumple waste paper for use as packing material.

➤ Consider selling or giving away unneeded goods for reuse.

➤ Use a rechargeable metal fire extinguisher instead of a plastic one.

➤ Use a fire blanket instead of a fire extinguisher—they're washable and reusable.

➤ Reuse salvaged lumber and other materials from old buildings for new construction projects (check your local building codes first).

➤ Secondhand tools are often as good (or better) than new ones and are less expensive.

➤ If your vehicle needs a replacement part, you may be able to find it at an automotive junkyard for less than the cost of a new part.

Finally, there's one more reuse strategy that not only saves money, but can actually make you some money. Buying antique furniture and housewares is one reuse strategy where the value of the items probably will go up, rather than down, over time. And they just don't make things like that anymore.

We'll take a look at the antiques market and all the other used markets in the next chapter. Sound like fun? You bet.

The Least You Need to Know

➤ Business, government, and industry can also save money with reuse.

➤ The office provides many opportunities for reuse strategies.

➤ Reusing last year's model computer can save you big bucks and still gets most jobs done.

➤ Refurbished office furniture often looks as good as new—and costs less.

➤ You can use many office and shipping supplies over and over again.

Chapter 16

The Used Marketplace

> ## In This Chapter
>
> ➤ Why used markets have become so popular
>
> ➤ A look at traditional and online auctions
>
> ➤ What about classifieds?
>
> ➤ The growth of secondhand stores
>
> ➤ Why tag sales are still a great deal

Shopping in secondhand stores used to be viewed by many as a slightly dubious activity practiced mainly by eccentric tightwads or low-income people who just couldn't afford to buy new stuff. But not anymore. The used marketplace is out of the closet and going mainstream. And everyone seems to be getting in on the action.

There are probably a number of reasons for this striking recent trend. Perhaps one is the growing realization among some consumers of the environmental costs of our throwaway society and a desire to get more use out of existing products. At least that's what I'd like to think.

But the main incentive for most people is primarily economic—they're simply looking for a good deal. Happily, regardless of the motive, the net effect for the environment is the same; it keeps a lot of reusable stuff out of landfills and incinerators and cuts down on new purchases.

In this chapter, I'm going to tell you about these exciting new reuse trends in some very old markets. But we're also going to look at some wild new trends in some very new markets as well. All set? Let's go. You might want to bring a few extra dollars along.

Used Markets

The used marketplace has undergone a dramatic transformation in recent years. Part of this is due to a deliberate attempt on the part of the industry to improve its image. Many stores have been cleaned up and brightened up and some now offer displays and amenities such as coffee bars that rival major chain stores. Some secondhand stores, in fact, have actually become chains with new branches in affluent suburbs.

But that's not all. The proliferation of Internet auction sites such as eBay have given a lot of exposure and added high-tech glitter to a very old business. The result has been that sales at such stalwarts as pawnshops, secondhand stores, and antique stores have been growing dramatically.

The most remarkable part of this is that, with the decade-long economic boom, most people can afford to buy new, but still are buying used. This represents a major shift in the way Americans view secondhand goods—and their markets. Let's look at those markets.

Earth Education

In recent years, the secondhand market has been growing almost twice as fast as the rest of the retail sector. In 1997, Americans spent about $12 billion on goods from these secondhand retailers, a 30 percent increase from 1992, according to the Census Bureau. And preliminary figures indicate that the secondhand retail market grew another 23 percent to $17 billion in 1999.

Auctions

One of the most time-honored secondhand markets in this country is the public auction. Although there are many variations on the auction theme, we're going to look at the two main categories: traditional and online.

Both types bring buyers and sellers together and facilitate the sale of goods to the highest bidder. But it's important to remember that merchandise sold at auction is normally sold "as is," and unconcealed damage and needed repairs are the buyer's responsibility. It's also important to remember that all auctions or auctioneers (with the exception of benefit auctions) charge a commission based on the amount of the sale.

Regardless of which type of auction you use, it's a good idea to do your homework ahead of time, because it's easy to get carried away in the excitement of competitive bidding. But if you are well informed, disciplined, and careful in your bidding, auctions can provide significant bargains on a wide range of secondhand goods.

Notices for traditional auctions often appear in the classified sections of newspapers, and you can check with auctioneers listed in the Yellow Pages for schedules of their upcoming auctions.

Traditional Auctions

Traditional auctions are still very much alive in this country, especially estate auctions, bankruptcy auctions, and—unfortunately—farm dispersal auctions. But that's not all. There are countless art auctions, car auctions, boat auctions, antique auctions, rug auctions, benefit auctions; you name it, there's probably an auction for it.

I've spent quite a few pleasant summer afternoons attending local auctions that are as much about good entertainment as good prices. Especially in the hands of an experienced auctioneer who can coax money out of people's pockets for almost any item—and leave them feeling good about it.

Green Tips

A painting by Pablo Picasso, *The Dream*, sold at auction in 1997 for $48.4 million. But you don't need to spend a lot of money to get some pretty good buys on a wide range of items at an auction.

And you never know what you might find at an auction. In fact, I bought one of my prized possessions, a 1954 Electrolux Model E vacuum cleaner, for a few dollars at a local auction. When I brought this slightly battered veteran home 10 years ago and plugged it in, it worked! And it's still going strong.

Traditional auctions offer a number of advantages that online auctions—despite their phenomenal popularity—don't provide. Here are the main benefits, according to the National Auctioneers Association:

➤ Full service—Many traditional auctioneers offer appraising, inventory, packing, moving, marketing, selling, and settling.

➤ Speed—Traditional auctioneers can deal with sellers who need entire collections or numerous possessions out of a house on short notice.

➤ Preview—Bidders have the chance to fully inspect each item of interest in person before the auction.

➤ Salesmanship—This is the most important ingredient, at least from the seller's point of view.

Finally, a well-run traditional auction provides an unparalleled social event that simply isn't available online. And it's a great way to give a lot of sturdy old stuff a new lease on life. Traditional auctions will almost certainly continue to serve a segment of the auction market for many years to come.

Online Auctions

The growth of online auctions has been phenomenal. The first online auction company, eBay, was founded as recently as 1995. Today it's the largest and most successful

Planetary Perils

If you are not careful, when you participate in an online auction you may not get what you thought you were bidding on, or you may not get it at all. Internet auctions have quickly become the number one source of consumer fraud complaints in this country. In 1997 the Federal Trade Commission received only 100 complaints. By the end of 1999 that figure had skyrocketed to about 10,000.

Green Tips

Paying for online auction purchases with a credit card is one of the safest payment methods because the charge can be disputed if there is a problem with the transaction. If the item in question is fairly expensive, consider using an escrow service such as i-Escrow (www.iescrow.com). Your payment is sent to the service, and they don't release it until you are satisfied with the item.

personal auction site. Currently, eBay hosts over four million new auctions and 450,000 new items *every day*.

But they're not alone. It seems like everyone is jumping on the online-auction bandwagon. Dozens of other auction sites such as Yahoo, Amazon, and Ubid sell everything from automobiles to kitchenware, computers to toys—and everything imaginable in between. Although some of this stuff is new, much is used, so online auctions are Reuse Heaven.

Of course, there's a dark side to all of this. A lot of people are simply continuing their unhealthy consumption patterns online. And that's not what I'm advocating at all. What I *am* suggesting is using the advantages of modern information technology to streamline the reuse process.

And online auctions are a remarkably efficient way of linking buyer with seller. If you are a prospective buyer of a used item, particularly an obscure used item, you'll probably find what you're looking for at an online auction. And if you are careful—and patient—you'll probably get it for a fair price.

Classifieds

Another traditional method of connecting buyer and seller is classified advertising. Most newspapers contain classified ads for just about every kind of used goods. Though you must pay a charge for placing most printed classified advertising, it offers the advantage of eliminating the fees charged by auctioneers, brokers, consignment shops, and so on. Prices are normally listed right up front and are often negotiable.

And like just about everything else these days, many classified listings have gone online. Some are simply online versions of their printed originals, while others are totally electronic. Web portals like Excite and Yahoo! now offer free classified listings for their users, and there are many other online classifieds as well. If you do a little research, you'll find dozens of options.

Though you don't have to worry about competitive bidding, the same general cautions that apply to online auctions apply to online classifieds—let the buyer beware! Regardless of whether you're using a printed or online version of classifieds, they offer a good general picture of how to price most items.

Exchanges

There are two main types of exchanges: materials exchanges and waste exchanges. We'll look at both. In either case, these exchanges allow for the use or reuse of products, materials, or resources that otherwise would probably go to waste—and end up being landfilled or incinerated.

Materials Exchanges

Materials exchanges are a creative way to match production scraps, overruns, samples, rejects, and returns from retail outlets with nonprofit groups, schools, and other organizations. Though some of this stuff is used, a surprising amount is brand new—yet, for a wide variety of reasons it has no value to its owner and would end up being thrown away if it were not for the active intervention of a materials exchange.

Materials exchanges offer some unique advantages. Businesses that contribute items save money on disposal costs and frequently are eligible for tax deductions, while the receiving organizations get items they would not otherwise be able to afford. This helps everyone involved as well as the environment.

Probably the largest exchange in this country is the National Association of Exchange of Industrial Resources (NAEIR) located in Galesburg, Illinois (www.naeir.org). NAEIR collects and processes donations of new, top-quality merchandise from American companies, and then redistributes those goods to qualified schools and nonprofits across the country. Since its founding in 1977, NAEIR has collected and redistributed over $1 billion worth of new, donated supplies and equipment.

Smaller materials exchanges are located in various parts of the country with a variety of missions. Some solicit retail rejects, while others collect old office furniture, display fixtures, construction materials, and household furnishings. Still others focus on art supplies. Most exchanges, however, aren't fussy, and will take almost anything with reuse potential.

Earth Education

Some large retailers have actually been known to throw away new clothing and other products that have been returned by customers because it was easier than reentering the items into their inventories. Materials exchanges offer a far more environmentally responsible alternative, and help a lot of worthwhile organizations at the same time.

Earth Education

North American industry generates around 11 billion tons of
nonhazardous solid waste as well
as 700 million tons of hazardous
waste every year. Finding ways to
transform some of this waste into
useful production inputs for
other industries is the main focus
of waste exchanges.

Waste Exchanges

Although waste exchanges operate on the same general principle as materials exchanges, the focus is primarily on industrial trash, or waste. As I've mentioned
previously, industry in this country generates huge
amounts of waste every year. Traditionally, most of
this ended up in the waste stream.

However, in recent years there has been an initiative
to match one industry's waste with another's raw material needs. This exciting new reuse strategy has saved
huge disposal costs for some companies while turning
their waste into a free or low-cost supply of materials
for another business. The potential for this simple but
elegant reuse strategy is enormous.

Dozens of active national and state waste exchanges
across the country find new uses for thousands of
items, everything from copper wiring to textile rem-
nants, and coal ash to solvents. The Environmental Protection Agency (www.epa.gov)
has an extensive listing of these exchanges. Try a search for "commodities, materials,
waste, exchanges" at their Web site for the most current lists.

Flea Markets

Flea markets and swap meets are the usual descriptions for a wide range of reuse
events. Some are large, regularly scheduled events that take place in the same location year after year, while others are smaller, informal one-time affairs in parking lots
or at the roadside.

Regardless of their size or frequency, these markets generally follow the same strategy:
Sellers rent spaces to set up their displays while shoppers stroll around looking for
bargains. Most of the goods at many flea markets are used, but some can be new. A
number of these events focus on specific areas of interest such as sound recordings,
classic auto parts, or amateur radios, to name just a few.

Flea markets, swap meets, tailgate parties, etc., generally offer an eclectic selection
of good used merchandise—and a lot of junk. But, then again, one person's trash is
another person's treasure. Check out the Flea Market Guide of U.S. Flea Markets
(www.fleamarketguide.com) for a comprehensive current listing of flea markets
around the country.

Reuse Yards

Reuse yards (mentioned previously in Chapter 13, "Reuse Strategies") are the locations at recycling centers and waste transfer stations where people are encouraged to leave reusable items for others to take home. You can find a wide range of items from old furniture to appliances, and windows and doors to metal roofing. And a lot of other items that are normally free (or almost free) for the taking.

Though this stuff is offered "as is," it's not unusual to find items that need little, if any, repair to return them to a usable condition. And you can't beat the price. This is a great way to keep reusable items out of the waste stream.

Secondhand Stores

Thousands of independent thrift stores nationwide still accept donations or consignments that help raise money for various worthy causes. A number of nonprofit secondhand organizations such as the Salvation Army and Goodwill Industries have chains of stores all over North America.

Earth Education

Urban Ore, a successful urban materials reuse operation in Berkeley, California, sold $1.4 million worth of "garbage" to local residents that it salvaged from the city's waste stream in 1995. About 95 percent of materials that the organization handles is actually sold for reuse, while 4.5 percent is sold to recyclers. Only one-half of 1 percent is land-filled.

But some of the hottest action in the used-merchandise market is taking place in glitzy new secondhand franchises like Play It Again Sports, Once Upon A Child, Computer Renaissance, Music Go Round, ReTool, and Plato's Closet. These franchises, developed by Grow Biz International of Minneapolis, Minnesota, buy, sell, trade, and consign new and used merchandise.

Although Grow Biz has experienced some growing pains recently, the fact that they have around 1,100 stores throughout the U.S. and Canada, selling a broad selection of used goods, is a stunning example of the growth of the secondhand market. Grow Biz is not alone. Many other companies are trying to cash in on this phenomenon. And the future of these businesses generally looks promising.

At a time when many discount stores tend to have a reputation for carrying second-rate merchandise, secondhand stores are gaining a reputation for high-quality goods at low prices. And the strong economy of the past decade has actually increased the supply of top-quality used goods that people want to dispose of—in favor of even more high-end items.

So, if you're looking for some good deals on used sports equipment, children's clothing, toys, computers, musical instruments, tools, or whatever, you might want to check out your local secondhand store. Chances are you'll find what you're looking for.

Surplus

Although surplus outlets may not be the first things to come to mind when people think of the used marketplace, they are worth a look. Government and industry surplus items that might otherwise end up in a landfill are frequently auctioned off or bought by dealers for resale.

Surplus goods include an eclectic array of things from electrical components to machinery, and plumbing fixtures to office supplies. The best part is that many of these items sell at deep discounts from their original cost.

Be forewarned, however, that this is an area where you need to know what you are doing—before you do it. And there's a steep learning curve. But, if you are willing to do some homework, you might be able to find some excellent reuse opportunities in surplus materials.

Tag Sales

No discussion of the used marketplace would be complete without tag sales. A wide range of reuse events fall under the tag-sale category, including garage sales, lawn sales, yard sales, and moving sales. Despite the different names, what these events have in common is that households (or friends or neighbors) organize them for the private sale of personal goods.

Rummage sales fall under the same broad category, but are generally organized by groups to raise money for a particular cause, and they tend to be held in public, rather than private locations.

Tag sales and their variants generally offer some of the best bargains on used goods because, in most cases, the sellers are not professional dealers and simply want to get rid of what they are offering. This is especially true of moving sales, in which a few dollars will often buy some real bargains.

Now, don't get me wrong. I'm not suggesting you should spend yourself into oblivion on used merchandise at tag sales—or any other used market. But if you have a genuine need for something truly useful, buying secondhand makes a lot of sense. And the many secondhand markets out there offer plenty of opportunities. Who knows? You might even find an Electrolux Model E hiding amidst the trash.

A yard sale.

(Photo copyright Greg Pahl)

The Least You Need to Know

➤ Used markets offer great prices and a chance to get the most out of older products.

➤ Online auctions offer unparalleled opportunities to purchase used goods—but let the buyer beware!

➤ Classified listings, both printed and online, are a great way to connect buyers and sellers of used goods.

➤ Flea markets usually attract large numbers of sellers—and buyers—to a single location.

➤ You can still find some of the best deals for used items at tag sales.

Part 4

Recycle It

We've finally made it to the third—and probably the most controversial—of the Three Rs—recycling. We'll start with a brief look at recycling's past, present, and future, and try to put it all in its proper perspective. And I'll explain what all the debate about recycling is really about.

Then, we'll sort our way through a large pile of recyclable materials. We'll look at the most common items—paper, metals, glass, and plastics—and learn how to deal with each of them. I'll also tell you about hazardous wastes and some other problem items as well.

After that, we'll look at nature's own recycling method—composting—and I'll explain why it's becoming so popular nationwide. And finally, I'll tell you about closing the loop—buying recycled products—and why it's so important.

Chapter 17

Recycling Basics

In This Chapter

➤ A look at recycling, past, present, and future

➤ The recycling debate explained

➤ Recycling basics

➤ How to recycle at home

Although recycling is the third and least effective R of the environmental movement, it's also been the most visible. Reacting to the perceived garbage crisis of the late 1980s, many communities and states set up recycling programs. These initiatives quickly helped to turn recycling into a high-profile citizen movement that was viewed by many as the solution to our waste problems. It wasn't. And it still isn't.

That's not to say that recycling isn't important. It is. But as I've explained before, it's only part of a much larger group of interrelated activities including reduction and reuse that, combined, will help us deal with many of our environmental woes. But recycling has also probably been the most controversial of the Three Rs, due mainly to its high visibility and a number of economic factors. And, unfortunately, that controversy continues.

In this chapter, I'll sort through the garbage that surrounds recycling and try to help you understand what's really going on. We'll begin with a short history of recycling. I'll also explain recycling's current status and its prospects for the future. Then, I'll go through the basics of the recycling process.

Recycled History

Recycling is the oldest strategy of all. The Earth, and everything on it, in fact, is essentially recycled stardust. Even you and I. And, as I've mentioned before, all of the ecosystems in our environment function in healthy, sustainable ways when there is a constant give and take of resources that are more or less in balance. And recycling, whether it is done by us or by nature, helps keep things balanced.

Recycling by humans is nothing new. In fact, thousands of years ago some of our distant ancestors routinely ground up broken pieces of pottery to add to the ingredients of new pottery. Gold, silver, and bronze items were often melted down and made into new items. Jewelry was transformed into golden calves. Swords became plowshares.

In the eighteenth and nineteenth centuries in this country, people regularly sold old rags, bones, and scrap metals to traveling peddlers who bought the waste from households and then resold it to waste dealers, who in turn sold it back to manufacturers. The manufacturers recycled the rags into paper, the bones into gelatin, ammonia, or fertilizer, and the scrap metal into new metal products. This pattern of materials recycling is referred to as a *closed loop*.

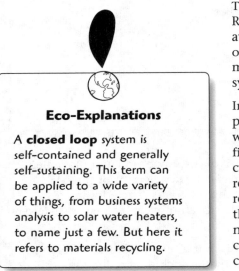

Eco-Explanations

A **closed loop** system is self-contained and generally self-sustaining. This term can be applied to a wide variety of things, from business systems analysis to solar water heaters, to name just a few. But here it refers to materials recycling.

Then, as I mentioned in Chapter 12, "Choose to Reuse," in the early 1900s there was a deliberate shift away from reuse and recycling to a throwaway economy, and the disposal of solid waste became a major municipal function separate from the old closed-loop system.

In the 1960s and 1970s, recycling was revived by hippie activists. Around 3,000 voluntary recycling centers were set up nationwide to roughly coincide with the first Earth Day in 1970. Since then, the growth of recycling has been dramatic. There are now over 10,000 recycling drop-off centers and almost 9,000 curbside recycling programs across the country, according to the Environmental Protection Agency. These programs now serve 51 percent of the population. And the percentage of municipal solid waste (MSW) that is recycled (including composting) has increased from 7 percent in 1970 to 31.5 percent in 1999.

But, unlike many Western European countries, (which tend to be way ahead of us on environmental issues), there is no national U.S. program, and recycling here has been pretty much left up to the individual states. Consequently, there are wide variations in participation. Minnesota leads the nation with a 45-percent recycling rate, according to a 1999 BioCycle Journal survey. At the other end of the spectrum, Montana and Wyoming (with vast open spaces available for landfills) have recovery rates of only 5 percent.

Clearly, there is still plenty of room for improvement. Especially when you consider that although we are recycling 31.5 percent of MSW, this means that 68.5 percent is still *not* being recycled and mostly ends up in landfills.

The Great Debate

Although some have hailed recycling in this country as "one of the most significant environmental success stories," others have attacked it as being unnecessary, expensive, and too much trouble. These opposing views can be very confusing. Let me explain what's really going on here.

The "garbage crisis" of the late 1980s that gave recycling such a boost also motivated a group of mainly private solid waste companies to build a large number of huge new landfills. These landfills were located primarily in economically depressed rural areas where land prices were low and struggling local communities needed the revenue that the facilities would generate.

It's also important to understand that, by the late 1980s, municipal solid waste hauling—once accomplished by thousands of independent companies—was dominated by just four big firms. In recent years, thanks to deregulation and further consolidation in the industry, landfills have come under the control of just a few large companies.

It's also instructive to understand who is making the most noise when it comes to anti-recycling campaigns. There are a number of prominent think tanks in various parts of the country that have been especially vocal. But if you follow the money, you will find that many of these organizations are funded, at least in part, by companies in the packaging, consumer products, and waste management industries.

Although landfills are promoted by their supporters as a solution, these landfills basically are part of the problem, especially if you take the long-range view of solid waste management. Landfills *can* play a useful role in a balanced solid waste management program, but far too often "solid waste management" has simply meant "landfills." And efforts to keep a steady stream of MSW—and income—flowing into these landfills has unquestionably hurt recycling efforts.

Let's get one thing straight. No matter what landfill supporters claim, spending large sums of money to bury huge quantities of resources in a hole in the

Earth Education

In 1989, there were 7,900 landfills in this country, but in 2000 that number had declined to 2,216. The landfills that remain are huge mechanized operations with enormous capacity. Solid waste and landfills have become big business, and these big solid waste companies lose money every time something is recycled instead of going into one of their landfills.

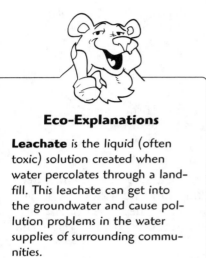

ground is simply not good for the environment in the long run. Virtually all landfills—whether they are lined or not—will eventually leak and pollute nearby groundwater with *leachate*, although most newer landfills have systems that are supposed to minimize this hazard. Landfills also emit significant amounts of greenhouse gases—36 percent of all methane emissions in the U.S., according to a 1996 EPA study.

But perhaps more important is the fact that one of the main goals of recycling is to reduce environmental damage caused by the extraction of virgin raw materials for the production of new products. A number of studies conducted by the U.S. Department of Energy, the Stanford Research Institute, and others have found that recycling-based systems offer substantial environmental advantages over virgin materials systems. And burying recyclable materials in landfills eliminates those potential benefits.

But recycling has had another hurdle to overcome. Critics have also charged that recycling is not cost effective and that it should pay for itself. But waste disposal, regardless of what form it takes, doesn't pay for itself. It's a cost that society must bear. Nevertheless, the cost issue has taken on new life in the past few years.

The dramatic reductions in the price of crude oil and other commodities, caused by the collapse of the so-called Asian Tiger Economies in 1997 and the Russian monetary crisis of 1998, also caused the prices paid for recyclables to plummet in this country (oil prices have recently rebounded to new highs). Since then, markets for many recycled products have generally been poor. This has tended to raise the costs of recycling. At the same time, costs for landfills have remained comparatively low, and some cash-strapped communities have opted to send all of their trash to landfills. In some cases this has diverted recyclables from existing recycling programs.

Finally, it's generally acknowledged that the original forces that motivated this country to start recycling in the 1970s and 1980s have been played out. And it's unlikely that there will be a dramatic event any time soon that will change that picture.

The combined effect of these problems has slowed the steady increase in recycling in this country to a crawl. In some locations recycling has even begun to decline, and officials at the EPA and in a number of states have begun to backpedal on their commitments to recycling targets. This is not the direction we should be heading in.

Although landfills may offer short-term financial advantages, especially during periods of low prices for recyclables, they do not help us develop the long-term thinking or solutions needed for sustainability.

In the long run, necessity is going to require much more comprehensive recycling than we are currently practicing. So the current situation is best viewed as a temporary plateau where we pause briefly to catch our breath before continuing to expand and improve our recycling efforts. Unfortunately, while we pause we are losing precious time. Meanwhile, the recycling debate goes on and on.

Recycling 101

Despite the problems with recycling, it remains an important environmental strategy to help us achieve a sustainable economy. And because roughly half the population of this country still is not recycling—even after all these years—I think it will be helpful to explain the basics. If you're a seasoned recycler, please bear with me.

So, what is *recycling?* Many people think of recycling as collecting things like bottles and cans. That's true. But this is only part of the picture. A more accurate and complete definition is: "The collection of waste materials, which are then reprocessed into new materials, and then sold as new products."

Eco-Explanations

Recycling is the collection of waste materials, reprocessing them into new materials or products, which are then sold again. Aluminum beverage cans are one of the most obvious items on the grocery store shelf that are continually recycled.

Okay, that's what it is, but why should we recycle? Here are the five main reasons:

1. Recycling saves natural resources—By making products from recycled materials instead of from virgin materials we conserve land and reduce the need to mine minerals and drill for oil.

2. Recycling saves energy—It normally takes less energy to produce recycled products; recycled aluminum, for example, needs 95 percent less energy than new aluminum made from bauxite ore.

3. Recycling reduces pollution—Making products from recycled materials generally creates less air and water pollution than making them from virgin materials.

4. Recycling conserves landfill space—Recycled products go back into the materials stream rather than into landfills.

5. Recycling creates jobs and saves money—Recycling creates far more jobs than landfills or incinerators do, and well-managed, fully-utilized recycling programs can be the least-expensive waste-management method. Why dump money into a big hole in the ground when we could be spending it on more productive things?

In addition, when recycling reduces energy consumption it also reduces acid rain and global warming. If all of this sounds just slightly familiar, you're right. Remember all

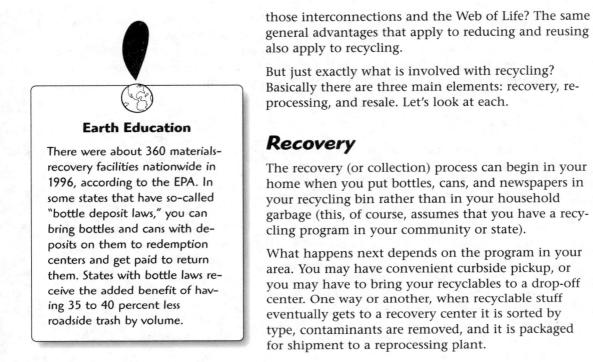

Earth Education

There were about 360 materials-recovery facilities nationwide in 1996, according to the EPA. In some states that have so-called "bottle deposit laws," you can bring bottles and cans with deposits on them to redemption centers and get paid to return them. States with bottle laws receive the added benefit of having 35 to 40 percent less roadside trash by volume.

those interconnections and the Web of Life? The same general advantages that apply to reducing and reusing also apply to recycling.

But just exactly what is involved with recycling? Basically there are three main elements: recovery, reprocessing, and resale. Let's look at each.

Recovery

The recovery (or collection) process can begin in your home when you put bottles, cans, and newspapers in your recycling bin rather than in your household garbage (this, of course, assumes that you have a recycling program in your community or state).

What happens next depends on the program in your area. You may have convenient curbside pickup, or you may have to bring your recyclables to a drop-off center. One way or another, when recyclable stuff eventually gets to a recovery center it is sorted by type, contaminants are removed, and it is packaged for shipment to a reprocessing plant.

Reprocess

When the recycled items arrive at a reprocessing plant they are converted into a reusable product. Glass is melted down into new bottles, aluminum cans become new aluminum cans, paper is reprocessed into paper, and plastics are chipped and melted down into a variety of new products.

To complicate things just a bit, there are three kinds of reprocessing: primary, secondary, and tertiary.

➤ Primary recycling is the reprocessing of materials into the same product, which can be recycled again, such as glass bottles into more glass bottles.

➤ Secondary recycling is the reprocessing of materials into a different but similar product, such as corrugated cardboard boxes into cereal boxes.

➤ Tertiary recycling is the reprocessing of a material into a product that is not likely to be recycled again, such as mixed office paper into bathroom tissue.

Regardless of which type of reprocessing is used, there is one more crucial part to the recycling process.

Resale

The third, and most important, part of recycling is resale of the recycled product. Without strong markets for recycled products, the entire process comes to a screeching halt. Early in the recycling revival of the 1970s, this is precisely what happened.

Enthusiastic novice recyclers nationwide collected huge quantities of paper, bottles, and cans. But the supplies of recyclables quickly overwhelmed the existing markets (which were limited, if they existed at all). Predictably, the law of supply and demand came into play and prices for recyclables plummeted. Many early recycling centers failed as a result.

Although we still have a long way to go, substantial progress on developing markets for recycled products has been made since the 1970s. I'll tell you more about this important development in Chapter 20, "Completing the Circle."

Planetary Perils

Without adequate markets for recycled products, even the best-organized recycling program will fail. To keep that from happening, we need to become better-educated shoppers. Read product labels carefully, and insist on products or packaging that contain recycled ingredients.

Is It Really Recycled?

Over the years, there has been a lot of debate about what a "real" recycled product is. This is because there are so many possible combinations of ingredients—and ways of interpreting them—for some products. But basically two main kinds of recycled material can be used to make a recycled product: "pre-consumer waste" and "post-consumer waste." Let's look at both.

Pre-Consumer Waste

Pre-consumer waste (also called internal waste) refers to waste that is generated during the manufacturing process that would otherwise have been dumped in a landfill (this does not include waste that would have automatically been "put back in the pot" at the factory).

Some purists insist that pre-consumer waste doesn't really qualify as recycled because it never actually entered the waste stream. But because there is roughly 25 times more pre-consumer waste than post-consumer waste, it's hard to ignore. Federal and state regulators now accept pre-consumer waste as recycled as long as it is properly identified.

Post-Consumer Waste

Post-consumer waste (also called external waste), on the other hand, refers to waste materials that have been generated after consumers have used them. When packaging, for example, is discarded after it is opened, it then becomes post-consumer waste. The same is true after you have finished reading your newspaper. Empty bottles, cans, and other containers also qualify as post-consumer waste.

Numerous federal and state regulations require recycling claims to be backed up with verifiable data. Although state regulations vary, the Federal Trade Commission, in particular, has strict guidelines for manufacturers to follow on descriptions for many recycled products.

Green Tips

When you buy recycled products, try to find those that contain the largest amount of post-consumer waste; this helps create more demand for recycled products. Generally speaking, the higher the content of post-consumer waste in our products, the closer we come to achieving a self-sustaining closed-loop materials flow through the economy.

Composting

Finally, no description of recycling would be complete without mentioning Mother Nature's original recycling method—composting. Composting is one of the best methods of keeping solid waste out of landfills. In fact, about 30 percent of household trash in North America is made up of yard clippings and kitchen waste. And it's all prime compost material, so there's plenty of stuff to work with. I'll have a lot more to say about composting in Chapter 19.

Can You Recycle It?

As I mentioned earlier, buying recycled products is probably the most important part of the recycling process. But how can you tell if a product is made from recycled materials and if it is recyclable?

This is not always an easy question to answer because it tends to vary from product to product. But many products contain information on them, or on their packaging, about their recycled content and whether the product itself is recyclable. I'll go into more detail about this in the next chapter as I describe the various kinds of recyclable materials.

Which Stuff Goes Where?

Okay, we know what recycling is and what its advantages are. But just how do you recycle on a day-to-day basis? For those of us who have been recycling for years, it seems so simple that we hardly give it a second thought anymore. And that's one of the key points—recycling just isn't the Big Deal some opponents try to portray it as.

It's mostly a matter of changing a few basic habits at home about which stuff goes where—and that's about it. Yes, it does require a little (very little) thought about which bag (or box or other temporary storage container) the particular item of waste goes into. But this isn't rocket science. Your three-year-old son or daughter will probably be able to do it for you—and tell you why it's good for the Earth, too.

Green Tips

Although it does take a few minutes to recycle household waste, most people find it less of a hassle than sorting through their mail, and the environmental benefits are substantial. Because it happens as you go through your daily routine, it really doesn't take more than a few seconds per item. It's not like you have to sit on the floor and sort through a day's worth of garbage every evening.

Sort It

Before we get into the details, I need to point out that there are differences between recycling programs in various parts of the country (no coordinated national program, remember?). So, what I'm going to describe here is based on what we do in my household. But it's pretty generic, and many other programs are similar.

Here's how it generally works. Instead of just tossing everything in the kitchen garbage you take maybe a second to think about where the item in your hand needs to go. Bottles, cans, and some plastics are rinsed, labels are removed, and then they go in the recycling bin. Mixed paper (mostly junk mail in our household) goes in a reused paper grocery bag, newspapers go in a separate bag, and cardboard in another. Food scraps temporarily go into a reused yogurt container and eventually end up in the compost bin.

Put It Out

Then, every week (every other week in our case) you put your recyclables at the curbside for pickup. That's it. If you have to take your recyclables to a drop-off center, it's admittedly a bit more involved (but at least you can catch up on the local community news while you're there).

It's Simple

I would say that, on average, I probably spend one minute a day on recycling-related activities. Too much trouble? I don't think so. And we have cut our garbage (and our garbage bills) roughly in half. The money we save on garbage admittedly gets spent on recycling pickup, but I figure that's a fair tradeoff.

Recycling does require a little thought and effort. But not much. And the advantages for the environment are substantial. Can you spare a few minutes a day for our future? For your children's future?

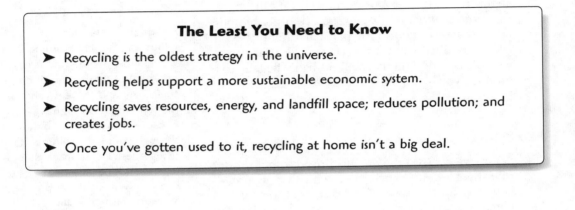

The Least You Need to Know

➤ Recycling is the oldest strategy in the universe.

➤ Recycling helps support a more sustainable economic system.

➤ Recycling saves resources, energy, and landfill space; reduces pollution; and creates jobs.

➤ Once you've gotten used to it, recycling at home isn't a big deal.

Recyclable Products

One of the biggest recycling success stories in this country is the aluminum can. In 1999 a staggering 102 billion aluminum cans were manufactured. Of that total, a remarkable 62.5 percent, or 63.7 billion cans, were recycled. This means that we are recycling almost two out of every three aluminum cans we use. That's pretty good, considering that recycling rates for some other products like PVC plastic are around 1 percent.

The striking differences in recycling rates between different materials just goes to show that, although we're making progress in some areas, there's still plenty of room for improvement in others. While recycling common materials is not that difficult, trying to figure out what to do with obscure items can sometimes be a real challenge. We'll cover both types in this chapter.

I'll start by telling you about the most commonly recyclable materials that you will find in your home. Then I'll explain why plastics are a bit harder to deal with. We'll also take a look at hazardous waste and how you can recycle it. Finally, I'll help you figure out what to do with obscure and hard-to-recycle items.

Commonly Recycled Materials

Five main categories of commonly recycled materials are found in most homes: aluminum, glass, paper products, steel, and plastics. These are the things that folks regularly put in their recycling bins.

Then there are hazardous wastes, such as antifreeze, motor oil, and paint. And, finally, there's a group of miscellaneous items such as compact disks, floppy disks, batteries, and so on, that can be a bit of a pain to deal with. Let's look at all of them.

But before we dive into the recycling bin, I need to mention again that because there is still no coordinated national recycling program in this country, the specific details of the program in your area (if any) may differ a bit from what I describe here. If you're not sure how to deal with something, check with your local program coordinator.

Earth Education

The can-making industry introduced the first aluminum can in 1957. Recycling aluminum cans saves 95 percent of the energy it takes to make aluminum from bauxite ore, the main reason why this is such a popular strategy with the industry. Using recycled aluminum cans also cuts down on air pollution.

Aluminum

Aluminum cans are the most widely recycled metal product. They're also the most common aluminum item found in most homes. And the aluminum industry obviously wants them back to recycle into new cans, or they wouldn't have paid nearly $1 billion for them in 1999.

Aluminum cans are easy to identify by their shape, and if in doubt, try the magnet test: Aluminum isn't attracted to a magnet. And the aluminum can you recycle today could be back in your hand in the form of a new filled can in as little as 90 days. Now, that's an efficient recycling system.

Other aluminum items such as pie plates, foil, and broken lawn furniture should be recycled if possible. Check first with your local program to find out if these items are accepted.

Glass

Glass is one of the most recyclable materials because it essentially never wears out. You can recycle glass endlessly into new glass products. And it's an efficient process. One ton of glass returned for recycling produces one ton of new glass. So, a ton of resources are saved for every ton of glass that is recycled.

A ton of new glass manufactured results in around 28 pounds of air pollution, but using recycled glass can reduce that pollution by 14 to 20 percent. In 1998, 35 percent of all glass containers in this country were recycled, according to the Glass Packaging Institute.

When you recycle glass, there are a few things you need to know:

➤ Recycled bottles and jars need to be separated by color: clear, green, and amber. (Some curb-side pickup programs allow glass containers of all colors to be mixed in the same recycling box, and they are separated later.)

➤ Broken glass containers should not be recycled.

Also, wash glass containers enough to prevent odors, but don't waste water trying to get them squeaky clean. It's also not really necessary to remove labels from glass jars—they get vaporized when the glass is melted down. But follow your local program's instructions.

Paper and Paper Products

More paper is recovered in this country for recycling than all other materials combined. And more paper is now recovered in this country than is landfilled.

The American Forest and Paper Association has a number of symbols that help to identify recycled fiber content in paper and paperboard products. These symbols normally are accompanied by a percentage figure that indicates the amount of recycled fiber.

Although most types of paper can be recycled, paper fiber can only be recycled about seven times before the fibers become too short. And there are a lot of different kinds of paper, so recycling paper is not as simple as recycling aluminum. The key is clean, well-sorted, uncontaminated dry paper. Here are the main categories and what you need to know about them.

Planetary Perils

Other types of glass, such as window glass or glass tableware, are made from a different type of glass and must not be mixed with recycled bottles because they will contaminate the bottle glass. Just a small amount of contamination can ruin the value of otherwise perfectly good recyclable materials.

Earth Education

The paper recovered for recycling in the past 10 years would fill more than 3.5 square miles of landfill space packed 50 feet high. In 1998, 45 percent of all the paper Americans used was recovered—45 million tons, an all-time record, according to the American Forest and Paper Association. More than one third of the raw material fiber U.S. papermakers use comes from recycled paper.

Paper recycling symbols.

100%

100 Percent
Recycled Symbol

25%

Recycled Content
Product Symbol

Newspapers

Newspapers have been recycled profitably for decades. The entire newspaper, including inserts, is recyclable, except for product samples and rubber bands. The easiest ways to deal with newspapers are to put them in a large brown grocery bag or tie them in bundles with natural twine.

White Office Paper

White office paper is the most valuable of recyclable papers if it's clean. If there is no separate category for white office paper in your area it can be recycled with mixed paper (after you've used both sides to print on, of course).

Green Tips

When in doubt about whether to mix an obscure type of paper in with mixed paper, throw it out instead. A number of things should not be included: stickers, napkins, tissues, waxed paper, milk cartons, carbon paper, fast food wraps, oil-soaked paper, drink boxes, neon paper, thermal fax paper, and plastic laminated paper.

Mixed Paper

Mixed paper is a catch-all category for most other types of paper, including: junk mail, magazines, photocopies, computer printouts, cereal/shoe boxes, and sometimes phone books. But it must still be clean, dry, and free from food and other contaminants. Staples are okay.

Corrugated Cardboard

Corrugated cardboard isn't accepted by all recycling programs, but if it is, it needs to be clean, dry, and broken down for easy handling. Some programs require that cardboard be free of plastic shipping tape, but staples are okay. Alas, greasy, pizza-stained cardboard is not okay.

Steel

Steel can be recycled again and again, and is used for a wide variety of products. But the largest uses are for auto bodies and so-called "tin cans" (mostly steel, very little tin). Virtually all steel products in this country contain some recycled (scrap) steel.

Each year, in fact, more than half the steel the domestic industry produces is recycled. In 1999 about 67 million tons of steel scrap were recycled, for a 63.9-percent-overall recycling rate, while the recycling rate for steel cans was 57.9 percent, according to the Steel Recycling Institute.

In most households, empty cans are the main steel items in the recycling bin. As with glass, it's only necessary to rinse cans enough to eliminate odors (dirty dish water is more than adequate).

Plastics Are (Almost) Forever

From an environmental standpoint, plastics offer a real dilemma. They are made from nonrenewable fossil-fuel-based ingredients, they generally aren't biodegradable, and because they come in so many different, incompatible varieties, they have not been easy to recycle.

Despite this, the growth of plastic products—especially containers—has been enormous. This rapid growth in new container production, combined with the slower growth in recovered containers, means that the recycling rate for plastic bottles has dropped steadily despite an annual increase in the number of pounds recycled. The recycling rate for plastic bottles has stabilized around 24 percent in the past few years. The recycling rate for all plastic packaging is around 9.5 percent, far below the rates for other major packaging materials.

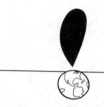

Earth Education

Plastic, unlike glass, aluminum, or steel, can only be recycled a limited number of times—often just once. What's more, when plastic actually is recycled it drops to a lower grade and still does not break down in the environment.

It is unrealistic to believe that plastic is going to disappear any time soon. Even if production were halted tomorrow, plastic would still be with us—or with our distant descendents—for hundreds of years. Like it or not, we're stuck with plastic for the foreseeable future, so we might as well make the best use of it. And recycling the stuff whenever possible, instead of dumping it in landfills, makes sense.

Whatever you may think about their motives, you have to give the plastics industry credit for at least trying to develop viable recycling programs and products. And, in most cases, these products are genuinely useful. The sturdy compost bin in my back

Earth Education

Currently more than 1,300 plastic products with recycled content are on the market. This includes everything from lawn furniture to boat docks. Read product information carefully for recycled content information.

Eco-Explanations

A **resin** is a sticky substance from which most plastics are made. Different types of plastic contain different formulations of resin.

yard is made out of recycled plastic. The recycled plastic lumber industry is growing steadily, and they're even experimenting with plastic railroad ties. But there's still plenty of room for more progress.

None of this would have been possible if the plastics industry hadn't figured out a system of sorting out the tangle of different types of plastic it was producing in such huge quantities. What they came up with were resin codes.

Identification Symbols

Back in 1988, responding to numerous requests from recyclers around the country, a series of *resin* identification codes were developed by the plastics industry to help identify the resin content of bottles and containers commonly found in the residential waste stream.

These triangular-shaped markers with a number in the middle are found on the bottom of almost all plastic containers. The numbers run from one to seven, and each one refers to a different type of plastic. The letters below the symbol are an abbreviation of the name of the plastic.

As a practical matter, the most commonly accepted plastics for most residential recycling programs are types one and two in container form.

Plastic resin codes.

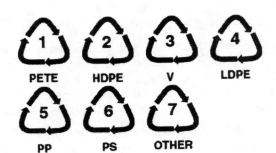

How to Recycle Plastics

Make sure the container is of a type accepted by your recycling program. Rinse it out. Dispose of the cap, as caps are often made of a different kind of plastic from the container.

"Degradable" Plastics

No discussion of plastic would be complete without mentioning degradables. A lot of research has gone into *degradable plastics*. And quite a lot of hype. In 1992, after the Federal Trade Commission announced an order prohibiting the manufacturers of some disposal diapers from advertising their products as "degradable," a lot of the hype stopped. But the research has continued.

There are now two main categories of degradable plastics: those that are petroleum based, and those that are not. In the long run, the nonpetroleum-based variety, known as biopolymers, have a lot to offer from an environmental standpoint.

Biopolymers are produced through the transformation of agricultural or marine feedstocks such as starch and cellulose, or by harnessing enzymes found in nature. In addition to being nontoxic, the processes used to create biopolymers minimize energy consumption and waste generation. Biopolymers can be composted into the soil and consequently are not part of the recycling system used for most other plastics.

Eco-Explanations

Degradable plastics are designed to eventually break down and disintegrate due to bacterial action or when exposed to sunlight or water.

Hazardous Waste

Even after years of public educational campaigns, many people are still rather careless when it comes to handling toxic and hazardous materials at home. Businesses would be fined for some of the things that individual homeowners do with toxics in their homes and gardens.

Items such as paints, solvents, automotive fluids, herbicides, and so on should never be disposed of in your household garbage. When these things are mixed in with regular garbage they either end up in landfills, where they may eventually end up polluting groundwater, or in incinerators, where they end up in the air we breathe.

One of the best ways to minimize hazardous waste is to only buy what you know you are going to need. But if you do have extra toxic materials to dispose of, check with your recycling program or garbage hauler to see if your area has a household toxic drop-off site or day.

Planetary Perils

Motor oil contains heavy metals and other toxics and is considered a hazardous waste. Motor oil should never be dumped down the drain or in your backyard. Do-it-yourself oil changers dump more oil every year than the Exxon *Valdez* spilled into Alaska's Prince William Sound. One quart of motor oil can kill fish in thousands of gallons of water.

Let's look at a few of the most common hazardous materials found in the home and what you can do with them.

Motor Oil

Used motor oil is recycled by heating it to remove impurities. Two and a half quarts of recycled motor oil can be made from one gallon of used oil. By comparison, it takes 42 gallons of virgin crude oil and a lot of energy to make $2\frac{1}{2}$ quarts of new oil.

Recycling used motor oil is fairly easy. Just put it into an empty plastic milk jug (reuse of jug!) and mark it as "used motor oil." Then take it to a location that accepts it. Your local recycling program coordinator can usually tell you where to take it. Many quick-lube franchises take used oil (Jiffy Lube, Valvoline Instant Oil Change Centers). Many auto stores take used oil as well, including Grand Auto, R&S Strauss, Pep-Boys, and Wal-Mart.

Antifreeze

About 80 percent of antifreeze bought in this country is used by individuals, some of whom, unfortunately, don't dispose of it properly. You can generally take containers of old antifreeze to a garage that has an antifreeze-recycling program.

Paint

Old paint should not be dumped down the drain. Most recycling programs have a household hazardous waste day or site where paint can be brought in. Check with your recycling coordinator or garbage hauler for details.

Problem Items

Then there are those miscellaneous items around the house that you don't quite know what to do with when they break, stop working, or are no longer needed. You know—floppy disks, CDs, batteries, and so on.

Compact Disks (CDs)

Trying to figure out what to do with old compact disks (CDs) can be a real puzzle. Even new CDs that come in the mail for online service provider solicitations can add up pretty quickly. And they don't even make good Frisbees.

But now music, CD-ROM, and even write-once disks and their cases are recyclable. They are pelletized by the reprocessor, and the CDs end up as automotive parts, while the cases can become egg cartons.

Send CDs and cases prepaid by UPS Ground or third-class mail to Plastic Recycling Incorporated, 2015 South Pennsylvania, Indianapolis, IN 46225. Call them at 317-780-6100 for more information.

Batteries

The dramatic proliferation of laptop computers, cell phones, pagers, and numerous other portable devices has given the battery industry quite a boost. Unfortunately, batteries contain metals, acids, and other compounds that cause numerous problems if they are released into the environment.

Here's how to deal with most batteries:

➤ Alkaline and carbon-zinc ("heavy duty") dry-cell batteries are sometimes collected as part of community recycling programs. If this doesn't happen in your area, you may have no practical alternative but to put them in your garbage (unless you are specifically prohibited by local regulations).

➤ Button-cell batteries, the small, round batteries that power cameras, watches, hearing aids, and so on, contain mercury, silver, cadmium, lithium, or other heavy metals. They are recyclable at many shops that carry watch, hearing aid, or camera batteries.

➤ Nickel-Cadmium batteries should be recycled because of the toxic cadmium they contain.

➤ Nickel Metal Hydride (NiMH) and Lithium Ion (Li-Ion) batteries from laptop computers may be recycled by sending them via mail or

Earth Education

End users throw away approximately three to four million failed or surplus computer disks every day—well over one billion each year. GreenDisk of Redmond, Washington, now recycles floppy disks. Unsold software is disassembled and separated into paper, plastic, and disks. The disks are erased, formatted, labeled, tested, and sold. Check out the GreenDisk Web site at www.greendisk.com for more information.

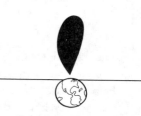

Earth Education

Enough disposable cameras have been thrown out, rather than recycled, to circle the planet when placed end to end. Anyone who actually does use a disposable camera should at least take it to a developer who absolutely promises to recycle the remaining parts after the film has been developed. Many don't.

UPS Ground to IGO, Attn: Battery Recycling, 9393 Gateway Drive, Reno, NV 89511. There are some restrictions. Call 1-888-205-0064 for more information.

➤ Automotive batteries contain lead, which is both toxic and valuable. In the U.S. more than 95 percent of all automotive batteries are recovered and recycled. Just about any place that sells them will take them back.

If you can't figure out what to do with a particular type of battery, your local recycling program coordinator or trash hauler should be able to help you.

Computers

Has that old 386 computer you bought a few years ago become an expensive doorstop? Now there's a better alternative: A growing number of computer-recycling programs around the country will take old computers and try to match them with new users. Computers that are not functional are usually disassembled and the materials are reused or recycled.

Earth Education

Twenty-nine tons of used computers were collected in Madison, Wisconsin, for recycling/reuse as part of the 1998 America Recycles Day program. Computer-recycling programs help you get rid of your old computer. They also provide jobs for the people who work for the recyclers, and offer computers to people or organizations that might not otherwise be able to afford them. Check out the PEP National Directory of Computer Recycling Programs at www.microweb.com/pepsite, where you'll find a good listing of programs by state.

In addition to helping people, these programs help the environment. It's a win-win situation. But don't wait too long to donate, or your old computer may become totally obsolete.

The Least You Need to Know

➤ Aluminum, glass, paper products, steel, and plastics are the most commonly recycled items in the home.

➤ Recycling aluminum saves a lot of energy.

➤ Glass can be recycled endlessly for bottles and jars.

➤ Plastics are harder to recycle because there are so many different kinds.

➤ You should recycle or properly dispose of hazardous wastes.

Chapter 19

Composting

> ### In This Chapter
>
> ➤ What composting is and why it's important
>
> ➤ How to make compost happen
>
> ➤ A look at various composting systems
>
> ➤ What to do when compost doesn't happen
>
> ➤ How to use your compost

Compost happens. It's the result of a natural process to recycle organic matter that's been going on for millions of years. That process is what eventually turns fallen leaves, twigs, or needles in the forest into rich, dark, crumbly soil.

You can use this same process in your own back yard to help reduce municipal solid waste (MSW) and help your immediate environment at the same time. And the best part of all is that it actually involves very little work. Mother Nature and a lot of her little helpers will do most of it for you. In this chapter, I'll tell you how to keep those little helpers happy.

First, I'll explain what compost is and why it's so important. Next, I'll tell you what you need to make it happen. We'll also look at various composting strategies and how they affect the length of time the process takes. Then, I'll offer some advice on what to do when things go wrong. Finally, I'll suggest a number of ways to use your compost effectively.

Nature's Way

So, what is compost and composting? Composting is the natural process of decomposition and recycling of various organic materials (plant matter) into a *humus*-rich soil amendment called compost. Insects, earthworms, and microorganisms help in this process.

Eco-Explanations

Humus is a dark organic material in soils produced by the decomposition of organic matter. It's a valuable additive for your lawn or garden.

Composting by humans is an ancient practice that dates back at least 2,000 years when Marcus Cato, a farmer and scientist who lived in Rome, advocated the composting of all food and animal waste before adding it back to the soil. In this country, most farmers were aware of composting by the nineteenth century.

Okay, so why is composting important? There are several reasons. Yard and food wastes make up around 30 percent of MSW in this country. And composting most of this material would trim the amount of MSW requiring disposal by almost one fourth. This would substantially reduce the amount of this material that is currently going to landfills and incinerators.

But what's so bad about dumping yard and food waste in landfills? The main problem (aside from filling up landfills more quickly than necessary) is that these materials break down very slowly due to lack of oxygen when they are landfilled. And as they decompose, they produce methane gas and acidic leachate, both of which cause environmental problems.

What's more, as I mentioned in Chapter 17, "Recycling Basics," recycling efforts aimed at other parts of the waste stream have begun to run out of momentum. Many people in the recycling sector now view composting waste—especially food waste—as one of the best ways of giving recycling rates a badly needed boost at a time when many communities are struggling to meet their recycling targets.

Compost has many advantages. When it is added to gardens it improves soil structure, texture, aeration, and helps to hold moisture. When compost is mixed in, heavy clay soils are lightened while sandy soils retain water better. Best of all, compost is essentially a free gift from Mother Nature. You help her, and she'll help you—and your garden.

Which Method?

Okay, we know what composting is and why it's important. But, just exactly how do you go about it? There are entire books written on this subject, so I can only offer a brief overview in one chapter. But this should be enough basic information to get you started.

Before we go too far, you need to decide which of the two main strategies you want to follow: low maintenance or high maintenance. Low-maintenance composting (sometimes called "passive" or "cold" composting) is probably best for beginners, especially for those who are motivated mainly by a desire to cut the amount of waste they send to landfills but don't have a lot of time to spare.

The high-maintenance approach (sometimes called "active" or "hot" composting) is for compost connoisseurs (usually experienced gardeners) who want to produce a large amount of top-quality compost for their gardens. You can start out with the simple approach, and as you gain experience you can always graduate to more sophisticated strategies.

What You Will Need

So, what do you need to make compost? Actually, a basic compost system only needs three main ingredients: greens, browns, and water. Greens (which provide nitrogen) are almost any type of fresh, moist plant matter, food scraps (avoid meat, fats, fish, and grease, which attract scavengers), while browns (which provide carbon) are dry materials such as leaves, wood chips, straw, and grass.

You follow just three simple steps to get your first compost pile started:

1. Collect as many greens and browns as you can. The larger the pile, the better it holds moisture, and the faster the decomposition process.

2. Take approximately equal quantities of greens and browns and put them in a pile, and be sure to cover food scraps with other compost matter.

3. Sprinkle enough water on the pile to make it roughly as damp as a sponge after you have squeezed the water out of it. Then, cover the pile with a tarp, plastic, or straw to keep it from getting too wet from the rain.

Earth Education

Over six million homes in North America are composting, and the number is increasing all the time. Composting recycles nutrients back into the soil, helps control soil erosion, reduces the demand for water by plants and trees, suppresses some plant diseases, and can reduce or eliminate reliance on petrochemical fertilizers. It can also extend the growing season and reduce stress from drought and freezes.

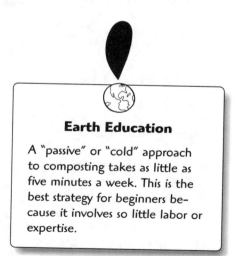

Earth Education

A "passive" or "cold" approach to composting takes as little as five minutes a week. This is the best strategy for beginners because it involves so little labor or expertise.

That's it. Mother Nature (and her little helpers) takes care of the rest. If it's very hot and dry, you may have to add a little moisture occasionally.

Now, I have deliberately described the most basic, low-maintenance method to illustrate just how easy this can be. And if you're really lazy (or smart), you can place this pile exactly where you want to do some gardening next season and you won't even have to move the compost anywhere when it's ready.

If you live in an apartment and don't have a backyard you can still get involved in composting on a small scale. Worm composting is perfect for apartment dwellers. An earthworm composting container can be kept under your sink or some other handy location to dispose of most organic kitchen waste. For additional information about earthworm composting, check out the Compost Resource Page (www.oldgrowth.org/compost) and click on "vermicomposting" for an extensive list of links. Worm Digest (www.wormdigest.org) is another great online resource.

I'll also tell you about some of the more involved backyard composting strategies in a moment. But first, let's take a look under the tarp and see what's going on in the compost pile. Let the kids have a look, too. Most school-age children love composting. They find the whole idea of turning trash into rich soil to be fascinating. And it is.

Green Tips

If your compost pile cools off too much in the winter, you can get things going again by adding an extra layer of insulation, such as straw, to help retain heat. You can also take a number of steps to speed up the composting process: chop the materials into smaller pieces, alternate layers of greens and browns, mix the pile occasionally by turning and stirring, and water the pile once a week.

How It Happens

This is where Mother Nature's little helpers come in. You provide the food, and they provide the labor. There's a whole army of microorganisms—including three groups of bacteria—that secrete enzymes to digest the waste in the compost pile. They are assisted by large numbers of fungi and enzymes that work to break down materials inside woody matter.

The microorganisms generate heat as they decompose the organic matter. A compost pile with temperatures between 90 and 140 degrees Fahrenheit is working properly. Generally speaking, the higher the temperature, the faster the process, while the lower the temperature, the slower the process. Compost piles often give off steam in cold weather.

But there are even more little helpers. Next are the earthworms that are very good at recycling decomposing organic matter into humus. And, finally, a large number of insects help by chomping their way through the compost pile, leaving aeration tunnels and digested matter behind them. It's a real team effort.

The length of time it takes Mother's little helpers to produce finished compost varies from perhaps a year for the passive approach to a month or so for the active approach. A compromise strategy between passive and active is to keep adding materials to the top of the pile, watering occasionally, and removing finished compost from the bottom (the strategy we use in our household). This should give you compost in three to six months.

Do You Need a Bin?

Many people ask whether a compost bin is necessary. It isn't. The basic compost heap I described earlier will work just fine. You can also just bury your compost in a hole or trench in the ground. Just be sure to bury it with at least eight inches of soil to discourage animals from digging it up.

But many people—especially in an urban setting—find that a bin keeps things neater and helps to retain heat. And, depending on the type of bin, it can also speed up the composting process. Let's look at your many bin options.

The Pallet Bin

Here's a simple strategy that combines reuse with composting. Take four old pallets, stand them on edge, with the tops of the pallets facing inward, to form a square bin that looks like a small animal pen. Tie the four corners together with rope, chain, or wire. You can cover it with an old tarp or plastic to keep out the rain. If you want to make a lot of compost, you can set up a second pen nearby and alternate between them.

Wire Fencing Bin

Take about a 12-foot length of sturdy medium-gauge wire fencing (new or used) and tie the ends together to form a circular bin. It's simple, it breathes well, and it will hold over a cubic yard of waste when it's full. You can cover it to keep out the rain. And it's easy to disassemble and move.

Planetary Perils

Don't place your compost bin or pile next to a wooden fence or building because it will encourage rot in those structures over time. And since a compost pile may occasionally give off an odor (especially if it isn't working properly), you might want to place it some distance from your home.

Trash Can Bin

Here's another great reuse idea. If you have a plastic trash can that you use to haul leaves and grass clippings out to the curb, it can be converted to a compost bin (since you won't be needing it for curb disposal service any more). Saw or cut off the bottom and drill a series of quarter-inch holes, spaced about six inches apart, in the side to help air circulation. For a more stable bin, set it in a hole in the ground (this has the added benefit of encouraging the helpers I mentioned earlier to get to work on your waste more quickly). The trash can lid acts as a rain cover.

Other Bins

You can also construct a bin with old cement blocks or even bricks. The materials you use don't make much difference. There are even more sophisticated multiple-bin systems that you can build if you decide to get more involved in this.

A commercial compost bin made from recycled plastic.

(Photo copyright Greg Pahl)

Green Tips

If you are in a real hurry to make compost, try a rotating compost bin, which can produce a finished batch of compost in less than a month. But be aware that this method also requires a little more time and energy than the "passive" or "cold" approach.

In addition, many commercial compost bins are available in a wide variety of shapes and sizes. Most are made from plastic—many from recycled plastic. Check with the manufacturer for details about the bin you are looking at.

Some of these bins are fairly simple, while others are rather sophisticated. A few actually rotate and thoroughly mix the materials, speeding up the process substantially. Other bins come with locking doors and tops that are intended to be rodent resistant.

Which brings up an important point: Because of problems with scavengers—especially rats—some municipalities may have restrictions on composting. A number of cities like Miami, Portland, San Francisco, and Toronto actively encourage composting but distribute rodent-resistant compost bins. Be sure to check your local regulations before you set up a compost pile.

What Else Do You Need?

Composting is a pretty low-tech activity. All you really need is a shovel to remove the compost from your pile or bin. You might find a pitchfork handy for turning the pile if you take the active approach. If you really want to get into it, a compost thermometer, a long probe that measures the inside temperature of the pile, might be helpful.

Troubleshooting Tips

Okay, let's say you've started a compost pile in your back yard, but things don't seem to be happening. Or maybe some strange things are happening. What to do?

If your compost pile is not heating up very well, there are a number of possibilities:

➤ The pile is too small—make it larger.

➤ There isn't enough water—add more water or cover the pile to retain moisture.

➤ Not enough air—turn the pile over to get things going.

➤ Not enough greens—mix in food scraps, grass clippings, or manure.

➤ Cold weather—add an extra layer of insulating material.

On the other hand, if your compost pile smells bad, there are several possible problems:

➤ If it gives off a rotten odor, it is probably too wet—turn the pile, or add dry brown matter such as leaves or straw.

➤ Or it may simply be too compact—turn the pile to loosen it up.

➤ If it smells like ammonia, it has too much green (nitrogen) in it—add more brown (carbon) like leaves, wood chips, or straw.

Finally, if your compost pile is attracting scavengers such as rats or raccoons, you probably have meat, fish, or fatty food scraps in there somewhere. Remove the scraps or use a pest-resistant bin.

Green Tips

If your compost pile is heating up too much (above 140 degrees), it simply may be too large. Try reducing its size or turning it over.

Old Family Recipes

Composting is a bit like cooking. If you start with a good recipe, the results will be even better. Here are a few old family recipes that will give you good results if you are starting from scratch with a new pile. They begin with a basic, slower-acting mixture and work their way up to "hotter" or faster-acting combinations.

Mild:

- ➤ 50 percent dry leaves
- ➤ 50 percent fresh grass clippings

Spicy:

- ➤ 50 percent dry leaves
- ➤ 25 percent food scraps
- ➤ 25 percent fresh grass clippings

Extra Hot:

- ➤ 50 percent dry leaves
- ➤ 20 percent fresh garden weeds
- ➤ 20 percent fresh grass clippings
- ➤ 10 percent food scraps

Planetary Perils

Never add feces from cats or dogs to your compost pile because of the possibility of contamination from disease pathogens and parasites. Also avoid adding dairy products, meat and bones, diseased plants, and noxious weeds and plants. If you use the active or hot method of composting, the higher temperatures should be enough to kill the noxious weed seeds, but if you want to be absolutely sure, don't compost them.

You may develop your own special recipes based on what you have available after a little experimentation. Compost connoisseurs tend to be fussy about the carbon-nitrogen ratio, but if you remember to keep a reasonable mix between greens and browns then it should work most of the time. You can also add a little of one or more of the following ingredients to spice things up a bit:

- ➤ half-shovel of garden soil—high in microorganisms
- ➤ half-shovel of finished compost—high in microorganisms
- ➤ half-shovel of bone meal—high nitrogen source
- ➤ shovel of firewood ash—high in potash and carbon

If you really want to heat things up, you can add a little manure from grass-eating animals such as cows, goats, sheep, horses, and so on. But don't use feces from meat-eaters like cats and dogs.

Or, if you prefer to keep it simple, you can just add whatever materials happen to be handy—even paper towels and tissue—to the top of your pile on a regular basis—and forget it. This is one recycling activity where it's virtually impossible to fail, because no matter what you do wrong, compost will eventually happen. It just may take longer.

Back to the Garden

Whether you have followed the right backyard composting procedures or not, you will eventually end up with some usable compost. But how do you know when it's ready? And, what can you do with it?

Your compost is ready when it finally cools down and looks dark and crumbly and feels like rich garden soil. It should have a sweet, clean aroma. You may want to sift out the odds and ends that didn't compost completely with a homemade screen that you can construct from two-by-four lumber and 3/8" hardware cloth. While sifted compost helps root vegetables, it's not really necessary.

Compost won't burn plant roots, so you can use it at any time in many different ways:

Green Tips

Compost is excellent mulch, and you can use it around trees and shrubs or in your vegetable garden. Apply compost to your garden several times a year if you have enough. The more the better. It's virtually impossible to add too much. The earthworms in your garden will love it, and so will your plants.

➤ Dig some into your flower bed or vegetable garden—use as much as you want.

➤ Work compost into the soil before planting a new lawn.

➤ Use screened compost as a great top dressing for existing lawns.

➤ Give trees, shrubs, and nursery seedlings a better start by planting them in a half-soil, half-compost mixture.

➤ Work the compost into the top few inches of soil around a plant for an excellent side dressing.

For additional information about composting check out the Compost Resource Page (www.oldgrowth.org/compost), which offers lots of basic and advanced composting information, tips, products and services, compost poetry (I'm not kidding), and links for additional information.

The Least You Need to Know

➤ Compost is nature's free soil-improvement product.

➤ Making compost can be a simple or a complex activity, depending on your time, energy, and goals.

➤ Microorganisms, fungi, enzymes, earthworms, and insects do most of the work in producing compost.

➤ You don't need a compost bin to make compost.

➤ Compost turns waste into a valuable resource, and you can use it almost anywhere to improve soil, conserve moisture, and prevent soil erosion.

Chapter 20

Completing the Circle

I'm sure you've heard the old saying, "A chain is only as strong as its weakest link." In the 1970s, the weakest link in the recycling chain was the lack of markets for recycled products. Although we have made substantial progress in this important area, it remains the weakest link.

The dramatic fall in prices for most recycled materials that followed the collapse of the Asian economies in 1997 dramatized the fragile and unpredictable nature of these markets. But one way to help even out these price swings is to increase consumer demand for products that contain recycled material—especially post-consumer waste. Even though you may be carefully recycling your household waste every week, you really aren't recycling until you are buying recycled products just as regularly.

And that's what we'll be focusing on in this chapter—closing the loop for recycled materials. First, I'll explain why it's so important to buy recycled products. Then, we'll take a look at the fine print on recycled packaging. I'll also tell you about some of the main programs that promote the buying of recycled products. After that, we'll look at some of the many products that contain recycled materials. Finally, I'll tell you about a few companies that have discovered that buying—and selling—recycled is good for business.

Why Buy Recycled?

There are many reasons why we should all be buying recycled products or products that have substantial amounts of recycled content in them. When you choose a recycled product over its nonrecycled alternative, you are encouraging the manufacturer to make more, which increases demand for the recycled materials that went into the product, which makes it easier to run recycling programs—and so on.

Green Tips

Every time you buy a recycled product, or a product with recycled content, you strengthen the markets for recycled materials. This purchasing of recycled consumer goods will help change the materials flow in our economy from a quick one-way trip to the landfill to a more sustainable flow that resembles a loop. This transformation is essential if we are to move toward a sustainable economy.

Close the Loop

The easiest way to describe this process is to take another look at the recycling logo. As you will recall, it has three arrows that chase each other's tails. Think of each of these arrows as one part of the recycling loop.

The first arrow represents collection. This is where you and I put our recyclable materials in our recycling bin or bring them to a local drop-off center. Then, the materials are sorted and sold to a reprocessor.

The second arrow is the manufacturing process in which recycled materials are crushed, melted down, or otherwise converted into new products and then shipped back to stores as new consumer goods.

The third—and most important—arrow is when you and I purchase the products made with recycled content. When we "buy recycled," we close the recycling loop.

Buying Recycled Saves

Buying recycled has numerous economic and environmental benefits. When we buy recycled products we ...

➤ Save natural resources because products made from recycled materials instead of virgin materials reduce the need to cut down trees, drill for oil, and dig for minerals.

➤ Save energy because it usually takes less energy to make recycled products.

➤ Cut down on air and water pollution because making products from recycled materials generally creates less pollution.

➤ Save landfill space because recycled materials don't go into landfills.

➤ Save money and create jobs because the recycling process creates far more jobs than landfills or incinerators do. And when properly set up and fully utilized, recycling can be the least expensive waste management method.

Sound familiar? You're right. The benefits of buying recycled products are virtually the same as the benefits of recycling. Which, as we have also seen, are very similar to the benefits of the two other Rs of the environmental movement, reduce and reuse. All those interconnections again.

Read the Fine Print

Okay, so now you're all fired up to buy recycled. Right? But be careful. Just because a product in the store displays a recycling logo does not really guarantee much of anything—except that it has a logo on it. The product may or may not contain recycled materials, and may not even be recyclable in your community—or anywhere else for that matter.

Buy Recycled Programs

There really has been a major shift in our attitudes about buying products with recycled content in recent years. Once viewed as a fringe activity for ardent environmentalists, buying recycled is going mainstream. Some of this has been the result of individual consumer demand. But a lot has been the result of a number of major initiatives by federal, state, and local governments and businesses. These organizations can have a substantial impact because of the huge quantities of materials and supplies they purchase.

Planetary Perils

Read packaging and product labels carefully—some products that look "green" aren't. Does the logo refer to the product, the packaging, or both? An awful lot of "greenwash" has been splashed around by various companies who want to cash in on increasing environmental awareness among consumers. And the difference between pre-consumer and post-consumer content is crucial to understanding most recycling claims.

Earth Education

Federal, state, and local governments as well as businesses have purchased billions of dollars' worth of recycled products in recent years to encourage their manufacture.

Part of this has been motivated by a desire to give recycling markets a boost—especially during periods of low commodity prices. But much of the incentive has been purely economic. Businesses, in particular, have discovered that they can save money while helping the environment—and improving their company image at the same time.

By and large, recycling has a good deal of consumer support nationwide, and businesses and governmental agencies have found that an increasing number of consumers want to deal with companies and agencies that use or sell recycled products. A number of high-profile national programs promote the buying of recycled. Let's look at a few.

Buy Recycled Business Alliance

The Buy Recycled Business Alliance (BRBA) was formed by and for the U.S. business community. The Alliance is a group of organizations committed to increasing the purchase of recycled content products through education. It also encourages leadership by example.

The Alliance supports and develops education and information programs that provide useful information to purchasers of recycled content products. BRBA was formed as an initiative of the National Recycling Coalition in 1992, in partnership with 25 major American businesses. Seed funds were provided by the U.S. Environmental Protection Agency. Since then, the Alliance has expanded to include a wide range of organizations. Check out its Web site at http://brba. nrc-recycle.org for more information.

WasteWise

WasteWise (www.epa.gov/wastewise) is a free, voluntary program sponsored by the Environmental Protection Agency that helps organizations eliminate municipal solid waste, while benefiting their bottom line and the environment. WasteWise is a flexible program that enables its participants to design their own solid waste reduction programs tailored to their particular needs.

Since its inception in 1994, WasteWise has grown to include more than 900 corporations, government agencies, universities, hospitals, and other organizations that are committed to cutting costs and conserving natural resources.

Earth Education

Some of the recycled-content products most often purchased by WasteWise partners include copier paper, paper towels, and toilet paper. WasteWise participants purchased more than 450,000 tons of recycled-content products in 1998, spending $4.7 billion. Many organizations also manufactured new products with recycled content or increased the percentage of recycled content in existing manufactured products, diverting 158,000 tons of waste in the process.

The EPA also has a Comprehensive Procurement Guideline (CPG) program that promotes the use of materials recovered from solid waste. Although it was originally developed for federal agencies, it can be used by state, local, and private agencies. You'll find more information about the guidelines at www.epa.gov/cpg.

Other Programs

Hundreds of other programs, buying cooperatives, and other initiatives encourage the purchase of recycled products in this country. All 50 states now have "buy recycled" programs, and at least 500 local governments encourage "green purchasing" of a wide variety of products, from paper to paving, and office supplies to mulch.

These programs are aimed at developing stable and competitive markets for products that can be made with post-consumer materials diverted from local waste streams. By using local materials, shipping costs can be kept low, and energy does not need to be wasted for transport over long distances. Most of these programs have created thousands of new jobs all across the country.

What's Available?

But how can you locate recycled products? It's easier than you might think. There is an excellent online Recycled Content Product Database, created by the California Integrated Waste Management Board, which offers sophisticated recycled product searches. Check it out at www.ciwmb.ca.gov/RCP. I think you'll be surprised at what you find. Look at the keyword classifications first to get some search ideas.

Just a few minutes of poking around on the Recycled Content Product Database will demonstrate that an awful lot of recycled items are available in almost every category imaginable.

It's pop quiz time again. Put on your thinking cap. What is the easiest way to determine the difference between a virgin product and a recycled product?

a. Chemical testing

b. Visible testing

c. None of the above

Earth Education

Over 5,000 products that have recycled content in them are currently available in this country. You need to know three important things about recycled products: They're definitely available now, they're competitively priced, and they're quality products. In most cases, it's difficult to tell the difference between virgin and recycled products.

The correct answer is c. None of the above. This just emphasizes the fact that it's very difficult to tell the difference between most recycled content products and their virgin alternatives.

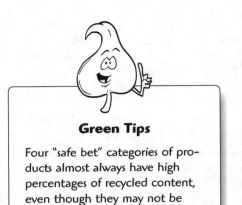

The one exception I can think of is facial tissue. I have yet to find a recycled brand that is as soft as its virgin alternatives. I still use the recycled stuff, but I sure wish they could get it right. There's an opportunity there for someone, I'm sure. Otherwise, recycled products generally meet or beat specifications for most virgin items.

Lots of Choices

So many other products are made with recycled content today that it's impossible to name them all. But here's a short list of some of the things you're most likely to run into at the store that offer recycled content in their packaging, the product—or both:

➤ cereal, cookie, and cracker packages

➤ canned beverages and foods

➤ detergent and cleaning supply containers

➤ shampoo and beauty products

➤ paper towels, facial and bathroom tissue

Here are some additional products that often have recycled content that you'll find at other retail establishments:

➤ writing paper, note pads, greeting cards, wrapping paper

➤ tools

➤ steel appliances

➤ carpeting

➤ wallpaper

➤ plastic garbage cans, recycling bins, flower pots

➤ corrugated boxes

➤ insulation in ski jackets and sleeping bags made from recycled PET plastic bottles

➤ garden hoses

➤ mulch

➤ patio furniture

There are many more products such as trash bags, rulers, mouse pads, cups and glassware, plastic lumber—even boat docks. And the numbers of products and categories continue to grow exponentially.

Plastic Lumber

Plastic lumber? That's right. This stuff, generally made from recycled HDPE (high-density polyethylene), is an interesting development. It's especially well-suited for damp installations where preservative-treated lumber is normally used—like outdoor decks.

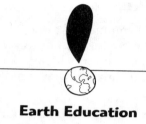

Earth Education

Picnic tables, benches, porch swings, rocking chairs, planters, playground structures, and signs can all be made from plastic lumber. A growing number of companies are beginning to manufacture plastic lumber in a variety of sizes, shapes, and colors.

Plastic lumber has the advantage of not needing toxic preservatives, it is impervious to moisture and insects, it doesn't splinter, and it also doesn't need maintenance except for an occasional washing. It's a great use of old milk jugs.

Buying—and Selling—Recycled

But turning plastic milk jugs into lumber isn't the only creative recycling idea. A growing number of businesses in this country (and around the world) are catching on to the advantages of buying—and selling—recycled products.

Clothing from Soda Bottles

One of the pioneers in this country is Patagonia. This well-known California clothing manufacturer has been making fleece garments out of post-consumer recycled (PCR) plastic bottles since 1993. The bottles are melted down, and then spun into polyester fiber. Patagonia was the first company in the U.S. to do this. A few others have followed their lead.

Every time you buy one of their vests, jackets, or other garments, you help to keep around 25 discarded two-liter soda bottles out of a landfill. The company estimates that its use of PCR since its inception has conserved about 20,000 barrels of oil and has kept about 10,000 tons of toxic emissions out of the atmosphere.

Patagonia's environmental ethic has expanded to include many other aspects of its business, including switching to organic cotton, trying to minimize the environmental impact of its procurement and manufacturing activities, and incorporating green design elements into its facilities whenever possible. And Patagonia isn't alone in applying environmental thinking to the business world.

Carpet in, Carpet Out

Interface, the world's largest commercial carpet manufacturer, used to try to sell as much carpet as it could, moving tons of nonrecyclable carpet fibers, glues, and backing through the economy—and eventually into landfills—every year. But not any more. This Atlanta-based company reinvented itself in the early 1990s to become a carpet *service* provider.

Under Interface's Evergreen Lease program, the company agrees to maintain the tile carpeting it installs over the term of the lease. When the carpet needs repairs, it usually means only replacing the carpet tiles in high-traffic areas, rather than the entire carpet. These repairs are normally accomplished overnight with minimal disruption of the office. Interface takes back the worn carpet tile and recycles it—ideally into new carpet as part of its larger program to become a sustainable manufacturing operation.

Earth Education

In 1998, Interface, an Atlanta-based commercial carpet manufacturer, reclaimed 433,000 yards of carpeting. Although Interface leads the industry in this initiative, they admit that they still have a long way to go in their recycling efforts.

The company has recently developed a new polymeric flooring material called Solenium that can be completely remanufactured into more of itself when it becomes worn, creating a closed-loop materials flow. This unique "resilient textile flooring" has a lot of other attractive low-maintenance features as well, and represents a dramatic breakthrough in recyclable floor coverings. Solenium is installed and maintained under a lease arrangement similar to the one used for the company's carpet tiles (we'll take another look at Interface in the next chapter).

Patagonia and Interface, of course, are not the only companies who have seen the (green) light. There's going to be a lot more of this sort of creativity in the near future as increasing numbers of businesses discover the advantages of buying—and selling—recycled products.

Additional Resources

A lot of good information is available on recycled products. In addition to the California Integrated Waste Management Board Web site I mentioned earlier, The Pennsylvania Resources Council has an excellent 1998 Buyers Guide to Recycled Products that lists more than 700 products and 200 companies. It's now available online. Check it out at www.prc.org. Or, the printed version is $4 for Pennsylvania residents and $6 for nonresidents (see "Pennsylvania Resources Council" in Appendix D for the mailing address).

The EPA's Web site has a comprehensive Buy-Recycled Resource Guide (www.epa.gov/ wastewise/buyguide.htm) that lists dozens of resources for recycled paper, office products, plastics, construction and landscaping materials, transportation products, parks and recreational products, textiles, vehicle products, and more. Although it's mainly aimed at business, a good listing of other Web sites is at the end.

Another interesting resource is Recycler's World (www.recycle.net), a worldwide trading site for information related to secondary or recyclable commodities, by-products, used and surplus items or materials. There are some good links to other sites as well.

With a little research, you can find all sorts of products that contain recycled materials that you might not have thought of before. So the next time you're in the store, look for these products. And if you don't see them, ask the owner or manager to stock them. Remember, you're not really recycling unless you're buying recycled.

The Least You Need to Know

➤ Buying recycled products closes the recycling loop.

➤ Without markets for recycled products, recycling does not work.

➤ Hundreds of federal, state, and local programs promote the buying of recycled products.

➤ Thousands of products contain recycled materials.

➤ Buying recycled products is a great strategy for individuals, businesses, organizations, and governmental agencies.

Part 5

A Sustainable Future

Now we've come to the most challenging—and exciting—issue of all—trying to ensure a sustainable future for our children and grandchildren. I'll begin by explaining what sustainability means, what the obstacles are, and offer some solutions, as well as examples of successful strategies.

Next, we'll look at the exciting world of renewable energy—solar power, wind power, water power, ocean energy, geothermal, biomass, and hydrogen. We'll also look at a wide range of transportation and living pattern issues, and how they relate to sustainability.

Then, we'll take a good hard look at population growth—and I'll explain why it's so important for us to get a handle on this difficult issue. I'll also tell you about green plans, and why they are such an exciting development. In addition, I'll mention some other, less tangible, issues that we need to work on if we are going to achieve a sustainable future. And finally, I'll leave you with some suggestions on how to get involved.

Chapter 21

Sustainability

In This Chapter

➤ What is sustainability?

➤ Why is it important?

➤ A look at the problems we face

➤ Figuring out the solutions

➤ Who's going to make it happen?

Victor Hugo, a nineteenth-century French poet and novelist, said, "Greater than the tread of mighty armies is an idea whose time has come." And sustainability is an idea whose time has definitely come.

The whole point of the Three Rs that we have looked at—reduce, reuse, recycle—is to encourage a shift toward a sustainable economy—and by extension, a sustainable future. And without a sustainable economy, there won't be a future. At least not one you would want to live in.

Working toward a sustainable world involves enormous challenges. But it also involves enormous opportunities. This is the most exciting part. The changes we're going to have to make in our economy and society to achieve sustainability are going to be radical. But the potential benefits will be huge. And that's what the rest of this book is about.

I'll begin this chapter by explaining what sustainability is and why it's so important. Then, I'll briefly review the problems we need to overcome and describe some of the solutions.

Finally, we'll look at a few examples of companies that are working toward sustainability.

What Is Sustainability?

Okay, so just what is sustainability? Anything that is sustainable can keep on going or endure indefinitely. So, sustainability is acting in a way that enables life on Earth to endure into the future while providing for the needs of all people and other creatures, and, at the same time, maintaining the natural systems that support all life.

Another way of looking at it is: "What comes out is no more than what goes in." Actually, if you add this to the things you should have learned in kindergarten, "clean up your own mess," and "share everything" (from Chapter 1, "It's Our Home"), you've about got the idea.

In its landmark 1987 report, *Our Common Future* (also called the Brundtland Report), The United Nations' World Commission on Environment and Development said, "Sustainable development is development that meets the needs of the present without compromising the ability of future generations to meet their own needs."

Now, I admit that some people view "sustainable" and "development" as contradictory terms. I tend to agree with them. But if development can be viewed as a process that evolves into a less-destructive form of human activity, then pursuing sustainable development makes sense.

The concept of sustainability applies to many different aspects of our lives. According to *Caring for the Earth: A Strategy for Sustainable Living* by The World Conservation Union (www.iucn.org), United Nations Environment Programme (www.unep.ch), and the World Wide Fund for Nature (www.panda.org), the principles of a sustainable society include …

➤ Respecting and caring for the community of life.
➤ Improving the quality of human life.
➤ Conserving the Earth's vitality and diversity.
➤ Minimizing the depletion of nonrenewable resources.
➤ Staying within the Earth's *carrying capacity.*
➤ Enabling communities to care for their own environments.
➤ Creating a global alliance.

Although it's hard to believe today, the concept of sustainability has very deep roots in this country. Native Americans had an intimate relationship with nature. They saw themselves as part of nature and tried to act in harmony with it. And they also had a keen sense of responsibility for their actions.

The Great Law of the Six Nations Iroquois Confederacy stated, "In every deliberation we must consider the impact on the seventh generation."

Looking at our current economic system, it's hard to see how we even consider the impact of our behavior on the current generation, let alone the seventh. And that's a big part of our problem. But if we are to achieve sustainability, we're going to have to begin to take the long view about all of our actions. Figuring out ways of dealing with our shortsighted habits is hard enough. But there are other issues we need to consider as well.

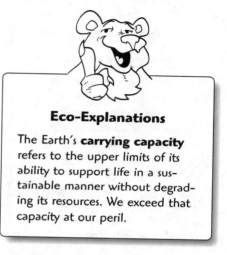

Eco-Explanations

The Earth's **carrying capacity** refers to the upper limits of its ability to support life in a sustainable manner without degrading its resources. We exceed that capacity at our peril.

The Problems

Part of the difficulty is that there are just so many problems. And, as we've seen earlier in the book, they're basically all interrelated. Try to fix one problem over here, and as an unintended consequence, a new problem pops up over there. Or, as the system becomes more and more strained, a series of cascading system failures become so severe that it's almost impossible to deal with any of them in an organized—or effective—way.

But among all the problems, three stand out: increasingly scarce resources, environmental degradation, and population growth. Any one of these by itself would be more than enough to try to deal with. Taken together, they're a real challenge. But if we are going to have a future worth living, we're going to have to face all of these problems head on, and come up with realistic solutions. Soon. Because, as a species, we humans have become like parasites that devour their host. And our host is planet Earth and its irreplaceable life-support systems.

So far, our response has mostly been to try to treat the symptoms. This is about as effective as using Band-Aids to patch the leaks in a dam that is about to burst. First, we've got to figure out how to lower the water behind the dam, and then how to overhaul the entire structure. And that's what's needed: a complete overhaul of our economic system. Impossible? Not necessarily. The process has already begun.

Planetary Perils

Reducing, reusing, and recycling by themselves are not enough to save our environment; we need to completely overhaul our economic system if we are to have a future worth living in. And we don't have a lot of time to figure out ways to do this. Every day that we delay makes it that much harder to repair the damage we've already done.

The Solutions

While all of the strategies that I have told you about earlier in the book—reduce, reuse, recycle—are important, frankly, they're not enough. Now, don't let me discourage you from practicing them daily in every way you can think of. Every little bit helps. But that's the problem. It's too little. And it's too late. We're simply not going to save the planet (or ourselves) by recycling another aluminum can. Or another billion.

The huge problems we face require solutions to match. So, in addition to the Three Rs, what we're going to have to do is nothing less than reinvent our exploitive, unsustainable economic system from the ground up. Then, we need to address a whole series of related social issues. The solutions, like the problems, are all interrelated.

Now, admittedly, this is a very tall order. But we really don't have much choice, unless squatting in some parched desert somewhere with billions of other wretched people, trying to eat sand, appeals to you.

To begin this process, we will need to follow four main strategies to reinvent the economy:

1. Copy Mother Nature
2. Dramatically increase resource productivity
3. Shift to a service economy
4. Repair the environmental damage we've already caused

Each of these strategies includes an incredible range of activities. We'll cover some of them in the remaining chapters. For now, let's start with the basics.

Copy Mother Nature

Happily, we really don't have to begin from scratch, because we have a model of how this system could work. And we don't have to look very hard to find it, because it's all around us. Most of what we need to know about the basics of a sustainable economic system was perfected by Mother Nature millions of years ago.

Eliminating waste in its many forms is one of the key ways of developing a sustainable economic system. In nature nothing goes to waste. After something has been used by one life form, it becomes an input for another. Even when things die, they decompose and are reused or recycled again and again. As long as things stay more or less in balance, the system functions indefinitely.

If industrial systems were redesigned to follow this pattern, there would be a constant reuse of materials in continuous closed-loop cycles. This would not only reduce the exploitation of many resources at the input end, it would also eliminate most problems associated with wastes at the other end. This sort of approach is part of a strategy generally referred to as *industrial ecology*.

And we're already making some progress in this direction. The many recycling initiatives we've already looked at are the first halting steps toward developing a circular materials flow. But we still have a long way to go. Reducing our use of non-renewable resources, like oil, is another important part of this strategy. And we've only just begun that process.

Some of these basic ideas have been incorporated into a new field of study called "ecological economics," which combines environmentalism with economics. Eco-economics looks at the relationship between ecosystems and economic systems and tries to help achieve a sustainable world by putting a value on our natural resources. Until recently, most of these resources have been treated as if they were free and inexhaustible. They're neither.

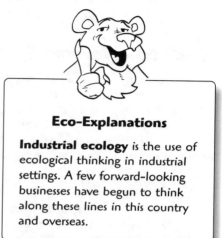

Eco-Explanations

Industrial ecology is the use of ecological thinking in industrial settings. A few forward-looking businesses have begun to think along these lines in this country and overseas.

Increase Resource Productivity

The second part of this new economic model concerns efficiency. In practical terms, transforming our present economic system into a sustainable one also means dramatically reducing our use of materials and energy by a staggering 75 to 90 percent. While that may sound unrealistic, our present system is so wasteful that it really is possible. Our energy network, transport system, and even our living patterns are all incredibly inefficient.

Unfortunately, at the national level, not much is being done to address this situation. The governments of Austria, the Netherlands, and Norway, on the other hand, have already committed to pursuing 75-percent-reduction targets for materials and energy. Other countries are following their leads.

Earth Education

The U.S. economy, overall, is grossly inefficient. It is estimated that only 6 percent of our huge materials flow ends up as products. Some observers maintain that the figure is much lower. The other 94 percent is wasted in numerous ways at all levels of our economic system. The materials used by all industrial processes in this country amount to a staggering one million pounds per American every year.

Another important part of this strategy is to put an end to laws, policies, taxes, and subsidies that encourage wasteful resource consumption. This includes subsidies to mining, oil, coal, fishing, and forest industries. In the Netherlands, Germany, Britain, Sweden, and Denmark, tax reforms designed to eventually accomplish this have already been enacted. Similar initiatives are being proposed throughout Europe (more on this in Chapter 26, "Green Plans").

Shift to a Service Economy

The third part of a new sustainable economy involves a fundamental shift in the relationship between producer and consumer, in which consumers primarily buy services rather than goods. This requires not only a shift in thinking at the manufacturing end, but at the consuming end as well. Companies need to discover the advantages of offering services, while consumers need to understand and appreciate the benefits of receiving quality services rather than acquiring more stuff.

A Swiss industry analyst, Walter Stahel, and a German chemist, Michael Braungart, proposed this basic idea in the mid-1980s. They proposed a service economy in which consumers lease or rent goods rather than buying them. The advantage of this strategy is that it would be in the leasing company's best financial interests to offer sturdy, well-designed, long-lasting goods that could be upgraded indefinitely. Stahel referred to this process as a "cradle-to-cradle" approach.

Companies such as Xerox with their leased copiers, and Interface with their leased carpet tiles, are two good examples of American companies that have successfully adopted this idea (more on them in a moment).

Repair the Damage

The fourth and final part of a new sustainable economic system involves repairing the damage we have already done to our environment to ensure a sustainable future. That damage is enormous and continues to mount daily.

Problems related to environmental destruction have spurred the mass migration of refugees across the world—12 million at last count. In many cases, these refugees pose a very real threat to the stability of their host countries. The longer we wait to do something to reverse these trends, the higher the eventual costs, and the longer it will take.

Earth Education

Violent weather in 1998 caused over $90 billion in damage worldwide, more than the weather-related losses for the entire decade of the 1980s. Deforestation and the resulting floods and mudslides, for example, have killed tens of thousands and have displaced hundreds of millions of others from their homes. Famine caused by overgrazing, over-consumption of water, and increasingly unpredictable weather in other areas, combined with growing conflicts over dwindling resources, have caused social instability in many countries. Just tune in to the evening news on any day of the week to see the latest painful examples.

A Team Effort

Okay, this is an awfully ambitious program. Who's actually going to take on this huge task? Because of its size and complexity, it's going to have to be a team effort. Perhaps the most interesting thing is that environmental activists aren't going to be the main players. They do have an important role to perform as cheerleaders and—especially—as watchdogs. But environmentalists are going to have some help, a lot of help in fact, from an unlikely ally—business.

Green Business

Business? That's right: big corporations. Why? Because business has seen the light—the green light. Not every business, mind you, but the smart ones. The ones that are going to be the leaders in the new industrial revolution that's about to take place.

More and more businesses around the world are finally catching on to the fact that if we continue to pillage the Earth, the ecological foundations that support life on this planet will eventually collapse—and so will the global economy. No economy. No profits. It's pretty simple, actually. But what to do about it isn't so simple.

As I've said before, this is going to be the environmental century because, for better or worse, environmental factors are going to be the dominant issues of the next 100 years. We're either going to figure out how to create a new economy that follows Mother Nature's example of sustainable activity—or we won't.

If we don't, we—or more accurately, our children and grandchildren—can kiss the Good Life goodbye. But if we do, the process of converting our consumption-obsessed, incredibly inefficient economic system into one that is environmentally sustainable offers the greatest investment opportunities in history. And forward-looking businesses, governments, and individuals have caught on to this.

It's no great secret that some of the big oil companies have recently been investing heavily in sustainable solar and wind-energy ventures (more on this in Chapter 22, "Renewable Energy"). A few large timber companies have abandoned clear-cutting and adopted selective tree harvesting instead. There are even some sustainably managed forestry programs in the Amazon Rain Forest in Brazil, where some of the worst logging abuses have taken place in recent years.

I want to emphasize that this is not going to be a simple or easy process. Wall Street still single-mindedly pursues "shareholder value" while ignoring the long-term costs. And some businesses will fight moves toward sustainability tooth and nail. But the smart ones will come around once they see the long-term advantages.

> ### Earth Education
>
> The process of converting our present unsustainable economic system into a sustainable one offers the greatest investment opportunities in history. Many foreign businesses are already positioning themselves to take advantage of those opportunities.

Forest Stewardship Council (FSC) certified logs being sustainably harvested in the Amazon in Brazil.

(Greenpeace)

Governments

Governments also have a productive and important role to play in creating a sustainable future. They need to identify and defend environmental limits. And they need to do that, both independently and cooperatively, with other nations, because global environmental problems don't respect national boundaries.

But governments also need to give businesses enough slack to develop their own solutions. This is because, whatever else you may think of them, the huge multinational corporations of today have pockets deep enough to pay for the huge new investments that are going to be needed. And the complexities of the problems we face are simply beyond the ability of governments to manage entirely on their own.

Some governments have already taken on the challenge, and are beginning to make progress. Costa Rica hopes to generate all of its electricity from renewable energy sources by 2010, and the Danish government has banned the construction of new coal-fired power plants.

And some countries, like the Netherlands, New Zealand, and Mexico have taken bold steps to coordinate and formalize their commitment to sustainability by adopting national Green Plans (more on that in Chapter 26).

So where is our government in this picture? Good question. Of all the major industrial nations, the United States probably has the poorest understanding of these initiatives and ideas. That needs to change.

Earth Education

Germany has announced plans to become the first nation to completely phase out its nuclear electrical-generation facilities over a 30- to 35-year period. The country also plans a major tax restructuring that will reduce income taxes, while raising energy taxes.

Groups and Individuals

Last, but by no means least, is another group of players that will take part in the race toward sustainability. This includes nonprofit organizations ranging from international environmental groups to local community action committees to churches—and everything else in between.

Supporting everything is an informed citizenry. That's where you and I come in. We can help this process by voicing our opinions, voting with our ballots and our dollars, and taking direct personal action when necessary. And if you come up with a great new idea for a sustainable product or service, go for it! Opportunities in the new economy are not necessarily limited to big business.

All of these groups and individuals will be the eyes, ears, and conscience of the movement. And we do have an important role to play. Our assistance will be needed constantly to encourage, prod, cajole, and otherwise push or drag government and business forward toward a sustainable future. We can't do this by ourselves. But we can do it together.

It's Already Happening

Now, I admit this all sounds crazy and hopelessly optimistic. It is optimistic. But it's not completely crazy; it's already happening, mostly in other countries, which is why it seems so outlandish from an American point of view. I'll tell you more about what is going on overseas in the chapters that follow.

But right now I want to mention a few examples of U.S. companies that have caught on to the huge potential that sustainability offers.

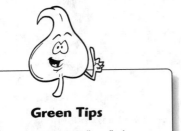

Green Tips

The companies that "get" the message of sustainability will be the leaders of tomorrow. The ones that don't will be history.

Green Carpet

One company that "gets it" is Interface of Atlanta, the carpet manufacturer I mentioned in the previous chapter. The company's innovative recyclable carpet tile leasing program was a stroke of sheer genius (although, when you think about it, you wonder why someone didn't come up with the idea sooner). Then, the company went on to develop a whole new category of floor covering with their "resilient textile flooring" called Solenium, which, as I mentioned, is endlessly recyclable into more of itself. But they haven't stopped there.

Since about 1994, the company has been actively reinventing itself—from the floor up—and now has adopted the ambitious goal of becoming the world's first truly sustainable enterprise. The main idea is to close all materials loops, take no virgin materials from the Earth, add nothing harmful to the biosphere, reduce manufacturing costs, and increase profit margins—all at the same time.

The Document Company

Xerox, which now bills itself as "The Document Company," has reinvented itself as a copy service provider rather than a copying-machine manufacturer. As you may recall, Xerox has reduced its purchases of a wide variety of copying machine parts by reclaiming, refurbishing, and reusing existing parts, while saving several hundred million dollars in purchases annually. What's more, its latest green-designed copier, with all parts either recyclable or reusable, is expected to save the company $1 billion via long-term manufacturing. The new copier uses 100 percent recycled paper, too.

Varying Shades of Green

There are other examples. The forest products giant, Weyerhaeuser Company of Washington State, has taken significant steps to cut pollution at its mills. United Parcel Service is cutting energy consumption, saving 2,200 trees, and eliminating about 550 tons of solid waste a year with greener packaging. Even DuPont, the huge Delaware-based multinational, says it has a zero-emission, zero-waste goal, although it has yet to set a deadline.

Many environmentalists remain skeptical. Considering the poor environmental records of some of these companies in the past, that's not surprising. But there is no question that more and more businesses are catching on to the fact that they can save money and make their products more competitive while helping the environment.

And there is a growing realization among both the business and environmental communities that the interests of these two long-time adversaries are beginning to come together. Not everywhere. Not always. And it's admittedly a wary relationship, but one that offers hope for possible productive cooperation in the future.

Earth Education

When the Boeing Corporation retrofitted the lighting systems in its design and manufacturing areas, it cut its lighting energy use by 90 percent and recovered the costs in two years. Many other businesses across the country are beginning to discover similar opportunities for saving energy—and money.

And all of this demonstrates that we are slowly moving in the general direction of a more sustainable economy and sustainable world. There is no doubt that sustainability is an idea whose time has come. The main question now is, will it come in time?

The Least You Need to Know

➤ Many Native Americans carefully considered the impact of their actions on future generations before making important decisions.

➤ Working toward sustainability involves enormous challenges—and huge potential rewards.

➤ The United States needs to take a much more active role in developing a sustainable economy.

➤ Shifting to a sustainable economy is going to require a cooperative effort between government, business, environmentalists, and informed citizens.

➤ American business is slowly beginning to move toward sustainability.

Chapter 22

Renewable Energy

In This Chapter

➤ Renewable energy explained

➤ How deregulation is helping renewable energy

➤ The role the sun plays in renewables

➤ A look at the many different kinds of renewable energy

➤ How you can help the shift to renewables

Millions of years ago, dinosaurs roamed the Earth. Today, fossil fuels from that era provide 90 percent or more of the energy in most of the industrial nations, and 75 percent of energy worldwide. The burning of fossil fuels is the main reason for the buildup of greenhouse gases in the atmosphere. And, as long as we rely on nonrenewable fossil fuels—coal, oil, and natural gas—as our main fuel sources, the trend toward global warming is only going to get worse.

Responding to these problems, many countries are beginning to switch to nonpolluting, renewable sources of energy such as the wind, the sun, rivers, and oceans. Not only is this good news for the environment, it's also an exciting development for both consumers and suppliers of renewable energy.

In this chapter, we'll look at what's happening in the hot new renewable energy market. I'll start by explaining what renewable energy is all about. Then, we'll explore its potential in a sustainable economy. After that, I'll tell you about solar power, wind power, water power, ocean energy, geothermal power, biomass power, and hydrogen. Finally, I'll explain how you can help the move toward renewables and a sustainable future.

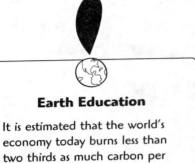

Earth Education

It is estimated that the world's economy today burns less than two thirds as much carbon per unit of energy produced as it did in 1860, but because economic and population growth have been so rapid, overall atmospheric concentrations of carbon dioxide have risen steadily. Reduction and eventual elimination of fossil fuels is a vital part of moving toward a sustainable world.

Beginning of the End

Although it's hard to believe it today, we're seeing the beginning of the end of the fossil fuel industry around the globe. It's only a matter of time before the shift to other, nonpolluting energy sources takes place. It won't happen overnight. But most observers believe it will have taken place before the end of the twenty-first century.

Although it's not a fossil fuel, nuclear power also needs to be eliminated. Nuclear energy, once viewed by many as a limitless source of cheap power, is now viewed by most people as being neither. It has proven to be far too dangerous and expensive, and the issue of what to do with the huge quantities of radioactive waste has yet to be resolved. Nuclear energy is almost certainly going to be phased out in many countries before the end of this century. Germany has already taken the first steps to do so within the next 30 to 35 years.

Renewable Energy

Okay, our current energy sources have some problems. What's the alternative? Renewable energy is the obvious answer. As its name implies, renewable energy (or "green power," as it is often called) is a source of energy that does not run out. Most renewable energy comes either directly or indirectly from the sun.

Because dwindling resources are already causing problems around the globe, anything we can do to shift to renewable energy will help reduce the potential for future international conflict over energy supplies. Renewable energy has the added benefit of not seriously polluting the environment the way coal, oil, natural gas, and nuclear power do.

There are six main categories of renewable energy: solar, wind, water, geothermal, biomass, and hydrogen. We'll look at each of them shortly. But first, it will be helpful to understand why green energy is finally becoming more popular.

Green Power Is Hot!

The current trend toward deregulation of the electric utility market both here and abroad has given the green power sector a huge jolt of fresh energy and renewed optimism. What's more, recent studies have questioned previously held assumptions about the efficiencies of large-scale electrical generation plants. As a result, a significant number of decentralized, smaller-scale generation facilities—most notably wind turbines—have begun to pop up in some pretty unlikely places—such as in the corn fields of Iowa.

Earth Education

In most cases, choosing a "green" electricity supplier will only cost a few dollars more per month on an average electric utility bill. Electricity markets have been opened to competition in California, Maine, Massachusetts, Rhode Island, Pennsylvania, and New Jersey. A number of other states, such as Montana, Illinois, New York, Delaware, Arizona, and Michigan are phasing in competition, enabling some customers to choose their electricity supplier. Many other states will be following soon as this trend gains national momentum.

As more and more states deregulate their electric utilities, the options for consumer choice will expand to include a wide range of possibilities. You and I will soon be able to vote with our dollars for the kinds of fuels we want to see used by our electric suppliers. At first this will generally mean somewhat higher bills for "green power." But because electricity generation is the largest industrial polluter in the country, encouraging clean energy with our dollars is worth the price, in my opinion.

There are three main reasons why green power is generally more expensive than fossil fuels:

1. Renewables are not fully developed and do not yet benefit from economies of scale.

2. Renewables are not supported by the huge subsidies that fossil and nuclear fuels have received.

3. The damage to the environment and human health caused by fossil fuels and nuclear power is not presently included in electricity prices.

Planetary Perils

When choosing a "green-energy" supplier, be sure to carefully check the earth-friendly claims; they're not necessarily true in all cases. Look closely at utility marketing claims for the percentages of their power that comes from each fuel source and how this compares with other suppliers or the regional average. Also check to see if the company is really planning on investing heavily in additional renewable energy projects.

But as more and more consumer demand and money flow toward renewables, consumer pressure to level the playing field for green power will also grow, and the expensive and wasteful subsidies to nonrenewables will gradually be eliminated. It won't be easy, because the politically powerful forces that guard those subsidies are firmly entrenched in our nation's capital. But this is another idea whose time has definitely come.

But Is It Really Green?

The electricity that flows into your home over the distribution lines is generic. There is no way of really telling where the electrons came from. But you can make a choice in where the money that you pay for electricity goes. That's the main point of deregulation. But how can you tell if the supplier you have chosen is really "green"?

This is where being an informed consumer is important. There is an increasing amount of greenwash being splashed around by some suppliers who claim to be earth-friendly. But when you look past the glossy ads and pretty Web pages at the real facts, you may find that it's just business as usual—with a thin green wrapper. Be skeptical. Ask questions.

Green-e

If you live in California, New Jersey, Pennsylvania, or Connecticut, you can easily check out your potential green-energy suppliers before you make a decision to switch. The nonprofit Center for Resource Solutions has established the Green-*e* Renewable Electricity Certification Program that covers these four states. New England and the mid-Atlantic region will be added soon, as the states are ready. More states in other parts of the country are expected to follow in the next few years.

Inspired by the success of the recycling logo, the program uses a "Green-*e*" logo to identify suppliers of electricity that have met the minimum environmental and consumer protection standards established by the Center for Resource Solutions. The project is the nation's first voluntary certification and verification program for "green" electricity. For more—and the most current—information on Green-e requirements, call 1-888-63-GREEN or visit their Web site at www.green-e.org.

Green-e

Green-e logo for the Renewable Electricity Certification Program.

(Center for Resource Solutions)

Here Comes the Sun

The sun is the planet's greatest source of energy. Every day, more solar energy strikes the Earth than all six billion of us consume in equivalent electric power in 27 years, according to the U.S. Department of Energy's National Renewable Energy Laboratory (www.nrel.gov). Ironically, this inexhaustible supply of energy has remained all but untapped. But that's changing.

We can use solar energy in two main ways: passively and actively. Passive solar energy is captured mainly through the design and orientation of a building, or through some of its elements, to take advantage of exposure to the sun. Active solar systems, on the other hand, involve installing special equipment that uses energy from the sun to heat water or living spaces or to generate electricity. I'll be focusing on active solar.

Most widely available active solar systems fall into one of two categories: photovoltaics (PV) that produce electricity from sunlight, and solar panels that produce heat for domestic hot water. The costs of these systems have dropped substantially since they were first introduced in the 1970s. In a move reminiscent of the period following the 1973 Arab Oil Embargo, a number of municipal, state, and federal programs are actively encouraging homeowners to add solar panels or photovoltaic systems to their roofs.

The Sacramento (California) Municipal Utility District's PV Pioneer program, for example, provides 2,000-watt rooftop solar energy systems to its customers at discount rates ($4,740 vs. $10,140 full price). Any excess electricity generated by the rooftop systems is returned to the main power grid, and homeowners receive credit through what is called *net metering*. Rooftop systems generally supply about half an average home's power needs in the Sacramento area. This will vary in other areas.

Eco-Explanations

Net metering enables electrical customers to sell back electricity at a retail price to the main power grid—by spinning their meter backward when their photovoltaic system is generating more then they are consuming.

Earth Education

The correct term for a wind-powered electrical generator is "wind turbine" rather than "wind mill." Worldwide, there were 38,700 wind turbines in operation at the end of 1998. And the potential for additional wind generation in the United States is enormous. North Dakota and the five surrounding states offer so much wind potential that wind energy experts call the area "the Saudi Arabia of wind power."

Whether you live in a state that has deregulated its utilities or not, there is a good chance that some type of solar energy system could be installed on the roof of your home. Photovoltaic solar panels that look like standard shingles or metal roofing are now available from a number of manufacturers.

In addition, a good deal of new commercial-scale solar energy activity is taking place in various parts of the country. Large new PV panels are even being used as architectural elements in a number of major new building projects. One recent example can be found at the University of Wisconsin in Madison, where a 3,000-square-foot atrium houses a large photovoltaic system that generates power.

The Winds of Change

Although solar energy probably offers the greatest long-term potential for renewable energy sources, the most excitement has been generated recently by wind power. I should point out, however, that wind is caused largely by the unequal heating of the air by the sun, so wind power is really just another form of sustainable solar energy.

Wind turbines have come a long way since they were first developed by Poul la Cour, a Danish meteorologist in 1891. Early wind turbines were capable of generating a few kilowatts, enough to power a house or two. Now they are a thousand times larger. The biggest ones being installed today are 1.65 megawatt giants with blades the wingspan length of a Boeing 727. Even larger turbines—up to four megawatts—are on the drawing board. Wind power does not produce air emissions, generate solid waste, or use water.

During and after the Arab Oil Embargo there was a flurry of wind turbine activity in this country, and some real advances were made in the technology. But when the Reagan administration dismantled the energy tax credits and incentives that had encouraged the installation of alternative energy systems nationwide, the U.S. wind-power industry collapsed.

Denmark, on the other hand, understood the incredible long-term potential for wind power, and after a 20-year partnership between government and industry, has emerged as the world leader in the field. And they have been taking full advantage of that position. The fact that there were more Danish wind turbines (rather than U.S.-made units) operating in the United States in 1998 than in Denmark (7,694 vs. 5,279) is a graphic example of this situation. If you want to see what the Danes are up to, check out www.windpower.dk for some of the most comprehensive and interesting information available.

The $11 million Searsburg, Vermont wind farm went online in 1997.

(Photo copyright John Zimmerman and Green Mountain Power)

Although small-scale, backyard wind turbines are available from a number of manufacturers, for most people, the simplest and least expensive way to participate in the wind-energy boom is to wait until they are offered a choice of energy suppliers that includes wind power in the energy mix. For additional information on wind power, check out the American Wind Energy Association (www. awea.org).

Water Power

Water power (or hydropower, as it is often called) uses the energy of falling water. In order to understand the renewable nature of hydropower, it's helpful to look at the larger system—the *hydrologic cycle*—that makes it possible.

In a hydropower installation, the energy of falling water spins the electrical turbines that actually generate the electricity. Hydropower does not

Eco-Explanations

The **hydrologic cycle** is the perpetual cycle in which water evaporates from lakes and oceans, forms clouds, falls as rain or snow, and then flows back into the ocean and lakes. The energy of this water cycle (like wind power) is driven by the sun and can be captured with hydropower.

produce any emissions or solid waste, but can cause other problems, depending on the size and location of the power plant. Large dams can disrupt fish migration in rivers, displace people, and damage habitat. Smaller "run of the river" hydroelectric installations that don't back up large amounts of water behind them have lower negative impacts.

There are three main types of hydropower facilities:

1. Impoundment—uses a dam to store water.

2. Diversion—generally uses only a part of a river's flow, sometimes without a dam.

3. Pumped storage—pumps water from a lower reservoir to a higher reservoir during periods of low electrical demand and lets the water flow back the other way during high demand.

Earth Education

Hydropower presently accounts for about 80 percent of this country's total renewable electricity generation. Roughly 80 percent of U.S. hydropower comes from impoundment or diversion facilities, and the remaining 20 percent is from pumped storage facilities. The United States is the second largest producer of hydroelectric power in the world after Canada.

Although hydropower offers a lot of advantages, large dam projects have fallen out of favor in this country in recent years. The outlook for new, large-scale hydropower projects in the U.S. is not very encouraging, according to most observers. There is, however, quite a lot of continued interest in small-and large-scale hydropower installations in some foreign countries such as China and Brazil, and in countries where national electrical networks have not been fully developed.

Ocean Energy

Harnessing the energy of the oceans, although related to hydropower, has enough differences to merit a separate discussion. Most ocean-energy plants are currently small and experimental. But there is some interesting long-term potential for this renewable, generally nonpolluting energy source. There are three main ocean technologies: wave energy, tidal energy, and ocean thermal energy conversion. Let's take a quick look at each.

Wave Energy

There are three main strategies to harness wave energy. The first uses floats or pitching devices that generate electricity from the bobbing or pitching motion of a floating object. These small generators are only able to power a buoy or beacon light.

The second strategy uses oscillating water columns in which the rise and fall of water in a cylindrical shaft causes air in the shaft to spin an electrical generator mounted on the top.

The third approach uses wave surge or "focusing" devices constructed near the shore that channel waves into an elevated reservoir. When the water flows back out of the reservoir it generates electricity using standard hydroelectric methods.

Tidal Energy

Tidal energy generally involves building a dam across a tidal inlet and allowing the incoming tide to flow through a sluice or gateway. When the tide is at its highest level, the sluice is closed, and the water flowing back out generates electricity using traditional hydropower technology. However, tidal energy systems can have a negative environmental impact because of reduced tidal flow and build-up of silt.

Ocean Thermal Energy

A huge amount of energy is stored in the world's oceans. The oceans absorb enough heat on a daily basis from the sun to equal the thermal energy of 250 billion barrels of oil. If you have ever been swimming in the ocean, you probably noticed that the deeper you go, the colder the water gets. Power plants can be built to use this difference in temperature to make energy. There are a number of demonstration projects in Japan and Hawaii.

Geothermal

Geothermal energy is a hot idea—literally. But unlike most other renewable energy sources, geothermal is not directly linked to the sun. It uses heat from the interior of the Earth to produce clean, generally sustainable energy. Resources for geothermal energy range from just a few feet below the Earth's surface to several miles deep.

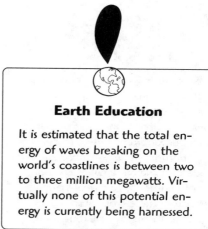

Earth Education

It is estimated that the total energy of waves breaking on the world's coastlines is between two to three million megawatts. Virtually none of this potential energy is currently being harnessed.

Earth Education

Geothermal energy is being used in many countries around the world, most notably in the United States, the Philippines, Italy, Mexico, Indonesia, and Japan. Most of the deeper sources of geothermal energy in this country are found in the western states, as well as in Alaska and Hawaii. Some geothermal power plants use steam, whereas others use hot water, to generate electricity.

Eco-Explanations

Biopower is the generation of electricity from trees, specially-grown organic materials, or organic wastes. Using trees or plants as fuel for biomass electrical generation does release carbon dioxide into the air. However, it does not contribute to global warming because these crops absorb carbon as they grow, creating a sustainable, closed loop.

But you don't need to live in a geologically active area to tap into geothermal energy. Within the top 10 feet or so of the Earth's surface, ground temperatures remain fairly constant year round at between 50 and 60 degrees Fahrenheit (excepting Alaska, where much of this surface area remains permanently frozen). Geothermal heat pumps can tap into this resource and can heat or cool a building through a system of ducts and pipes.

Geothermal exchange (or GeoExchange, as it is also called) works by moving heat either into or out of the ground, depending on the season and the heating or cooling requirements. In the winter, heat is extracted from fluid in pipes buried in the ground and is distributed to the home or building, usually by a series of ducts. In the summer, the process is reversed and the relatively cool fluid in the buried pipes conducts heat from the building into the ground.

Geothermal exchange is the most energy-efficient, environmentally clean, and cost-effective space conditioning system available, according to the Environmental Protection Agency. The U.S. General Accounting Office estimates that if GeoExchange heat pumps were installed nationwide, they could save several billion dollars annually in energy costs and would substantially reduce pollution.

Check out GeoExchange, the Geothermal Heat Pump Consortium Web site, at www.ghpc.org for more information.

Biomass

Sunlight causes plants to grow, and the organic matter that makes up these plants is known as biomass. Biomass can be used to make electricity, fuels, or chemicals. The use of biomass for any of these purposes is called bioenergy. Biomass electrical energy (also referred to as *biopower*) can come from crops grown especially for energy production, such as trees, or it can be from organic wastes, such as methane gas from landfills.

There are four main types of biopower:

1. Direct-fired—Most biopower plants use the direct-fired method. They burn the feedstocks directly to produce steam, which spins a turbine that generates electricity.

2. Cofiring—This is a strategy used mainly by coal-fired electric-generation plants to reduce emissions, especially of sulfur dioxide, by mixing coal and bioenergy feedstocks.

3. Gasification—These systems convert the biomass into a gas, which is then burned in a gas turbine that spins an electric generator. Methane gas from land-fills can also be used to generate electricity by fueling boilers that generate steam for turning electric generators.

4. Small, modular—These systems can be fueled by any of the above methods and are used in small-scale community or consumer installations.

Although the outlook for biomass is generally good, it currently only accounts for around 4 percent of the energy used in the United States. But it is an especially attractive option for the 2.5 billion people worldwide who presently live without electricity. Many of these people live in remote areas where large amounts of biomass are readily available for fuel. Small, modular biopower plants at the village level would be an excellent solution.

Hydrogen

Until fairly recently, hydrogen was seen as a rather distant option. But now many observers believe that it may become a viable major fuel within the next few decades.

Strictly speaking, hydrogen is not really a fuel source, but, rather, a renewable energy storage and transport medium that must first be produced from water in a process known as *electrolysis*. And that's a problem, because the electrical energy required for this process under existing technology is substantial. Hydrogen currently takes twice the amount of energy as other fuels to do the same amount of work. Hydrogen is also bulky to store and to transport at the present time.

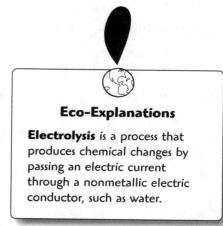

Eco-Explanations

Electrolysis is a process that produces chemical changes by passing an electric current through a nonmetallic electric conductor, such as water.

But hydrogen has some excellent qualities. It can be combusted like other ordinary fuels, or it can be converted to electricity in fuel cells, forming water or steam as an exhaust product with virtually no negative environmental impact. And there's no problem with supply—hydrogen is the most abundant element in the universe. Consequently, many of the major energy companies are looking seriously at hydrogen's potential. Royal Dutch/Shell, one of the world's largest energy companies, has already established a hydrogen subsidiary. Others are sure to follow.

Initially, it appears that hydrogen will be used in fuel cells for cars, trucks, and industrial plants, just as it already provides power for spacecraft. In the long run, however, hydrogen has the potential to provide a carbon-free fuel for general purposes. An awful lot of research money is currently being spent on hydrogen-related projects, and we can expect to see some dramatic breakthroughs in the next few decades.

Consumer's Choice

As you can see, there is quite a selection of renewable energy out there. Only time will tell which of these options will become the main replacements for fossil fuels. But one thing is certain: Fossil fuels eventually will be replaced. And the sooner we get serious about moving that process forward in this country, the better.

And that's where you and I come in. One of the best ways we can participate in this process is to exercise our choice as consumers to buy "green" energy when it becomes available. Initially, it may cost a bit more than "dirty" energy, but in the long run it will save us—and the environment—a lot more. Now that's real green power.

The Least You Need to Know

➤ Most renewable energy comes either directly or indirectly from the sun.

➤ Many people could install a solar energy system on the roof of their home.

➤ Before you switch to a "green" energy supplier, make sure it really is green.

➤ Denmark has become the world leader in the field of wind-turbine design and manufacturing.

➤ Biomass power plants offer a lot of potential for both large-scale and small-scale installations.

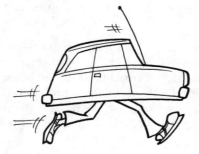

Transportation

We all need access to transportation. We need to get to work, to go shopping, to attend meetings, concerts, or sports events, and all the other activities that are part of our busy lives. But how we get there has an enormous impact on the environment, for better or worse, depending on the form of transportation that we use.

In the United States, transportation basically means cars. Americans love their cars. Automobiles offer comfort, convenience, and most of all, freedom of movement. But that "freedom" comes at a high price.

In this chapter, we'll look at our driving habits, and I'll explain what the consequences of our auto addictions are. Then we'll explore a number of alternative energy vehicles that offer some exciting possible solutions to some of the problems. Finally, I'll tell you about other methods of transport that need to be encouraged if we are to achieve a more balanced transportation system and sustainable lifestyle.

Car Talk

Ideally, a sustainable transportation system should meet the needs of everyone without seriously damaging the environment. Our present transport system—especially in this country—does neither.

Transportation currently accounts for about 20 percent of the annual six billion tons of carbon emissions from human activities that are leading to global warming. That's because most of our vehicles burn vast quantities of fossil fuels. Some burn more than others (more on that shortly). The ultimate solution to this problem, of course, is to switch from fossil fuels to renewable energy sources. We looked at those sources in the last chapter, and we'll look at ways of using some of them in vehicles in a moment.

But since this transition to a carbon-free transport system isn't going to happen overnight, we need to deal with current reality. Let's take a good, hard look at some of the other costs and consequences of our automobile habit.

Planetary Perils

Our heavy consumption of gasoline has kept us dependent on imported oil from politically unstable parts of the world, increasing the chances of military involvements. Our auto addiction has also turned most of our massive six- and eight-lane urban highway network into virtual parking lots during commuter rush hours—and at many other times as well.

The Costs

While the automobile has given us the freedom to live wherever we wanted, it also has resulted in vast areas of suburban sprawl that have spread out from city centers in a largely haphazard fashion, usually gobbling up prime agricultural land in the process (more on this in the next chapter). These sprawling bedroom communities are a threat to both human and environmental health. Vehicle exhaust is often the main ingredient in urban air pollution, which kills three million people worldwide every year.

Another negative impact of the automobile is that it tends to perpetuate social injustice and poverty. Low-income people tend to live in the inner cities. Many jobs these days tend to be located in the suburbs—in shopping malls and other locations that are difficult or impossible to get to by public transit. Recently in some cities this situation has been reversed, with low-income, inner-city residents being forced out of downtown areas that have suddenly become trendy. In either case, minimum-wage workers would have to spend roughly half of their entire income on a vehicle just to get to work—an almost impossible situation.

Hidden Subsidies

One thing that has encouraged our wasteful driving habits in this country is artificially low gasoline prices. Even at the all-time record prices of June 2000, Americans still pay half of what most Europeans do. And if we were to pay the true cost of gasoline—including all the subsidies, tax stabilization programs, environmental, health, and social costs—gasoline would be somewhere between $5.60 to $15 a gallon, according to the International Center for Technology Assessment.

Earth Education

The hidden costs of driving in the U.S. amount to at least $184 billion a year, including $40 billion for road costs not covered by fees and tolls and $56 billion for health damage due to air pollution.

Yet we have become so addicted to cheap gasoline, that almost any increase is viewed as an assault on our inalienable right to be wasteful. The spike in gasoline prices in June 2000, and the political furor it caused, is a case in point.

While everyone was busily pointing their fingers at somebody else, no one had the courage to place the blame where it rightly belongs—on the shoulders of the American people, and our wasteful driving habits. And the most striking symbol of those habits is the sport utility vehicle (SUV).

A Bad Sport

SUVs, described by some environmentalists as "rolling monuments to environmental destruction," have, among other things, had a severe impact on fuel efficiency in this country. In 1975, federal Corporate Average Fuel Economy (CAFE) standards were passed, requiring new cars to have a fuel economy of 27.5 miles per gallon, and new light trucks (including SUVs) to have a fuel economy of 20.6 mpg.

Those economy levels were reached by the 1980s, and have stagnated ever since, according to the Sierra Club. And in 1999, the average fuel economy for the U.S. fell to 23.8 mpg, the lowest level since 1980. And this is progress?

Groups like the Sierra Club and Friends of the Earth have been trying to close the so-called "SUV loophole" for years, but have been repeatedly blocked by Congress, which has passed provisions in the annual transportation-funding bill that forbids raising CAFE levels.

Planetary Perils

Under the 1975 federal Corporate Average Fuel Economy standards, SUVs are allowed to waste 33 percent more gasoline, emit 30 percent more carbon monoxide, and 75 percent more nitrogen oxides than passenger cars. The gross inefficiencies of these vehicles have contributed to Americans wasting 70 billion gallons of gasoline since 1990, according to environmental groups.

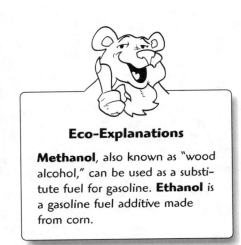

Eco-Explanations

Methanol, also known as "wood alcohol," can be used as a substitute fuel for gasoline. **Ethanol** is a gasoline fuel additive made from corn.

The American Council for an Energy-Efficient Economy recently updated its "Green Book: The Environmental Guide to Cars and Trucks." It lists the 12 greenest and the 12 "meanest" (from an energy-efficiency standpoint) vehicles for 2000. Guess what were at the bottom of the list? A group of SUVs and pickups from the major U.S. manufacturers, with efficiency ratings of 11 to 12 mpg in the city and 15 to 16 mpg on the highway (the manufacturers claim efficiencies a few mpg higher). Check out the list for yourself at www.greenercars.com.

Alternative Energy Vehicles

Sometimes when change comes, it seems to happen all at once. This is the case in the auto industry. After a decade when the biggest marketing news seemed to be how many beverage holders a vehicle had, alternative-fueled vehicles are suddenly all the rage. Recent high gas prices have unquestionably been an added incentive, but this is mainly another case of an idea whose time has come.

Alternative fuels such as *methanol, ethanol,* compressed natural gas, liquefied petroleum gas, and electricity produce less tail-pipe pollutants than conventional gasoline and diesel fuel. Using any of these fuels has the potential to improve air quality. But the most promising of these in the long run is electricity.

Three main types of alternative-fueled vehicles use electricity as motive power:

➤ Electric vehicles, or EVs, as they are called

➤ Hybrid gas-electrics, usually referred to as "hybrids"

➤ Fuel-cell-powered vehicles

Straight electric EVs, powered by heavy onboard batteries, have been available for a number of years in some markets. They boast zero emissions, but frequently need to be plugged in to an electrical outlet to recharge the batteries—a major disadvantage.

Hybrids use a combination of conventionally fueled engines and electric motors as their power source. Hybrids are a compromise between the zero emissions of electric motors and the longer range of a gasoline-powered engine. Hybrids are unquestionably one of the most significant developments to hit the auto market in decades.

But the most exciting development of all is the fuel-cell-powered automobile, which is the next step in the alternative-fueled vehicle process. All three of these new vehicle types are the forerunners of an enormous revolution in technology that unquestionably will have profound effects on the global economy. Let's take a look at all three.

Electric

Question: "What is the range of an electric vehicle?" Answer: "That depends on the length of the extension cord." This bit of cruel humor pretty much sums up the electric vehicle (EV) dilemma—lack of range. The problem is the batteries. Despite decades of research into lighter-weight, longer-lasting batteries, about the best that the most current EVs can manage is around 120 miles on a six- to eight-hour charge.

Don't get me wrong, I've driven an electric pickup truck—and I loved it. It was one of a number of Solectria EVs that are part of an ongoing demonstration project run by EVermont, the public/private organization that runs the electric vehicle program in Vermont.

But even enthusiastic supporters of the program admit that the lack of range limits the use of most EVs to short trips around town or relatively short commutes. Which means that they are not practical for many people as a long-distance, general-purpose vehicle. They are a good match, however, for fleets of local delivery trucks or vans that don't stray very far from their recharging stations.

Limited range aside, EVs offer some pretty nice features. They have zero tailpipe emissions (no tailpipe at all, actually), no oil changes, no tune-ups, no antifreeze or exhaust system replacements. They're quiet. And they handle pretty much like other vehicles—Toyota's popular new RAV-4 EV has a top speed of 79 mph, which is fast enough.

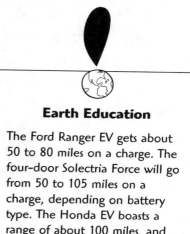

Earth Education

The Ford Ranger EV gets about 50 to 80 miles on a charge. The four-door Solectria Force will go from 50 to 105 miles on a charge, depending on battery type. The Honda EV boasts a range of about 100 miles, and the Nissan Altra EV will go up to 120 miles.

Planetary Perils

The long-term fate of some electric vehicles presently available is in question due to lack of consumer demand, but that may change, especially if large businesses and governments begin to buy these vehicles in quantity for their fleets.

There has been a lot of imaginative thinking going on in the EV field. One striking example is the Sparrow Personal Transit Module. The Sparrow, a single-passenger vehicle, is designed specifically for commuters and inner-city driving. Powered by 13 12-volt batteries, the three-wheel Sparrow provides an effective range of 30 to 60 miles and a top speed of 65 mph. It's easy to park in tight spaces, and has zero emissions.

Is there an EV in your future? That depends. EVs clearly do work, and rather well in some applications. They could easily be used for regular commuting by a lot of people, since the average commute in this country is 22 miles. Many families have a "commuting car" anyway, so why not an electric? Some companies and communities are actively encouraging EV use. Portland, Oregon, for example, has recharging stations for electric cars scattered throughout the downtown area.

The Sparrow Personal Transit Module.

(Photo copyright Greg Pahl)

Still, EVs tend to be pricey for their limited driving range. And the batteries are expensive to replace when they eventually wear out. You might want to consider a lease rather than an outright purchase (actually, many EVs are only available on lease). That would let you check it out for the duration of the lease and then you can decide whether you want to continue or not. EVs are currently available at dealerships in about 30 states.

For additional information about electric vehicles, take a look at the Electric Auto Association Web site at www.eaaev.org, the Electric Vehicle Association of America at www.evaa.org, and also www.evworld.com.

Hybrid

Now, you may have gotten the impression that environmental groups are always at odds with automakers. They're not. In fact, in January 2000, the Sierra Club actually gave its first-ever product award in its 108-year history—to a car! The new Honda Insight, a low-emission hybrid gas-electric vehicle that gets 61 mpg in the city and 70 mpg on the highway, was the lucky winner of the club's Excellence in Environmental Engineering Award.

The Insight is about to have a lot of competition. The four-door Toyota Prius hybrid gas-electric, which hit the U.S. market in July 2000, uses the same general technology as the Honda Insight. Due to its slightly larger size and better passenger carrying capacity, the Prius *only* gets 45 mpg city mileage, and 52 mpg on the highway, which is still excellent. And it has a driving range of about 600 miles before you have to stop for more gas.

Other automakers are feverishly working on hybrids of their own. Ford has promised that its P2000 will be available by the end of 2000, and General Motors is predicting a production-ready hybrid by 2001. Volkswagen is reportedly working on a 78-mpg hybrid, to be followed by 118- and then 235-mpg models. The race is on. Start your engines!

Hybrids are clearly the wave of the near future, and we're going to see a lot more of them on the road in the next few years, especially if gas prices remain high. But these hybrids are still only a transition to the obvious long-term solution—automobiles powered by hydrogen fuel cells.

Earth Education

Regenerative braking in gas-electric hybrids recovers some of the energy that is normally lost from the use of mechanical brakes in an automobile. When you decelerate, the electric motor not only acts as a brake, but it also acts as a generator and feeds electricity back onto the batteries.

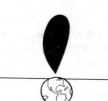

Earth Education

Electric propulsion is highly efficient and can convert over 90 percent of the electricity produced into traction. Electrically powered vehicles have the added advantage of being far simpler from a mechanical standpoint than their internal-combustion-powered competitors.

Fuel Cell

As I mentioned in the last chapter, most experts view hydrogen as the primary long-range fuel of choice in a sustainable global economy. And fuel cells are the primary means of using that hydrogen. Fuel cells produce electricity through the chemical reaction between hydrogen and oxygen. The result is power to run vehicles and other devices with little or no pollution. Water vapor and heat are the byproducts.

Fuel cells are about twice as efficient as conventional engines, they have no moving parts, and they require little maintenance. No wonder they are generating so much enthusiasm. By about 2050 it is possible that the hydrogen needed to power these cells may be produced from water using solar or wind-generated electricity. The hydrogen would then be sent to market via a network of pipelines.

Earth Education

In 1997 Daimler–Benz (the predecessor of DaimlerChrysler) teamed up with a Canadian company to create hydrogen-fuel-cell systems. At the time, Daimler predicted it would be producing 100,000 fuel–cell-powered vehicles by 2005. Shortly afterward, Toyota upped the ante, and said that fuel–cell-powered vehicles would seize one third of the world auto market by 2005. In June 2000, DaimlerChrysler announced that it would invest nearly $1 billion in low-emission vehicles.

But that's a long way off. In the meantime, there is a source of hydrogen closer to hand: natural gas. The first fuel cells can run on natural gas—which can be separated into hydrogen and carbon dioxide. While the carbon dioxide that is emitted is still a problem, the plentiful supply of natural gas (and an existing distribution system) makes it an attractive short-term choice to help jump-start fuel-cell use.

And the use of fuel cells to power electric vehicles is about to become a reality—soon—not some time in the distant future. It should come as no great surprise that DaimlerChrysler, Ford, General Electric, and Toyota are all actively investing in fuel cells. And automakers are working on vehicles to put them in.

Virtually all the automakers are jumping into the fuel-cell race. DaimlerChrysler recently announced that the first buses powered by fuel cells would be delivered in 2002, to be followed by passenger cars in 2003. GM is promising fuel-cell-powered versions of its EV1 by 2004.

Initially, these fuel-cell vehicles will probably be around 50 percent more expensive than their gasoline-powered versions, limiting their appeal. But DaimlerChrysler and Ford both say that they hope to be able to sell fuel-cell cars at just 10 percent above the cost of gas-fueled vehicles. Don't expect fuel-cell cars to be price competitive much before 2010, however.

While these are exciting possibilities for reducing auto emissions, I want to emphasize that they won't do anything to reduce traffic congestion on our highways. In fact, the new zero-emission vehicles are likely to make traffic much worse unless we take steps to make other types of transport more attractive. That means developing a more balanced transportation system.

The Plane Truth

As bad as the situation is on the ground, things are even worse overhead. Air travel is arguably more environmentally devastating than driving. This is because jets are so much less efficient. On average, they need 40 percent more energy than automobiles to move a passenger for each mile traveled.

Yet Americans love to fly. We are willing to stand in long lines at overcrowded airports and endure frequent delays for the privilege of being squeezed into tiny seats for uncomfortable flights to another overcrowded airport, often inconveniently located a long way from our intended destinations. That's if your flight wasn't cancelled altogether. So why do we put up with all of this aggravation? Basically, it's because the alternatives are generally even less appealing.

In an attempt to relieve a system that is fast approaching gridlock, Congress passed a $40 billion aviation bill in 2000. The bill would increase aviation spending in fiscal 2001 to $12.7 billion, up $2.7 billion from 2000. The money is intended to expand capacity and improve the efficiency of the system. Aviation, like highways, has long been favored by congressional generosity.

Planetary Perils

In 1998, airlines carried over 614 million passengers for 619 billion passenger miles (a passenger mile is one person transported one mile), according to the Air Transport Association. U.S. Department of Transportation figures show that 2,084 complaints were made by air passengers in April 2000, up from 1,316 the same month a year earlier.

Some communities near the ends of runways (or projected runways) are not pleased. Their concerns about noise pollution are understandable. But one could be tempted to ask: "Why are we spending billions of dollars to encourage such an environmentally damaging and inefficient mode of transport when there could be better alternatives?" Admittedly, there is no viable alternative for quick travel to overseas destinations, but domestic travel is another matter.

Mass Transit

Every time I travel in Western Europe I am reminded about how wonderful a good public transport system can be. Every time I return to the U.S., I am faced with the reality of how awful ours is.

Generally speaking, the state of public transportation in this country is an embarrassment. It's a patchwork, incoherent, uncoordinated mess that reflects our love affair with the automobile and many decades of neglect while Congress has been busy shoveling huge sums of money into massive highway construction programs and subsidies for the oil and airline industries.

But there are some signs of hope. Despite persistent efforts of public transit opponents to cut its funding, public transportation has begun to attract an increasing number of steady riders.

One way you can help is to encourage the development of new public transit initiatives in your state or region, and support the necessary funding. And if you are lucky enough to actually have a public transit system, use it. You'll generally save money over the cost of driving, and help the environment, too.

Earth Education

Ridership on public transit in the U.S. increased 15 percent between 1995 and 1999. In 1999, Americans took more than nine billion trips on public transportation, the highest ridership in nearly four decades. This represents the highest level since the beginning of the federal transit program, according to the American Public Transportation Association.

Riding the Rails

If public transit in this country is an embarrassment, then our lack of solid support for our national rail passenger system is a disgrace. I'm talking about long-distance trains now, as opposed to city subways or light rail systems. In this country, Amtrak is the sole provider of intercity passenger rail service. In 1998, Amtrak served more than 21 million passengers for a total of five billion passenger miles.

Unfortunately, Amtrak has persistently operated at a deficit—a $907 million loss for 1999 alone. And Congress has been threatening to force liquidation of Amtrak if it can't operate at a profit by 2003.

I'm not blaming Amtrak. They do the best job they can—under the circumstances. But instead of constantly trying to cut every last dollar of support for Amtrak, Congress should be trying to figure out ways of making rail travel even more attractive than it already is. Congress doesn't seem to have any problem coming up with $40 billion for airport and other improvements that will essentially subsidize airlines. So what's all the fuss about subsidizing Amtrak? And if there were better Amtrak service, more people might be tempted to take the train instead of clogging our already-overburdened airports.

Western European countries regularly spend huge sums of public money on their rail systems. It's simply viewed as part of a larger, integrated and efficient transportation system that serves all their citizens. The frequency of service, the comfort of the trains—and the huge ridership—proves that it's money well spent.

Amtrak is definitely one of the "greenest" under-utilized resources that this country has to offer. Discover it for yourself. For additional information on Amtrak call 1-800-USA-RAIL or check out their Web site at www.amtrak.com.

Pedal Power

But there's another important piece in an integrated transport system—the bicycle. I'm serious. If you think that bicycles are just for kids or a thing of the past, think again. Bikes are making a big comeback. Especially in cities. And for good reason. They're affordable, they don't pollute, they require little land, and they reduce traffic congestion and noise.

Many Americans will probably find this hard to comprehend, but anyone who has been abroad probably knows what I'm talking about. Especially if they've been to the Netherlands. Even though the Netherlands has one of the highest densities of cars per square kilometer in the world, because the Dutch have given a high priority to bike paths, the country also has one of the highest rates of bicycle use. In fact, some 30 percent of all urban trips there are made with bicycles.

Getting around on a bike in most American cities can be a hazardous activity. But it's great exercise, can actually be quicker than driving, and is good for the environment. A growing number of cities in this country are beginning to realize the advantages of bicycles over cars in downtown environments, and some are actually removing multilane highways and replacing them with green spaces, parks, and bicycle paths.

The Rails-to-Trails Conservancy, a nonprofit organization founded in 1986, is dedicated to creating a nationwide network of public trails from former rail lines and connecting corridors. In addition to bicycling, most of these trails also encourage walking, running, skating, horseback

Green Tips

Take the train on your next vacation trip and help cut pollution while you have a pleasant journey. Trains are one of the most efficient modes of mass transport, and move passengers for much less fuel-per-passenger mile than the competition. If for no other reason than that, rail transportation (long distance or local) deserves both our ridership and our support.

Earth Education

In 1969, 25 million bicycles and 23 million cars were produced worldwide. Recently, the annual production of bicycles has averaged 105 million while the average for automobiles has been 37 million. Although most of the bicycles in this country are for recreational use, the majority of those sold in other countries are used for basic transportation.

riding, or cross-country skiing. Check out their Web site at www.railtrails.org for more information.

Working to establish, improve, or extend bike paths or walking trails is one of the best things you can do for a more balanced transportation system—and a sustainable future.

The Least You Need to Know

➤ The automobile is causing serious environmental problems around the world.

➤ Americans have become addicted to artificially cheap gasoline.

➤ Electricity offers the best means of propulsion to cut vehicle emissions.

➤ Railroad passenger travel is one of the "greenest" forms of public transport.

Chapter 24

Living Patterns

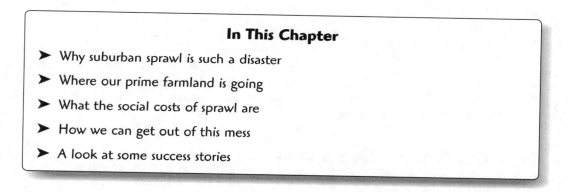

In This Chapter

➤ Why suburban sprawl is such a disaster

➤ Where our prime farmland is going

➤ What the social costs of sprawl are

➤ How we can get out of this mess

➤ A look at some success stories

There was a time when owning a house in the suburbs, with a green lawn to mow, used to be a basic part of the American Dream. But, now, being stuck in the middle of the vast wasteland of suburban sprawl, with no means of escape except your car, has turned that dream into a nightmare for many people.

The automobile—along with heavily subsidized highways and gasoline—made suburban sprawl possible in the first place. But as our highways grind toward total gridlock, and as the social fabric of our communities continues to unravel, more and more people across this country are waking up to the fact that our terribly wasteful and damaging suburban development patterns are simply not sustainable.

In this chapter, we'll take a look at our current living patterns and why they developed the way they did. I'll also explain why they are so damaging to us and to our environment. Then I'll offer some suggestions on ways to make things better, and I'll show you some examples of communities that have got it right or at least are heading in the right direction.

Nightmare on Elm Street

As you may recall from Chapter 5, "The Land We Live On," this country has the dubious distinction of having the most spread out, car-dependent cities in the world. This pattern began to show up after World War II with the development of suburban housing tracts such as Levittown on Long Island. Since then, this pattern has repeated itself all across the nation.

The result has been to create millions of largely isolated families who are forced to drive everywhere for even the most basic services—often to huge shopping malls with their impersonal big-box stores. Meanwhile, the children are bused to big-box schools where they may become lost in the crowd as well.

No wonder so many people are feeling lost these days. The sense of community that played such an important role in this country in the past has been bull-dozed away, along with the cornfields. The zoning laws that were originally designed to help people escape pollution have caused even more pollution. The automobile, which made all this possible, has turned on its former master and bitten the hand that feeds it. And the idyllic dream on suburban Elm Street has unquestionably turned into a nightmare.

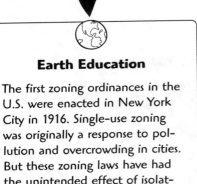

Earth Education

The first zoning ordinances in the U.S. were enacted in New York City in 1916. Single-use zoning was originally a response to pollution and overcrowding in cities. But these zoning laws have had the unintended effect of isolating huge numbers of suburban residents from the goods and services that are needed for everyday life.

The Trouble with Sprawl

So many things are wrong with our present suburban living patterns that it's hard to know where to begin. But I'll try. And part of the difficulty is that many of these problems are interrelated. Sound familiar? Web of Life, again.

Suburbia and our automobile-centered lifestyle are at the heart of a complex series of problems that affect virtually all aspects of our lives, from the environment to economic and social conditions. And, as is often the case, most people have been trying to apply Band-Aids to the symptoms without looking at the causes. Let's take a closer look at the problems. We'll start with the obvious stuff and work our way down from there.

Where Did All the Farmland Go?

The disappearance of open space in this country is really dramatic. If you haven't been back recently to where you grew up, you might not recognize it today. The loss of land to sprawl is staggering. Between 1980 and 1997, a total of 27 million acres were converted to development. And if you add another conservative 6 million to bring it up-to-date, that makes the total 33 million acres.

I realize that 33 million acres might be hard to visualize. Let me put it to you in a way that might help. The amount of land that has been transformed into suburban sprawl in the U.S. since 1980 roughly equals the combined areas of the states of Vermont, New Hampshire, Massachusetts, Connecticut, Rhode Island, Delaware, New Jersey, and most of Maryland.

The loss of land between 1992 and 1997 was the worst in Texas, where 1.2 million acres succumbed to bulldozers and backhoes, while the second worst was in Pennsylvania, where 1.1 million acres were converted. Georgia, Florida, North Carolina, California, Tennessee, and Michigan weren't far behind. But worst of all is the fact that most of this wall-to-wall housing and mega-shopping-mall building frenzy has gobbled up prime agricultural land in many parts of the country. And once it's been converted, it's essentially gone forever.

Planetary Perils

The rate of development of farmland, forests, and other open space in the U.S. has tripled in the late 1990s. Between 1980 and 1992, the rate of loss averaged less than one million acres a year. But between 1992 and 1997, it averaged a whopping 3.2 million a year.

Unfortunately, there are few parts of this country that are free of this kind of massive development. Even in relatively rural Vermont, land development has outpaced population growth by more than two to one, according to a recent study by The Vermont Forum on Sprawl. "This suggests that we are consuming land at excessive rates, and probably in excessive amounts," the report said.

Vermont has had a long-standing national reputation as being an environmentally enlightened place ever since the passage of Act 250, a controversial land use and development law, in 1970. But due largely to stiff opposition from landowners and developers, the land-use portion of the law was never implemented and was deleted in 1984. While other environmental legislation has subsequently been enacted, suburban sprawl has managed to spread like wildfire, particularly in fast-growing Chittenden County surrounding Burlington, Vermont's largest city. The sprawl, and the debate about how to deal with it, continues to grow.

These same general patterns—to a greater or lesser extent—are being repeated elsewhere around the globe. And, in a world where finding enough food and fresh water for our steadily growing population is becoming an increasingly urgent problem, the loss of so much prime agricultural land to parking lots and housing seems short-sighted at the very least.

Sprawl comes to Vermont.

(Photo copyright Greg Pahl)

Lost Ecosystems

As bad as the loss of farmland is, it gets worse. As highways, housing developments, parking lots, and shopping malls spread like a cancer across the landscape, entire ecosystems are disrupted or destroyed. It's not unusual for a new highway or subdivision to cut through sensitive natural areas and disrupt the flow of water or movement of animals. And some of these animals may be endangered species.

In a recent report, "Road to Ruin," by Taxpayers for Common Sense and Friends of the Earth, some of these problems were highlighted in a listing of 50 of the most wasteful highway projects in the country that are in the early stages of development. According to the report, 10 national parks and other protected lands would be impacted by some of the roads mentioned, including Denali National Park in Alaska, Everglades National Park in Florida, as well as the only coral reef in the continental U.S., also located in Florida.

And like prime farmland, fragile natural ecosystems are also lost for good once they have been paved over or otherwise developed. And when that happens, another little piece of the Fabric of Life has been torn.

Loss of Community

Though it's relatively easy to see the visual damage to the landscape caused by sprawl, the less-tangible harm caused to our social fabric is every bit as important. Our low-density, single-use land development strategy has unquestionably contributed to a series of social problems, related to the breakdown of community.

Parents—often both of them these days—spend so much time trying to commute to and from work on highways that resemble parking lots that they don't have any time left over for their children—or for themselves. Quality time for family activities is often the first casualty. Needless to say, there isn't much time left over for community building either. And all of this to pay for the cars that are needed to get to work to support a house in the suburbs and a rat-race lifestyle that leaves almost everyone feeling exhausted and cheated.

But sprawl, and the lack of equal access to transportation, also causes social inequalities. One third of the U.S. population is too young, too old, or too poor to drive, leaving them essentially stranded. Although many lower-income Americans who live in the inner cities have access to public transportation, most potential employers in the suburbs cannot be reached by subway or bus systems from the inner city.

Since 1986, Chicago has had a successful "reverse-commute" bus system designed to address this problem. It makes about 25,000 trips a day on more than 1,000 buses and vans to suburban office parks, malls, and other work sites. Washington, D.C., and a few other cities are experimenting with similar systems. But there's still plenty of room for improvement.

Sprawl has other ways of isolating those at the bottom of the economic spectrum from the rest of society, due to the lack of affordable housing in many suburban communities. Creating stable, mixed-income neighborhoods is one small step toward addressing this situation.

Planetary Perils

The loss of the sense of community is one of the most serious social consequences of sprawl. A lot of the trouble is due to the physical separation and dispersion that comes along with suburban planning. Many people who live in suburbia almost never see their neighbors, except through the windows of their cars.

The High Costs of Sprawl

Aside from these obvious problems with sprawl, recent research has turned up some additional disadvantages. In a study conducted by Northern Illinois University for the American Farmland Trust (www.farmland.org), it was found that urban sprawl has far higher costs than most people generally realize. The study found that new, scattered residential developments generally …

➤ Do not generate enough taxes to educate the children who live there.

➤ Fall short of paying to maintain the roads leading to and through their subdivisions.

➤ Where municipal water and sewer services are available, the costs of building those services may be paid by other taxpayers.

But there were some equally disturbing findings related to personal safety. The study showed that in these subdivisions …

➤ Police response times were as much as 600 percent longer, on average, than in the adjoining municipality.

➤ Ambulance response times were as much as 50 percent longer.

➤ Fire response times were as much as 33 percent longer.

While the study was conducted in the suburbs surrounding Chicago, the same general situation can be found in most other parts of the country as well.

And while the costs of additional schools, roads, utilities, police, medical, and fire services needed to cover new subdivisions are generally borne by existing and new residents equally, the extra coverage primarily benefits the new residents. If you live in a part of the country that has been subject to sprawl, and if you have seen your property taxes go through the roof, now you have a better idea why.

Planetary Perils

Every 100 rural homes built add anywhere from $4,780 to $19,760 a year in extra school busing costs, according to a recent Illinois study. Sprawl destroys prime farmland and open space, damages ecosystems, increases our dependence on the automobile, causes a sense of physical and social isolation, divides economic groups, is excessively costly to build and maintain, results in decreased public safety services, and, overall, is unsustainable.

Way to Grow!

Although zillions of acres of prime agricultural and forestland continue to be bulldozed as you read this, there are some signs of hope. Nationwide, concerns about suburban sprawl are growing.

What to do? Improving gasoline efficiency, or even completely eliminating fossil fuels in our transportation system, does nothing to resolve sprawl. It potentially just makes it worse (solve one problem, create another, remember?).

The real root of our problem is that most of us are living in the wrong places to begin with. We're scattered all over the countryside in living patterns that make viable alternatives to the automobile (regardless of the kind of fuel it runs on) almost impossible. We need to rethink those patterns in order to make the use of a car unnecessary in the first place.

Compact Centers

One of the best ways to do that is to encourage and plan development in traditional compact village and urban centers, leaving surrounding spaces open. Unfortunately, in some parts of the country, it's already too late to do that. In other areas—especially rural areas—there's still time.

But even in heavily developed regions, there are strategies that can make things better. While many people view the solution to sprawl to be mainly a question of creating better public transportation, I think we need to pay just as much attention to creating better neighborhoods. If people have basically everything they need right in their own neighborhoods, they don't need to go anywhere else in the first place.

Changing local zoning laws to encourage the creation of livable neighborhoods is a powerful tool. Back in the 1970s, Portland, Oregon, decided that it could cut gasoline consumption (and driving) by resurrecting the idea of neighborhood grocery stores. They did, and it worked. It's simple strategies like this that can be the catalyst for recreating community. This is especially important because the loss of community is one of the biggest problems generally associated with sprawl.

Zoning and land-use planning can also offer market-based incentives that reward the clustering of housing, jobs, and shopping in areas that can be easily reached on foot. And careful design can make these neighborhoods a pleasure to live in, with attractive buildings, welcoming green spaces, convenient sidewalks, and a full range of services that people want and need.

Transportation Options

You might be tempted to think that cities are bad enough already, and that encouraging even more urban population is just going to make matters worse. But densely populated cities don't have to be unlivable. European cities, which tend to be exciting, vibrant places, generally have four times more people living in central areas than we have in this country.

Earth Education

In Denver, 60 percent of residents cited sprawl as a top concern, as did 47 percent in San Francisco, and 33 percent in Tampa, according to a recent survey. In a survey conducted early in 2000 by the Pew Center for Civic Journalism, frustrations over sprawl and growth were shown to be edging out more traditional issues, such as crime, the economy, and education.

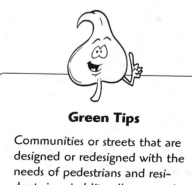

Green Tips

Communities or streets that are designed or redesigned with the needs of pedestrians and residents in mind literally come alive with people, which encourages even more attractive shops and services for local residents.

But because of the relatively small areas involved, most European city-dwellers can walk to where they need to go or take convenient public transit. In fact, about half of European urban trips are either made on foot, by bike, or by public transit. That compares with 87 percent travel by car in this country. Most Europeans have a number of viable transportation options. We generally don't.

Cities can also use zoning, land-use planning, and market incentives to encourage high-density development close to public transit routes, while discouraging development in areas located farther away. Arlington, Virginia, for example, has used new Metro stations as the focus of development. Real-estate values surrounding new stations typically increase, encouraging additional private development.

Earth Education

Car sharing in Berlin, Germany, cuts car ownership by 75 percent and commuting by almost 90 percent. In Stockholm, Sweden, a series of so-called "transit villages" have been deliberately encouraged by city government around suburban railroad stations. The result of this strategy was to reduce car trips by 229 kilometers (142 miles) per person between 1980 and 1990 while transit use increased, according to the Worldwatch Institute.

Good Examples

Some good examples of transportation and land-use decisions can be found in other countries. The clustering of development or redevelopment within easy walking distance of public transportation is a key part of the anti-sprawl picture. In Canada, a series of density bonuses and penalties have helped focus much of Toronto's development within a reasonable walking distance of subway or light-rail services.

Even in this country, there are a few signs of progressive thinking about sprawl and transportation issues. In Seattle and Boston, some expensive beltways that were built not that long ago are being removed. And, instead, these cities are beginning to put more money into practical alternatives, like growth centers that are connected by light rail, new buses with convenient and frequent schedules, and more bike paths.

A number of other cities and communities around the country have been involved in a variety of efforts to address a wide range of sprawl and sustainability issues. But the Pacific Northwest region has been particularly proactive—and successful—in these kinds of initiatives.

Stopping Sprawl

Portland, Oregon, is widely acknowledged as having the most successful coordinated effort to contain sprawl of any city in the nation. A 1973 state law required every city and town to establish a plan for future growth, but left it up to the individual communities to decide for themselves how to implement them. In response, the Portland metropolitan area set an outer boundary for future growth (known as an urban-growth boundary) that would protect surrounding agricultural and forestlands.

In order to make the area within the boundary more livable, Portland has been trying to encourage clustered, mixed-use development that is easily served by public transit. New rules mandate that 85 percent of new buildings must be within a five-minute walk of a transit stop.

Although many of these initiatives have been challenged repeatedly, they have remained popular with the majority of the state's citizens and have survived referenda and a variety of lawsuits. This is largely due to the widespread public participation in the planning process that led to the land-use laws in the first place.

As a result, downtown Portland, which had become a bit down-at-the-heels, is now a vibrant and thriving community. And the surrounding area, now served by an excellent light-rail system, is not suffering from the gridlocked traffic congestion afflicting most other metropolitan areas around the nation. And best of all, just 20 minutes from downtown, Portland residents have access to abundant natural beauty and green space.

Earth Education

Before enacting dramatic new land-use and planning laws, the state of Oregon used to lose 30,000 acres of agricultural land every year; now it is only losing 2,000 acres a year. This is a vivid demonstration of the power of imaginative, long-range planning and cooperative problem solving.

A Sustainable City

Although Portland has received a good deal of national attention for its managed growth success, some interesting things have been happening about 115 miles to the north in Olympia, Washington. Since 1993, Olympia has had a Sustainable City Initiative. This incredibly forward-looking municipal policy is a model for the entire nation. The introduction to the city's new philosophy says:

"The City of Olympia acknowledges its responsibility for leadership in creating a sustainable community—locally, regionally, and globally. A sustainable community is one that persists over generations and is far-seeing enough, flexible enough, and wise enough to maintain its natural, economic, social, and political systems."

Since the initiative was formalized, Olympia has used "sustainable community" as an integrating theme for a good deal of its planning. The city also initiated a Sustainable Community Roundtable, a nonprofit organization that uses a participatory process to facilitate the transition to sustainability in the region. The Roundtable releases annual reports of progress. Included in its 1995 update were initiatives to …

➤ Institute a regional land-use and transportation strategy aimed at developing urban core areas at a density that will support public transportation.

➤ Protect wetlands, agricultural, and forest lands.

➤ Promote waste reduction and recycling.

➤ Encourage new and expanded secondary-material manufacturing business.

➤ Expand Community-Supported Agriculture to around 1,000 participants.

279

The Sustainable City Initiative extends to many other projects and activities, but they all are basically related to building a better future for our children and grandchildren. While the initiative is unquestionably still a work-in-progress, it sounds like Olympia has gotten the message and is headed in the right general direction.

A growing number of communities around the nation are beginning to adopt similar strategies. Your community could be one of them.

Get Involved

If you would like to learn more about sustainable communities, here are some excellent resources. Check out Communities-by-Choice (www.communities-by-choice.org), the Sustainable Communities Network (www.sustainable.org), the U.S. Department of Energy's Center of Excellence for Sustainable Development (www.sustainable.doe.gov), or The Joint Center for Sustainable Communities of the United States Conference of Mayors and the National Association of Counties (www.usmayors.org/uscm/sustainable).

The Least You Need to Know

➤ Urban sprawl is an unsustainable and highly destructive growth pattern.

➤ Sprawl is gobbling up over three million acres of land in this country every year.

➤ Sprawl has made millions of Americans a slave to their automobile.

➤ Compact downtown areas can be livable, attractive, and vibrant places to live in.

➤ Some forward-looking towns and cities, both here and abroad, are developing practical strategies to build sustainable communities.

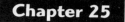

Chapter 25

Population

In This Chapter

➤ Why overpopulation is the single largest threat to sustainability

➤ What Thomas Malthus said about population

➤ Why we're not making much progress on population control

➤ What our options are

There is one final issue that, if left unresolved, has the potential to undo all the other positive environmental initiatives I've talked about so far. It's population. That's because population—or, more specifically, overpopulation—is at the root of most of our other interconnected environmental dilemmas and poses the largest obstacle to a sustainable future.

Our continued unchecked global population growth is the main cause of our overconsumption of basic resources such as food, water, and land. Though there are a wide range of opinions on the subject, one thing is becoming increasingly obvious in some of the war-torn, drought-stricken, disease-ridden countries in Africa: If we don't do something about runaway population and its accompanying poverty soon, Mother Nature will do it for us.

In this chapter, we'll take a look at the many different aspects of the population problem. We'll look back in time to put our current population levels in perspective. Then we'll look at some projections of where we might be in the future. Then I'll tell you why it's so hard for us to make any progress on these issues. Finally, I'll tell you what our choices are.

The Population Time Bomb

A time bomb is ticking. But unlike a hidden terrorist bomb that usually goes off with no warning, this one has been in plain sight for years. People talk about it, yet, like the weather, nobody seems to be able to do anything about it. But if we allow this bomb to explode, it's going to have a far more devastating effect on the planet than even the most vicious terrorist attack could possibly have.

Of course, I'm talking about overpopulation. Now, concerns about overpopulation are nothing new. As I mentioned earlier in the book, the ancient Greeks were concerned about maintaining the delicate balance between food supply and population, and both Plato and Aristotle were strong supporters of zero population growth.

Planetary Perils

Currently, around 1.8 billion people (30 percent of the global population) suffer from malnutrition, the largest number and proportion of the world population in history, according to the World Health Organization. In the time it takes you to read this sentence, approximately three children will have died somewhere on this planet from starvation or malnutrition.

But perhaps the most well-known opinion on the subject was put forward by British economist Thomas Malthus in his theory on population, *An Essay on the Principle of Population*, published in 1798. Basically, Malthus said that human population tends to increase faster than the supply of food, and that increasing population is only brought under control by famine, disease, and war. This pessimistic view of humanity was often used as an excuse to avoid helping the poor. But his vision of a species that is incapable of exercising common sense in regulating its own numbers has haunted us ever since.

Current population problems around the world tend to lend weight to Malthus's views. Let me help you to understand the magnitude of the present situation. In the time it takes you to read this sentence, approximately 30 babies will have been born somewhere in the world, many of them into abject poverty.

Here's another way to get some perspective on this. Check out the Census Bureau's World PopClock Projection at www.census.gov/cgi-bin/ipc/popclockw. After you've had a chance to look through the global population projections for the next year, jot down the big number at the top of the page and then hit the refresh button on your browser. You may be in for a surprise. That's how many more people were born around the world than those who died while you were looking at the Web page. For those of you who don't have Internet access, the numbers increase by about 148 people every minute, 8,880 per hour, 213,120 per day. And so on.

A Look Back

It's hard to put our current population figures into any meaningful perspective without looking to the past. It took several million years for human numbers to reach one billion around 1800. We hit the two-billion mark just 130 years later, in 1930. Thirty years after that, in 1960, there were three billion of us. Fifteen years later, in 1975, our numbers had grown to four billion. Twelve years later, in 1987, it was up to five billion. Twelve years after that, in 1999, we hit six billion. And the numbers continue to climb at about 77 million per year.

From these statistics, it is obvious that there has been exponential population growth until about 1975, when the pace of increasing numbers began to taper off a little. Part of this is due to the fact that in some countries population increases have leveled off or actually have begun to decline. But in other countries, especially in the developing world, it's another story.

Earth Education

China is the world's most populous nation with 1.2 billion inhabitants. By 2050, the population in India is expected to swell by almost 600 million, and Pakistan will more than double its numbers to 357 million. Nigeria's population will increase from 122 million to 339 million by mid–century, and Ethiopia will more than triple the number of its inhabitants from 62 million to 213 million.

A Look Ahead

United Nations projections show global population growing 3.3 billion by 2050. That brings the total to 9.6 billion. Unfortunately, as I've said previously, most of that increase will take place in the developing nations that can least afford to cope with it. Some of the most dramatic increases are projected for the Indian subcontinent and sub-Saharan Africa. These two areas are already home to some of the planet's hungriest people.

But not all the growth is going to be in the developing countries. The U.S. population has doubled during the past 60 years to 275 million, and at the current growth rate, may reach half a billion in the next 50 years. Each year our nation adds three million people (including legal immigrants) to its population, plus an estimated 400,000 illegal immigrants. In the long run, these relentless increases are ultimately not any more sustainable here than they are elsewhere.

If you want to see how may Americans there are right now, check out the U.S. PopClock Projection at www.census.gov/cgi-bin/popclock. In addition to the current population, the site also includes statistics for births, deaths, international migrants, and historical national population estimates. The U.S. population is increasing by one person every 11 seconds, according to the site.

Resource Demands

Continued population growth is the main reason for the growing pressure on our shrinking natural resources. And even though our standard of living is much higher in the U.S. than in many other countries (that, of course, is why so many people try to come here illegally), sooner or later it will begin to decline as more and more people put additional demands on our limited resources.

But the strain on resources is the most obvious—and the most worrisome—overseas. Although these resources include virtually everything from forests to minerals, I'm going to focus on food, because it's so basic to human survival.

Earth Education

In 1900, every farmer in this country produced enough food to feed seven other people. Today, each U.S. farmer feeds 96 people. Around the world, advances in agricultural technology have tripled cropland productivity in the last century. Despite all these dramatic improvements, we still cannot seem to provide adequate supplies of food for all the Earth's inhabitants.

Food

Malnutrition is a growing problem in many countries. One reason is that the global production of grains on a per-capita basis has actually been declining steadily since 1984. This is important because grains provide between 80 and 90 percent of the world's food supply. You don't have to be a mathematician to figure out that, under those circumstances, every additional mouth to feed means that much less food for everybody else.

The simple explanation is that the "wonders" of modern agricultural science have not been able to keep pace with population growth. Most of the dramatic gains in crop production that were made between 1950 and 1984 were due to advanced plant breeding strategies, expanded use of irrigation, and increased use of fertilizers. Though some additional breakthroughs in plant genetics are possible, most agricultural observers believe we have pushed the technology about as far as it practically can go.

Land

Another reason we should not expect dramatic increases in food supply is the land itself. Land is a finite resource. And, as real estate agents love to point out, "they're not making any more of the stuff." Consequently, the huge gains in soil productivity between 1950 and the 1990s were due mainly to increased use of chemical fertilizers. But don't expect that to be repeated in the twenty-first century. Some countries, including the United States, Mexico, Korea, and Japan are already seeing productivity gains tapering off. There's a point beyond which adding more fertilizer just doesn't help.

What's more, at least some of the crops grown during this period were on marginal lands that were made productive with the aid of fertilizers. Some of this land probably cannot be expected to stay in production in the long run, particularly if weather patterns become even more unpredictable in the future.

Water

But the main reason we should not expect any dramatic increases in food supply is water—or lack of water. World irrigation has about reached its upper limits, and in some countries it is expected to decline, as rapidly dropping water tables finally force cutbacks in excessive water use.

Both India and China can expect to face this situation in the not-too-distant future, which will seriously affect their ability to feed their huge—and growing—populations. India is expected to add 600 million to its current population by 2050, while its water table falls by three to ten feet per year. The same general pattern can be seen in China, where the water table under much of its agricultural land is falling at a rate of five feet per year. Most other nations will have to face this same reality sooner or later.

Planetary Perils

Currently, 40 percent of the world's food production comes from irrigated land, but the amount of irrigated land per person has declined since 1978 as the population has continued to grow faster than food supply.

Reaching the Limits

Although it should be pretty obvious that we are rapidly approaching the limits of a sustainable world population, there is wide disagreement on what those limits actually are. Some observers say we've already passed the limit. They're right, if everyone on the planet were to try to live the kind of lifestyle we enjoy in this country. But we've already seen that's simply impossible. Others say that the Earth could support nine billion. By 2050 we'll find out if they're right. Others say the number is 15 or 20 billion. And some cheery optimists even maintain that there really are no limits.

These are the folks who tend to believe that the "free market" and the wonders of modern science and technology are going to solve all of our problems. They remind me of the overconfident bioengineers and entrepreneurs in *Jurassic Park* (the book or the movie) who insist that all the sophisticated state-of-the-art technological safeguards they have so carefully constructed and installed will keep everything under control—just before all hell breaks loose.

Planetary Perils

Our democratic institutions and personal freedoms may ultimately be endangered if we do not come to grips with global over-population.

Some experts who follow population issues closely have warned that democratic institutions and societies that operate under the rule of law are in danger of becoming an endangered species under conditions of severe overpopulation—when the rule of law crumbles under the weight of the rule of numbers. This is already happening in developing nations where anywhere from 70 to 95 percent of housing in rapidly growing urban sprawl areas is being constructed "illegally." The sheer numbers involved makes any serious attempt to do anything about it virtually impossible.

There are two more issues about the planet's carrying capacity that makes all the debate about which number is correct seem pretty foolish. They are the issues of "overshoot and system collapse." You may recall from Chapter 1, "It's Our Home," that some scientists have warned of the possibility of an ecological disaster known as "system collapse." This is where our relentless damage to the Fabric of Life finally causes one interdependent ecological system to unravel after another in a chain reaction that spirals out of control until our life support system has been totally compromised.

That's bad enough, but then there's the problem of "overshoot" (remember Easter Island from Chapter 2, "Something Old, Something New"?). Basically what this refers to is that by the time we've passed the upper limits of the planet's carrying capacity, and we realize that we've passed them, it's already too late to do anything about it.

Part of the problem is due to what is known as "population momentum," in which today's children grow up to have their own children while their parents are still alive. And trying to do anything quickly about population momentum is like trying to suddenly change the course of a large ocean liner that is steaming ahead at full speed—when an iceberg suddenly appears directly in its path out of the fog. And we all know what happened to the *Titanic*.

The Need for a Policy

Okay, we have a problem. A rapidly growing problem. We're literally eating ourselves out of house and home. And in theory at least, the solution should be fairly straightforward—simply bring our population down to a sustainable level that matches our planet's capacity to meet our needs on a sustainable basis. But applying this common sense approach is anything but simple.

Too Much Talk

Everybody seems to have an opinion about population, but not much of anything gets done about it. United Nations Population Fund officials and others frequently complain that there is too much talk and not enough action when it comes to dealing with the population issue. They're right.

There are so many differing views on what to do about it—many of them totally contradictory—that trying to make any real progress is extremely difficult. Despite these difficulties, a number of environmental groups and other advocacy organizations including the Carrying Capacity Network, Environmental Defense Fund, League of Conservation Voters, National Audubon Society, National Wildlife Federation, Northwest Environmental Watch, and the Wilderness Society, try to keep the discussion going—or at least have developed policy statements on population issues.

One of the most active of these organizations, Negative Population Growth (NPG), a Washington, D.C.-based national organization, advocates a smaller and sustainable United States population to be accomplished through voluntary incentives for smaller families and immigration limited to 100,000 annually.

NPG cites strong support for action on population issues in a 1995 Roper Reports survey that they commissioned. The survey found that …

Planetary Perils

Our inability to talk openly and unemotionally about population issues is keeping us from making badly needed progress on overpopulation both here and abroad. In this country, the subject of population control has become so hopelessly entangled in the endless debates about abortion, and clouded even further by racial and religious factors, that many people seem incapable of having any useful discussion of larger population issues at all.

➤ 72 percent of Americans worry that overpopulation will be a serious problem in the next 25 to 50 years.

➤ 83 percent of respondents favored a lower number of immigrants than presently are permitted.

➤ 59 percent said the present population is already too big.

➤ 55 percent said overpopulation is a major national problem that needs to be addressed now.

Earth Education

Half of all Americans now see overpopulation trends as a threat to the nation's resource base, according to a Roper survey. Interestingly, the survey also found that one in three Americans now think that the U.S. needs to reduce its population to maintain a sound economy and environment over the long term. This runs counter to the widely-held view—actively encouraged by many in the business community—that a strong economy depends on continued population growth. Public opinion is clearly beginning to shift on this important issue.

For a complete description of NPG's program, as well as a listing of other organizations that are working along similar lines, visit their Web site at www.npg.org.

Babies as Usual

Unfortunately, many of the same sorts of divisive issues that have stymied any serious progress on population issues in this country are also to be found in many of the developing nations around the world. Though there has been some progress here and there, for the most part it's babies as usual. Some politicians in these countries bristle at the mere mention of family planning, pointing to the lack of population control initiatives in the U.S. Other politicians deny that there is a problem.

Many of the societies in these countries view big families as a necessity—a strategy that is often actively encouraged by religious leaders and long-held cultural traditions. And in some of these countries women are denied even the most basic rights—such as access to education and job opportunities—that we take for granted in this country. And it is the education of young people that is the key to moving toward smaller families. It's clear from the data that is available that the more education young people have, the fewer children they produce.

All of these problems have led to virtual gridlock on overpopulation solutions at a global level. The rich industrialized nations blame the developing nations for inaction. The developing nations blame the industrialized nations for lack of funding. Everyone blames everybody else. It's a mess. And while the world's leaders waste their time posturing and arguing about all this stuff, the digits on the population clock continue to spin, and the population bomb continues to tick. Maybe Malthus was right.

Tough Decisions

Okay, I can't leave the discussion there. Breaking the current deadlock on population issues is not going to be easy. At the very least, we need to start talking openly—and realistically—about these issues. And if the world can't reach a consensus on how to proceed, then, at the very least, each country needs to decide for itself what its own national carrying capacity is, and then work diligently to achieve it. But even that isn't going to happen as long as we keep our heads buried in the sand like ostriches, pretending there isn't a problem.

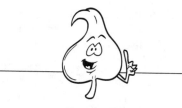

Green Tips

In order to attempt to solve the problem of global overpopulation we need to begin by admitting that we have a problem. Then, we need to face the many complicated issues squarely and try to find areas of agreement—such as trying to ensure a better world for our children—in order to begin a meaningful dialog. Then we need to figure out a strategy for a sustainable future for them.

What all of this boils down to in the end is that we have some choices to make. Difficult choices. And those choices depend on what kind of world we want in the future. If we want a world where everyone has a lifestyle like the one we have become accustomed to, then we better start seriously figuring out ways of reducing the global population drastically, because, as I've said previously, the planet can't support our lifestyle for even the present global population, let alone a larger one.

Another scenario is to continue our current lifestyle, and stand back and ignore the rest of the world as its population continues to grow exponentially while it descends into perpetual misery and conflict. To think that we could somehow remain apart and survive that scenario in the long run is unrealistic, however. We're having enough problems right now trying to keep illegal aliens out of this country. Can you imagine what it would be like if we were one of the only places left on the planet where there was enough food, water, and shelter? Forget it. And forget the Bill of Rights and just about everything else, too.

The most sensible scenario would be to lead by example. Cut back on our excessive consumption of resources. Face our own population issues openly—and resolve them. Then, help the rest of the world—especially the developing world—find ways to resolve theirs. These ultimately are global problems that call for global solutions. That's because, even if by some miracle we were to resolve our population issues tomorrow, the lack of progress overseas still threatens our future security.

We need to keep in mind one key point while we are trying to decide how to proceed. As the population of the Earth continues to go up, the average global standard of living goes down. And the longer we wait to act, the lower that living standard is going to be. And if we wait too long, the matter of choice will be taken out of our hands completely and Mother Nature will make our decisions for us. She's already giving us a preview of her methods in parts of Africa. That's not a future we should be leaving to our children and grandchildren.

It seems to me that instead of arguing endlessly about how many people the Earth *could* support, we should be thinking about the number it *should* support and work toward that goal. If we want to offer the global population a reasonable chance at a reasonably decent lifestyle, then we need to learn to live within our means—both nationally and internationally. And that means bringing global population to a sustainable level before we reach the point at which we don't have any choices left.

For more information on population issues check out the EcoFuture Web site at www.ecofuture.org/ecofuture and click on "overpopulation." For a more technical view of population, the United Nations Population Information Network is the place to go. Check it out at www.undp.org/popin. And if you like statistics, try Popnet (www.popnet.org).

The Least You Need to Know

➤ Overpopulation is probably the most difficult issue to resolve.

➤ Most of the increases in population in the next 50 years will take place in developing countries.

➤ Our inability to talk openly about overpopulation issues is keeping us from making needed progress.

➤ If we don't deal effectively with overpopulation, our children and grandchildren face a stark future.

➤ We still have time to make the difficult choices needed to resolve overpopulation.

Green Plans

The environmental problems we face are so huge and complicated—and there are just so many—that trying to solve them seems almost impossible. If someone could just figure out a way of dealing with these problems in a comprehensive, coordinated way we might actually make some real progress. Guess what? Someone has. And the strategy is called a green plan.

Green plans, or national environmental strategies, are the most effective—and only realistic—way of coming up with the large-scale solutions to solve our global-sized environmental problems quickly enough to avert the impending ecological meltdown that we're headed for.

And this exciting development is what I'm going to tell you about in this chapter. First, I'll explain what green plans are all about and why they are so important—and effective. Then, we'll take a look at some green plans in action, both overseas and in this country.

Green Plans

I've deliberately saved the most exciting part for last. And green plans are definitely the most significant development to appear on the global environmental scene because they are models of sustainability in action. Green plans are so exciting because they take a radical new approach to environmental decline: They don't just try to react to it; they attempt to solve it.

This may sound like an incredibly ambitious goal, but green plans include some incredibly powerful tools to get the job done. For starters, green plans are based on an optimistic spirit that basically says, "Yes, we can do this!" And the key word here is "we." Unlike most previous confrontational "us-versus-them" attempts to deal with environmental problems, green plans draw their strength from a cooperative approach that includes everyone working together toward a common goal. Cooperation is probably the most important feature of green plans.

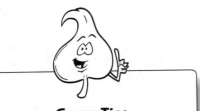

Green Tips

If the participants in a green plan all work together, they can accomplish many different goals simultaneously and more efficiently than if they tried to solve a wide range of environmental problems separately. This powerful new cooperative approach has been proven to work in many different parts of the world where green plans have been adopted.

The great strength of green plans is in their scope. People take hope from these large-scale efforts because they see that their government is really serious about the plan. And the sheer size of the environmental threat, and the magnitude of the response, brings people together and enables them to put their previous differences aside in order to achieve the new common goal.

What's more, almost everyone is willing to make the small sacrifices necessary when they realize that their efforts will result in a livable future for their children and grandchildren—especially when they understand that their entire community or society is working toward the same goal. Of course, this is the sort of thing I have been talking about throughout this book, but on a much more organized basis.

Green plans have the ultimate goal of achieving environmental and economic stability and a high quality of life for everyone. And the best part of all is that these plans not only work for nations, they are also an effective strategy for regions, states, or even cities and towns. Maybe yours.

Big Problems = Big Solutions

I spent the whole first part of this book describing the sorry state of our planet's ecosystems, so I'm not going to repeat all the depressing facts here. But I do want to point out that, until now, we have generally been trying to deal with our environmental problems in a piecemeal approach. We've been reacting to one problem after another by passing new laws or regulations, or by cleaning up messy oil spills, without really getting to the root of the problem.

Now, you might be tempted to ask, "How can we possibly solve the big problems if we can't even make progress on the smaller ones?" Good question. But that's the strength of green plans. Their "big picture" approach resolves a lot of the smaller problems almost automatically as you work on the larger issues.

Green plans are the only effective way to resolve the big problems because they treat the environment as it really exists—a single, interconnected ecosystem that can only be repaired through a co-ordinated, long-range plan of action. Green plans look past individual issues to the problems caused by the relationships between those issues. This ecological approach acknowledges that we cannot solve the individual problems without looking at the relationships between them.

Planetary Perils

By trying to deal with our many environmental problems individually, we fail to address the larger underlying problems. What is needed is a large-scale, comprehensive, integrated approach that is designed to solve the underlying problems completely. Green plans can do this.

Admittedly, this can get rather complicated. Green plans use a fairly sophisticated systems-analysis approach to divide complex problems into basic elements. This is the only way that an effective response can be developed that addresses all of the many interrelationships. This analysis is the basis for the development of the greenplan.

Here is an overview of how the process works from the Resource Renewal Institute in San Francisco (www.rri.org). A green plan …

➤ Anticipates problems rather than simply reacting to them.

➤ Establishes short- and long-term goals, as well as strategies and timelines for achieving them.

➤ Allows flexibility in determining how goals will be achieved, and it encourages innovation.

➤ Utilizes a mix of legal, regulatory, and voluntary measures.

➤ Includes provisions for monitoring and evaluating progress toward goals and reporting the results.

➤ Provides mechanisms for incorporating this feedback into the plan.

➤ Is flexible and can change in response to new information.

➤ Requires a sound database with solid agreement on the science behind it.

➤ Uses information systems and technologies to support decision-making.

One key element of most green plans that is not immediately evident from this list is the "polluter pays" principle. Basically, what this means is that the tax structure is changed to make polluters pay the true costs of their activities while encouraging environmentally beneficial activities with various incentives.

Another great strength of green plans is that they are designed to be flexible and can be updated as necessary to include new information and strategies. And finally, green plans can be customized to meet the specific environmental, economic, and social needs of a particular region.

A New Partnership

One of the greatest strengths of green plans is that they are a comprehensive strategy that gathers the whole galaxy of environmental and sustainability concerns under a single umbrella. This way, people who are concerned about rainforests, wilderness preservation, urban sprawl, wildlife habitat, toxic chemicals, human rights, population issues, etc., suddenly find themselves included as important parts of a larger coalition that is working to resolve all of these concerns. And there's strength in numbers.

But the partnership extends well beyond environmentalists and social activists. It includes the entire society from top governmental officials, to bureaucrats, to business and labor leaders, and regular citizens like you and me. Everyone has a productive role to play. And everyone participates in the design of the plan, making it relatively difficult for any one group to block or dismantle it.

Green Plans in Action

Of course, anything as totally new as this always has its critics and its doubters. "Show me that it actually works," is the usual attitude. Well, as it

Earth Education

In 1983, Huey D. Johnson, a former California Secretary for Resources, founded the Resource Renewal Institute to study and promote green plans. Johnson wrote an excellent book on the subject of green plans, *Green Plans: Greenprint for Sustainability*. Published in 1995, the book provides a comprehensive explanation, and is essential reading on the subject.

Planetary Perils

One of the biggest obstacles to successful green plans is short-term political thinking. Green plans require a new kind of leadership that is open to collaboration and is optimistic about the future. The kinds of major transformations that green plans entail require leaders who not only can see the eventual benefits that the plans offer, but also have the political courage and determination to see the process through the inevitable ups and downs along the way.

turns out, it actually does work; this isn't just some wild-eyed new theory. It's being used in a growing number of countries and locations around the world. And the most interesting part is that these different green plans are working successfully in countries with very different geographies, populations, politics, and cultures. Before we take a look at some specific examples, here's a little background.

The phrase "sustainable development" that plays such a key role in green planning gained world attention in the 1987 UN World Commission on Environment and Development report *Our Common Future*. Also known as the Brundtland Report after the commission's chair, Norwegian Prime Minister Gro Harlem Brundtland, *Our Common Future* emphasized the links between the problems of growth, economics, technology, and the environment. The solution that was proposed was sustainable development. As I've mentioned previously, this was defined as "development that meets the needs of the present without compromising the ability of future generations to meet their own needs."

Ever since the Brundtland Report, sustainable development has been a popular, widely discussed and debated idea. And both the report and many of the ideas it contained have been central to the development of green plans. Now let's look as some examples of green plans in action.

Earth Education

Agenda 21, signed by 154 nations at the Rio Earth Summit in 1992, contained many of the basic ideas originally spelled out in the Brundtland Report of 1987. The Earth Summit resulted in an ambitious agenda to address the environmental, economic, and social challenges that face the global community. While some progress has been made on a number of these issues, much remains to be done.

The Netherlands

You may recall from Chapter 1, "It's Our Home," the simple guidelines for responsible living that you should have learned in kindergarten are: share everything, clean up your own mess, and flush. Well, in the Netherlands, the Dutch have taken "clean up your own mess" to heart, and have made it the central theme of their national green plan—the National Environmental Policy Plan (NEPP), enacted in 1989.

The Brundtland Report contained an appeal for nations to stop shifting responsibility for environmental problems onto future generations and other countries. This was the basis for the Dutch decision to try to clean up their present environmental problems within 25 years, or roughly one generation. And they put their best and brightest minds to work on figuring out ways to do it. Faced with life-threatening environmental problems caused by congestion and heavy industry, the Dutch had their work cut out for them.

The NEPP encouraged a creative partnership between business and government. The government set the comprehensive 25-year environmental goals, but left it up to the various industrial groups to devise the specific strategies on how to meet them. This balanced approach between public and private sector roles enabled industry to come up with the most cost-effective ways of complying with the goals.

Earth Education

The Dutch National Environmental Policy Plan is the oldest, most comprehensive, and successful green plan in the world. In the past 10 years, the Dutch have made dramatic progress in many key areas. They have phased out ozone-depleting substances. Industry has reduced its waste disposal by 60 percent, and waste recycling has increased to 70 percent. And they have also reduced sulfur dioxide emissions from power plants by 70 percent, according to the Resource Renewal Institute.

In addition to the national plan, each of the 12 Dutch provinces was required to develop a plan of its own. It's interesting to note that the provinces have the responsibility for implementing and enforcing many of the government policies.

The Netherlands designed NEPP to be updated every four years, based on new information and feedback. And more frequent informational reports on progress and problems are made every year. This careful, constant monitoring of the plan enables the government to make prompt mid-course corrections as needed.

But perhaps the most exciting part is that the Netherlands have accomplished this (and much more) while the Dutch economy has continued to prosper—clearly demonstrating the inaccuracy of the widely-held view that economic prosperity and environmentalism are incompatible.

New Zealand

Meanwhile, on the other side of the planet, there have been some dramatic and exciting developments in New Zealand. Like the Dutch, New Zealanders have decided to "clean up their own mess" but have taken a different route to get to the same destination.

While the Netherlands is one of the most densely populated countries on the planet, New Zealand is one of the least. Consequently, New Zealand's green plan, the Resource Management Act (RMA) passed in 1991, is quite different. Nevertheless, the RMA was established using the same sort of nationwide input, negotiation, and compromise as the Dutch plan.

The guiding principle of the RMA is the sustainable management of New Zealand's considerable natural resources. But before actually tackling that job, the country took a long hard look at its existing governmental and regulatory structure and decided that it wasn't up to the task.

Enacting the RMA resulted in sweeping changes in the country's environmental management structure. The RMA replaced 57 overlapping management, urban-planning, and environmental laws with a single, comprehensive, coordinated plan. About 800 units of local government were reduced to fewer than 100 as a result of a local government reform process. And, finally, a number of watershed-based regions were established for resource management, rather than using previous political boundaries.

Under the framework of the RMA, some of New Zealand's cities have made substantial progress in developing sustainable and attractive urban environments for their residents. Waitakere City has probably made the most progress, and is seen as an international model of an "eco-city." The new city green plan calls for the overhaul of suburban sprawl, encourages cluster development, and creates a network of streamways and ecological corridors.

A recent evaluation of the RMA found that New Zealand has maintained broad-based consensus support nationwide. Remarkably, in less than a decade, New Zealand has managed to accomplish a bold cultural change and reform that probably would have taken other countries at least a generation.

Mexico

You might be surprised—as I was—to learn that a more recent addition to the growing green plan group of nations is Mexico. This is a significant development, because Mexico is one of the first developing countries to create a green plan.

The Mexican Environmental Program was set up in 1995. When legislation that included the main elements of the program was initially presented to the Mexican Congress, it became apparent that it lacked broad support from nongovernmental organizations (NGOs). Instead of trying to force its passage, the vote was postponed for a year in order to allow for a series of roundtable discussions on the bill with local, regional, and national representatives to build support for the legislation. Because of this effort, the legislation had much greater support when it went to Congress the second time.

Earth Education

Under New Zealand's earlier environmental regulations, landowners had to follow strict guidelines on what they could or couldn't do with their land. Under the country's new green plan, the emphasis has shifted to what kind of impact various activities will have on the environment. As long as the planned activity doesn't exceed certain set environmental standards, landowners are now pretty much free to do what they wish—one of the main reasons why the plan gained so much popular support. But with that relative freedom comes individual responsibility. Every New Zealander is now responsible for any negative effects that his or her activities may have on the environment.

Earth Education

When Mexico enacted its green plan, the Mexican Environmental Program, it suddenly leapt ahead of many wealthy industrialized nations in its environmental policy. The program is a comprehensive, forward-looking plan that identifies specific environmental problem areas and offers methods and tools to resolve them. Although the fate of the plan is not entirely clear under Mexico's new President, Vincente Fox, it remains a considerable achievement for Mexico and an example for other developing nations around the world.

Other Countries

Singapore is another country that has a green plan. Enacted in 1992, this comprehensive plan has been cited by the UN as a model for industrializing nations. A growing number of other countries have enacted various types of strong environmental legislation or policies that are close to—but not quite—green plans. These nations include Canada, Austria, Denmark, Norway, and Sweden. The European Union has also established an action plan, *Towards Sustainability*, that is similar to a green plan. This plan contains a set of environmental guidelines for EU member nations. It will be interesting to see what develops from these various green initiatives in the coming years.

Red, White, and Green

With all of this progressive and forward-looking activity going on in other countries—especially in the European Union—where does this leave us? Not in a very good position, I'm afraid. While these other nations are reshaping their economies and societies to become more efficient, sustainable—and highly competitive—we continue to drive around in our SUVs while we complain about the high cost of gasoline.

Needed: A Plan

If there is one country on the planet that desperately needs a green plan, it's the United States. And the planet desperately needs the United States to have one.

While we continue to pursue our inefficient and wasteful habits, we are losing our competitive edge in the new global economy. The Danish preeminence in the wind-turbine business is a prime example of our being asleep at the wheel. And the longer we stay asleep, the greater the danger that we'll run our SUVs off the road and into the ditch—where we'll stay hopelessly mired in the mud while the small, smart, nimble little green-plan countries around the world zip past us on the new Global Economic Highway.

As I've said previously, a growing number of U.S. companies are belatedly beginning to realize this danger, and, ironically, it may be the business community that ultimately saves us from—well—the business community. And from ourselves.

Good for Business

It's become increasingly obvious to forward-looking business leaders that sustainable business practices are good for the bottom line as well as for the environment. Businesses in countries that have developed efficient new green-energy policies have already gained a competitive edge over energy-inefficient U.S. manufacturers. Unfortunately, this helps to make foreign products less expensive and adds more momentum to the ongoing loss of American jobs to other nations.

However, more and more U.S. companies are changing their old patterns of thinking on these issues, particularly large multinationals like chemical giants Dupont, Dow, and Monsanto, which have learned some valuable lessons from their foreign divisions and affiliates.

And, as more and more U.S. companies see the light, the formerly solid base of resistance to change is beginning to crumble, leaving the coal, oil, and auto industries increasingly isolated—and stuck in their old ways of thinking. However, DaimlerChrysler, with its strong new German management influence, has recently abandoned the sinking ship of resistance to environmental enlightenment.

Planetary Perils

Our lack of comprehensive green planning in this country puts us in danger of falling behind many of our international trading partners. And because we consume a third of the world's resources, even if every small nation on the planet were miraculously to adopt a green plan tomorrow, their efforts would be totally overwhelmed by the negative environmental consequences of our over-consumption.

Will It Work Here?

Okay, green plans have a lot to offer. They seem to be effective in small nations. But can they work in a large and diverse country like the United States? The answer, quite simply, is "yes," because a few pioneering plans are already working at the state and local levels in this country.

Planetary Perils

Because we have failed to adopt comprehensive green planning in this country, many U.S. businesses now use twice as much energy as their competitors in some other nations.

Green plans function best when the people who are directly affected can have an opportunity to work on their creation and participate in their oversight and maintenance. Trying to come to a consensus on a national green plan would almost certainly be a time-consuming and frustrating process at the present time. Consequently, green plans developed at the state and local levels probably have the best chance for success in the near future. Once they have demonstrated their benefits, the rest of the nation will be more likely to accept them.

What about the federal government? Expecting long-range, visionary thinking from Congress at the moment is not realistic. Consequently, the most constructive role the federal government can play is to encourage local green plans with funding assistance and to revise federal laws that might stand in the way of those local plans. Here's a brief overview of some green plans in this country.

Earth Education

Minnesota, with its great natural beauty and progressive politics, has taken significant steps toward establishing a green plan. The Minnesota Legislature has allocated nearly $2.5 million for sustainable development initiatives and studies. In addition, the state has enacted a series of laws in recent years to address a wide range of issues, including sustainable forestry, redevelopment of contaminated urban industrial sites, and community-based planning for sustainability, among many others.

Minnesota

Minnesota has taken a bold leadership role in developing the first state green plan in this country. Former Governor Arne Carlson took the initial step in 1991 when he initiated a program called Minnesota Milestones. The program, which had input from thousands of residents, was intended to develop a long-term vision for the state for the next 30 years.

This was followed by the Minnesota Sustainable Development Initiative in 1993. The initiative focused on seven key areas of economic and environmental importance: agriculture, energy, forestry, manufacturing, minerals, recreation, and settlement. Two years later, the initiative published a plan, "Challenges for a Sustainable Minnesota," which included an overall vision, principles for making decisions, and recommendations for achieving the goals detailed in the earlier initiative. In 1996 the state legislature transformed the goals into state law.

Although Minnesota is still only in the relatively early stages of working with and refining its plan, it has made more progress than any other state in the country.

Oregon

In the late 1980s, Oregon began to experiment with some progressive ways to deal with issues of environmental and economic decline. In a program called Oregon Benchmarks, it developed ways to measure the quality of life in areas such as education, health, employment, and the environment.

Building on the success of the Benchmarks program, the state legislature approved a Green Permits program in 1997, which allows the state Environmental Quality Commission to use innovative permitting strategies. And in 1999, state legislators introduced a bill to establish a green-planning management framework for the state's environment. Although the legislation has not yet been enacted into law, the prospects for eventual passage are seen as reasonably good. All the signs tend to indicate that Oregon will continue on the long and winding road to eventually establishing a state green plan.

Chattanooga

At first glance, Chattanooga, Tennessee, might seem like an unlikely candidate for developing a green plan. In 1969, Chattanooga was noted mainly for having the worst air quality in the nation, tuberculosis rates that were three times the national average, and a seriously polluted Tennessee River that ran past an industrial wasteland. Under these circumstances, there was only one way to go—up.

Earth Education

In May 2000, Oregon Governor John Kitzhaber signed an executive order on sustainability for internal state operations, demonstrating the state's continued commitment to working toward a greener future.

A coalition of grassroots organizations, doctors, and members of the business community came together to start the enormous task of cleaning things up during the 1970s. Inspired by the progress that had already been made, a more ambitious initiative, Chattanooga Venture, tackled even more projects in the 1980s.

By 1988, the city's air was actually meeting federal air standards. And after years of hard work, the industrial wasteland along the riverfront has now been transformed into a park. Today, downtown Chattanooga is served by a fleet of free electric buses, and the city is well on its way to becoming an ongoing demonstration project for a successful sustainable community. Considering where they started from, if Chattanooga can do this, almost any city can.

A Long-Term Process

While these somewhat limited state and local plans scattered across the country are a far cry from the Dutch NEEP, they still clearly demonstrate that basic green plan principles can work almost anywhere. Now, I realize that in this country we tend to favor quick solutions to problems. Politicians love to suggest them—even if they don't really work.

Green plans, on the other hand, are fairly complicated to develop and manage, and are difficult for some people to understand because they are a long-term process rather than a short-term, limited program. Green plans require educated and informed citizens who are patient and wise enough to wait to see the results along the way as the process gradually unfolds.

Nevertheless, I'm convinced that it's only a matter of time before additional states discover the many advantages that green plans offer. All it really takes are people with long-range vision who are committed to building a sustainable community for themselves—and for their children and grandchildren. That could even be you.

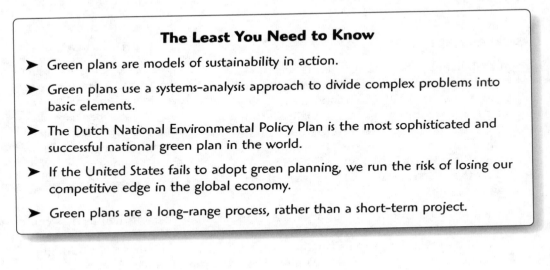

The Least You Need to Know

➤ Green plans are models of sustainability in action.

➤ Green plans use a systems-analysis approach to divide complex problems into basic elements.

➤ The Dutch National Environmental Policy Plan is the most sophisticated and successful national green plan in the world.

➤ If the United States fails to adopt green planning, we run the risk of losing our competitive edge in the global economy.

➤ Green plans are a long-range process, rather than a short-term project.

You Can Help

"An ounce of practice is generally worth more than a ton of theory," E.F. Schumacher says about environmentalism in his classic 1973 book, *Small is Beautiful: Economics as if People Mattered.* And that's what I've been talking about throughout most of this book—small, practical, everyday strategies you can use in your home, at work—just about anywhere—to help save our environment.

But, as we've also seen, saving our planet involves more than just recycling aluminum cans or using public transportation. A lot more. Although we've already covered a large number of subjects, I freely admit that I've only scratched the surface. That's because, as I've said many times, the Web of Life represents an amazingly complex tapestry of life on this planet. Look closely at one part, and you begin to see the threads that connect to the other parts.

In this final chapter, I'm going to briefly touch on a few more of those interconnected parts that need to be addressed if we are going to achieve a sustainable world that will be worth living in. Finally, I'll suggest some additional ways you can help.

Important Issues

If you've managed to get this far, you deserve some credit for fortitude. Thanks for hanging in there with me through some pretty depressing material: global warming, acid rain, falling water tables, dying trees, collapsing fisheries, nuclear disasters, disappearing species, toxic chemicals, oil spills, urban sprawl, and on and on.

Planetary Perils

Technology cannot fix all of our environmental problems. Continued scientific developments in agriculture may create more productive plants but can't create more arable land to grow them on. Advances in communication technology may speed up the dissemination of information, but can't guarantee that we will use it wisely. More fuel-efficient autos will not create more livable cities.

But we've also covered some pretty exciting, positive things such as Community Supported Agriculture, ecotourism, downshifting and voluntary simplicity, clothing made from recycled soda bottles, various types of renewable energy, electric cars, green plans, and more. Most of these give me reason to hope that we can indeed solve many of our environmental problems if we just pull together and put our minds to work on them.

However, while all these things are important, they do not represent a complete list of the necessary ingredients for a sustainable future. And there are some key issues that can't really be resolved by technology or innovative products. That's because these remaining issues concern matters of the heart, the mind, and the soul. And that's what we're going to focus on in the remaining pages.

Our Attitudes and Values

By now it should be clear that many of the changes we need to make in order to live more sustainably are not only going to require a change in habits, they're also going to call for a substantial change in attitudes. One of the key things that we need to come to grips with is to try to answer the question, "How much is enough?"

This seemingly simple question cuts right to the heart of the matter of our addiction to over-consumption. How much really *is* enough? The answer to this question is going to be different for different people. But instead of trying to come up with a long-winded discussion on this subject, I'm going to turn to the wisdom of the past—the third century B.C.E. to be precise.

The Ancient Chinese had an answer: "He who knows he has enough is rich." This comment from the Tao Te Ching pretty much hits the nail on the head just as squarely today as it did 2,300 years ago. In fact, many of the answers to our most vexing environmental, political, and social questions were offered thousands of years ago in the world's great religious traditions. We can look back to these rich traditions for inspiration to find ways to encourage the best human impulses instead of the worst.

But putting these simple guidelines into practice in a society totally dominated by a commercial culture, which urges us to put our faith in "things" instead of spiritual values, is a difficult task for us and for our children. Which brings us to another important part of the sustainability picture.

Education

One of the most powerful tools for helping to build a sustainable world is education. In developing countries, education often makes the difference between young people—particularly females—being hopelessly stuck in poverty or being able to make informed decisions that can lead to jobs and productive careers outside of the home. This has the advantages of improving their economic prospects as well as their minds, while simultaneously reducing soaring birth rates.

In this country, education can play a similar role. But the opportunities for advancement are far more plentiful—especially for college graduates. But if our children grow up to be heavy consumers like us, all this education will have been wasted if they blindly consume their way to oblivion later in this century.

Green Tips

Educating our children (and ourselves) about the environmental consequences of overconsumption is an important part of creating a sustainable future because it is our children, especially, who will be making the difficult economic, political, and social choices that will determine whether humanity has a future worth living in.

There is reason for both hope and anxiety at present. Most of our young children are strong supporters of environmental preservation, but at the same time many are avid consumers. Madison Avenue has been specifically targeting our kids with a vengeance to try to make sure they get hooked to hyper-consumption early in their lives. They seem to be succeeding. Spending by 4- to 12-year-olds has nearly tripled from 1991 to 1997. And the trend to entice cash-strapped secondary and high-school districts to sign ad contracts to allow commercial advertising in the classroom and on school property is a particularly noxious example of this initiative.

At the college level, there has been a hopeful counter-trend that has been aimed at bringing environmental sustainability into college curricula, procurement policies, and campus infrastructure. Colleges and universities have a rich tradition of pioneering cultural shifts, and sustainability is no exception. Several hundred university presidents from around the globe have been working together to help facilitate this initiative.

Planetary Perils

From the beginning of the Common Era to 1899, it is estimated that around 38 million people died as a result of war. The twentieth century was the most violent period in all of human history, with over 110 million deaths related to warfare in just 100 years. World War II resulted in an estimated 54 million military and civilian casualties.

Earth Education

There are still over 36,000 nuclear weapons in the world, despite the fact that the Cold War is supposed to be over. And these remaining weapons are still enough to totally destroy the planet and everything on it. Abolition 2000 (www.abolition2000.org) is an international organization that has been actively working to abolish these nuclear arsenals.

Peace and Disarmament

Ending violent conflict is another key part of our effort to build a sustainable future. Since the end of the Cold War, the prospects for armed confrontations between major nations have generally become less likely, but internal conflicts within nations have, unfortunately, become much more commonplace. Although some of these internal wars have been over dwindling (or unequally distributed) resources, many have been the result of ethnic tensions, intolerance, or repressive governments. These conflicts have been responsible for millions of casualties.

It's clear that if we are going to survive in a sustainable world, we need to develop ways of avoiding the use of force in the first place. The United Nations, originally established "to save succeeding generations from the scourge of war" has made some progress. It has participated in a large number of peacekeeping missions around the world—with varying degrees of success and failure. But perhaps its greatest contribution has been in the area of encouraging peace through its many other activities: anti-poverty and child survival programs, advocating women's rights, encouraging fair elections, and promoting sustainable development, and more. The UN needs our continuing support.

If we are to achieve a lasting peace, we need to gradually get rid of the means to wage war. We already have made some progress in disarmament. Military expenditures worldwide have declined by around 40 percent since their peak in the mid-1980s. Reflecting that decline, military arsenals, including nuclear weapons, have also been substantially reduced.

We need to continue the progress we have already made on disarmament. In particular, we must avoid any temptations to reverse the course we have been following; many people around the world are beginning to realize that weapons, more often than not, facilitate violence and destabilization rather than protect the peace.

What's more, on the assumption that "an ounce of prevention is worth a pound of cure," we also need to strengthen our efforts to develop better strategies for conflict prevention between nations, ethnic and religious groups, and individuals. That means learning tolerance, patience, forgiveness, and how to listen to those with whom we disagree.

One group that has been patiently working on this difficult task since the 1970s is The Alternatives to Violence Project (www.avpusa.org). AVP is an international association of volunteer groups working to encourage nonviolent lives in prisons, communities, and schools through community building, respect, cooperation, and trust.

Social Justice

Another issue that's closely related to peace and disarmament is social justice. Remember the second thing you should have learned back in kindergarten—share everything? This is an idea that seems to have been forgotten by a lot of people around the world. Some may have never learned it in the first place. But if we were to put this simple idea into practice, we could solve many of the worst problems that confront us—including most conflicts.

Now, I admit that poverty is probably not the first thing that comes to mind when most of us think of environmental problems. But global poverty represents one of the largest single threats to building a sustainable world.

Poverty, of course, is nothing new. Around 400 B.C.E., Plato observed that "any city, however small, is, in fact, divided into two: One, the city of the poor; the other, of the rich." That observation could have been made yesterday, except that the number of poor has grown dramatically since Plato's time.

In the recent past, most industrialized societies tended to think of poverty as being a Third World problem, and for the most part, tried to ignore it. This is no longer possible. That's because millions of these impoverished people are taking matters into their own hands by trying to migrate to any other nation that offers better opportunities for them and their children. You can't really blame them.

This has raised the very real specter of mass migration to the wealthy nations in Western Europe and North America that will make it increasingly difficult to maintain the lifestyles and freedoms to which we have become accustomed.

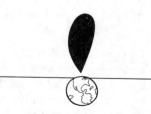

Earth Education

In 1987, 16 million people lived on less than $2 a day in Eastern Europe and Central Asia, but by 1998 the number of people struggling to live on that income had grown to 93 million. The World Bank estimates that 1.3 billion people live in absolute poverty, earning incomes of $1 a day or less.

Green Tips

One of the most effective strategies to reduce the number of illegal immigrants into rich industrialized nations is to help improve the conditions for the poor in their own countries before they become immigrants.

What all this boils down to is that we can no longer seriously talk about building an environmentally sustainable world economy without addressing the needs of the world's poor. And that requires a concerted effort on the part of the developed nations to help improve the lives of the poor where they live, rather than trying to stop them at our borders. So far, this has generally amounted to a lot of talk, but not much action.

More than 50 years ago, Aldo Leopold, one of the most important environmental voices of the twentieth century, got right to the heart of this matter when he said "all ethics rest upon this single premise: That the individual is a member of interdependent parts." And those interdependencies extend to the entire human family as well as to the natural world.

All Politics Is Local

We face an awful lot of enormously complicated challenges in the years ahead. This is going to require imaginative, courageous, and bold thinking on the part of a lot of people. However, expecting this kind of leadership from our nation's capital, though not hopeless, is hardly encouraging. Congress can't even recycle its own office paper, let alone provide leadership for something as progressive as a national green plan.

Of course, I realize that these folks are elected by us, so we're getting what we deserve—I suppose. Somehow, I can't help but feel that we deserve better. But that requires an educated and informed citizenry that votes. But then the dilemma of whom to vote for comes up—and it's a real problem much of the time. If the major parties can't offer us real choices, then perhaps it's time to look to third parties that can.

And one of the best places to look for alternative candidates for political office is probably right in your own state, county, or community. There's quite a lot of interesting political activity at the grassroots level these days. Pay attention to what's being said, and if you hear a candidate who is talking intelligently about sustainability issues (regardless of his or her party affiliation) you might want to consider supporting him or her, or his or her program. When it comes right down to it, green politics is local anyway, so that's where we need to begin.

Which brings up the most important point of all: Perhaps the person you need to put your faith in to make things better is the one who stares back at you in the mirror every morning while you brush your teeth. That's right: you.

There is an unfortunate tendency for people to look for inspired leaders who will save them—and the world—with brilliant programs or initiatives. And while we're waiting vainly for this to happen, our world is going down the tubes. And it's our world. So, instead of sitting at the breakfast table and complaining about our elected official's latest failures to do anything productive, get out there and do something yourself. You won't be alone.

Planetary Perils

One of the most dangerous strategies for saving the environment is to wait for someone else to do it. Don't wait. Get involved.

Groups and Organizations

And this is perhaps the most hopeful sign of all. An interesting phenomenon has been taking place that began in the early 1990s. While many of our elected officials—and even some traditional environmental groups—were dithering, more and more people at the local level got tired of waiting for someone else to do something about the destruction of our environment, and they began taking independent action. As a result, there has been a steady rise in the number of small ad hoc groups and organizations run by people who a decade ago would never have called themselves "environmentalists." You may know some of these people right in your own community.

These groups and individuals are hard to categorize because they have so many different concerns. There are wilderness preservationists, animal rights and anti-nuclear activists, green politicians, population control advocates, anti-genetic engineering protesters, agribusiness opponents, and a lot of people who are concerned about the effects of the globalization of the economy. Though these groups don't have a single message or theme, they do have a unifying concern for justice and a gritty determination to work for it regardless of the odds.

Battle in Seattle

And then, like a flash of lightning, all of this disorganized energy suddenly became focused in December of 1999 in Seattle, Washington, at the meeting of the World Trade Organization. Tens of thousands of demonstrators from all across the country descended on the city to try to shut down the planned meeting of the WTO. They succeeded. Outnumbered and unprepared, Seattle's 1,800-member police force was unable to deal with the size and scope of the demonstration on the opening day of the meeting.

Earth Education

There were roughly 40,000 non-violent demonstrators, including thousands of members of labor unions, religious groups, and a wide assortment of environmental organizations protesting the World Trade Organization in Seattle in December 1999. This demonstration is now viewed by many as a major turning point in global opinion about world trade and related environmental and social issues.

The next day, armed with tear gas, pepper spray, and riot clubs, the police tried to regain the upper hand and only managed to make a difficult situation worse in what has now come to be known as the "battle in Seattle." Though the small number of self-proclaimed anarchists who did a good deal of damage to the downtown business district got most of the media attention, the fact remains that the vast majority of the demonstrators did their best to maintain a nonviolent protest.

When the police tear gas had finally dissipated and the demonstrators had gone home, it was clear that the course of economic globalization had been changed forever. The WTO, which has traditionally conducted most of its business behind closed doors, had served as a lightning rod for the growing discontent over global economic trends that have left those most affected—just about everyone, but especially workers and the poor—shut out of the process. The WTO has now been put on notice that this is no longer acceptable behavior.

But, in addition, the demonstrators have managed to focus world attention on a whole series of important interrelated issues. The rights of workers to form labor unions and bargain collectively was high on the list of demonstrator's concerns, as was the issue of wide differences in environmental regulations around the world. They pointed out, quite correctly, that it's unfair to ask countries that have strong environmental protection programs to compete against countries with weak or no controls. And they have also made it clear that freer trade, regardless of how attractive it may be as a goal, will not be permitted to override all other human values.

Beyond Seattle

Energized by their success, many of the same demonstrators have gone on from Seattle to protests in Washington, D.C., and other cities across the U.S. and Canada aimed at the WTO, the World Bank, the Organization of American States, the World Petroleum Congress, and others. All of these organizations are now on notice that their activities are going to be watched very closely by a concerned and mobilized citizenry.

What all of these demonstrations have done is to make it abundantly clear that there needs to be far more public participation in the process of setting the rules for global trade and then monitoring it as it goes forward. Because they affect everyone, global trade issues are too important to be left in the hands of trade ministers and corporate lobbyists.

Although these demonstrations have undoubtedly served as a wake-up call for multinational corporations and international trade officials, I think there is just as much potential for using this new-found energy to work on domestic issues—especially green domestic issues.

As I pointed out in the last chapter, the greatest strength of green plans is in their ability to bring groups together to work cooperatively for a sustainable future. Green plans offer the obvious unifying framework that has been missing from the activities of most of the different protest groups in recent years. So, if demonstrating in the streets for a better future is not your style, you might want to consider sitting down with members of your community to develop a local green plan. There's an awful lot of renewable human energy out there just waiting to be harnessed.

Get Involved

So, where does all this leave us? It leaves us needing to make some choices. We can choose to continue to live our lives as if there were no limits, which will almost certainly carry us over the brink to systems collapse and disaster. Alternatively, we can choose to accept the fact that there are limits to our environment's carrying capacity, and that we must learn how to live within those limits.

Earth Education

Around 2,500 peaceful demonstrators marched to protest the World Petroleum Congress meeting in Calgary, Alberta, Canada on June 12, 2000. The protesters urged the use of alternative energy sources rather than fossil fuels.

Green Tips

The best way to help build a sustainable world is to match your background, training, personal strengths, and abilities to projects or initiatives that can make use of them. That might be limited to reducing, reusing, and recycling at home or at work, but it's a good start.

What's the best way to help? That's something you have to decide for yourself. There are so many things you could do. Here are a few ideas:

➤ Write letters to the editor in support of progressive environmental laws.

➤ Encourage a more balanced transportation network.

➤ Support and use public transportation.

➤ Work to stop the continued expansion of the superhighway system.

➤ Help fund, build, or maintain a bike path.

➤ Ride a bike.

➤ Walk more.

➤ Help protect endangered species of animals.

➤ Buy your food at a local co-op or farmers' market.

➤ Hold a community meeting to develop a shared long-range vision for the future.

➤ Get involved at some level in a local or state green plan.

➤ Work to keep commercial advertising out of your community's schools.

➤ Work for social justice.

➤ Teach and practice tolerance.

➤ Become a peacemaker.

➤ Live more simply.

➤ Plant a tree.

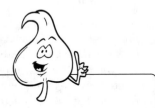

Green Tips

Regardless of what method you choose, it's important to remember that your efforts *really do matter*. Many hands make light work. As the green plans around the world have already clearly demonstrated, many hands pulling in the same general direction can have a profound—and positive—impact.

You might decide to do a number of these things. Or maybe something else. But all of these activities will help to create a sustainable future for everyone in lots of small ways that can really add up.

It's Up to Us

As I've said, one way or another, this is going to be the environmental century. We're either going to get it right—or we're not. And if we don't, our children and grandchildren are going to have to live with the unhappy consequences for the rest of their lives.

There is no law of nature that says they have to live in a world that degenerates into a harsh and dangerous wasteland filled with conflict, bloodshed, disease, and hopeless poverty. If that's what happens, we will only have ourselves to blame. And Thomas Malthus's dark vision of humanity will have been correct.

But on the other hand, if we get it right, the Third Millennium can be the green millenium, an age when we finally learn to live in harmony with our environment—and with each other. And that would be a bright and hopeful future we can be happy to leave for our children. The choice is ours.

So, the next time you see that picture of our beautiful blue and green Earth with its swirling white cloud patterns surrounded by the cold darkness of space, just remember, the Earth is our home. Our only home.

The Least You Need to Know

➤ Working toward disarmament and peaceful resolution of conflict is an important part of a sustainable future.

➤ An environmentally sustainable global economy is impossible without helping the world's poor.

➤ A lot of people have gotten tired of waiting for someone else to solve our environmental problems and are doing it themselves.

➤ You can do so many things to help create a sustainable future.

➤ Everyone has a constructive role to play in working for a better world.

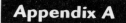

Environmental Timeline

2200 B.C.E.—Akkadian Empire falls, possibly due to a prolonged dry spell in the northern region of the Mesopotamian valley.

1500 B.C.E.—The first jars and bottles are made out of glass.

400 B.C.E.—The first municipal dump in the Western world is established in ancient Athens.

350 B.C.E.—The Greek philosophers Plato and Aristotle warn of the dangers of overpopulation and are strong supporters of zero population growth.

160 B.C.E.—Marcus Porcius Cato the Elder introduces composting as a way to build soil fertility in the Roman Empire.

1680—Easter Island society begins its descent into civil warfare and cannibalism after overshooting the island's natural carrying capacity.

1690—Paper recycling begins in America when the first paper mill is established near Philadelphia.

1776—Metal recycling in America begins when patriots in New York City topple a statue of King George III, melt it down, and turn it into thousands of bullets.

1803—Louisiana Purchase.

1848—Discovery of gold in California.

1849—U.S. Department of the Interior is created.

1854—*Walden,* by Henry David Thoreau is published.

1862—First Homestead Act is signed into law by President Lincoln.

1864—*Man and Nature* is published by George Perkins Marsh.

1867—Mining Law of 1867 encourages miners to explore for and extract minerals on public land.

1872—Mining Law of 1872 encourages even more mining on public land; Yellowstone Park created.

1885—The first garbage incinerator in the United States is built on Governor's Island in New York Harbor.

1891—Yosemite National Park is created.

1892—John Muir founds the Sierra Club.

1897—The Forest Management Act is passed, opening federal forest reserves to logging, mining, and grazing interests.

1904—First "junk mail" is authorized by the U.S. Postal Department.

1905—National Audubon Society is formed.

1908—The Grand Canyon becomes a national monument.

1910—The Pickett Act allows the president to remove public lands from development for oil and agricultural use, but not for mining use.

1916—National Park Service is created.

1935—U.S. Soil Conservation Service is created; the Wilderness Society is founded; National Wildlife Federation is created; first beer can is produced by Kreuger's Cream Ale in Richmond, Virginia.

1944—Dow Chemical invents polystyrene foam and calls it Styrofoam.

1945—First atomic bomb is detonated in New Mexico.

1948—Federal Water Pollution Control Act is passed; Aldo Leopold publishes his book *A Sand County Almanac*.

1955—The Clean Air Act is passed by Congress.

1956—Water Pollution Control Act is amended to fund water treatment plants.

1957—First commercial U.S. nuclear power plant starts up.

1961—Procter & Gamble begins test-marketing the disposable diaper.

1962—Rachel Carson's book *Silent Spring* is published.

1963—Congress passes the first Clean Air Act.

1964—Congress passes the Wilderness Act.

1965—The Water Quality Act and the Solid Waste Disposal Act are passed.

1967—The Environmental Defense Fund is established.

1968—Reynolds Aluminum starts recycling aluminum cans in California.

1969—Greenpeace is founded.

1970—First Earth Day is celebrated; the Environmental Protection Agency (EPA) is created.

1971—the first bottle-recycling law is passed in Oregon.

1972—The United Nations Conference on the Human Environment takes place in Stockholm, Sweden; the first buy-back centers for purchasing recyclables from the public are opened in Washington State.

1973—Endangered Species Act is passed; Alaskan oil pipeline is approved; Arab oil embargo.

1975—The first disposable razor is produced and marketed by Gillette.

1976—The National Academy of Sciences warns of the dangers that CFCs pose to the ozone layer; Toxic Substances Control Act is passed.

1977—Love Canal neighborhood in New York is evacuated when it is discovered that it is located on top of a chemical waste site; the nuclear reactor at Three Mile Island Power Plant in Pennsylvania melts down.

1978—The Amoco *Cadiz* spills its entire 226,000-ton (67 million gallons) cargo of crude oil into the Atlantic off the coast of Brittany; first two-liter plastic bottle is introduced.

1979—The *Atlantic Express* and *Agean Captain* collide in the Caribbean off Tobago, losing 370,000 tons (110 million gallons) of oil, the third largest oil spill in history; the *Ixtoc 1* oil well spews 140 million gallons into the Gulf of Mexico, the second largest oil spill in history.

1980—The "Superfund" Act is passed by Congress, requiring the EPA to follow a "polluters pay" policy for cleaning up abandoned toxic waste sites.

1981—EarthFirst! is established.

1984—The Union Carbide plant in Bhopal, India, releases a highly toxic chemical cloud into the air, killing 2,000 people and injuring 200,000 more.

1985—*The Rainbow Warrior*, a Greenpeace ship, is sunk off New Zealand by French agents to stop it from disrupting nuclear tests in the South Pacific.

1986—The Number Four reactor at the Chernobyl nuclear power plant in the former Soviet Union melts down and explodes, releasing a huge radioactive cloud, forcing the evacuation of 450,000 people.

1987—The Montreal Protocol is signed by 24 nations to reduce levels of ozone-destroying CFCs in the atmosphere; the infamous "Garbage Barge" incident takes place along the East Coast.

1989—The Exxon *Valdez* runs aground off the coast of Alaska, spilling 37,000 tons (11 million gallons) of crude oil into Prince William Sound.

1990—Twentieth anniversary of Earth Day.

1991—Near the end of the Persian Gulf War, Iraqi forces destroy eight oil tankers and onshore terminals in Kuwait, causing a 240-million gallon oil spill, the worst in history.

1992—United Nations Conference on Environment and Development (Earth Summit) in Rio de Janeiro.

1997—The UN Commission on Sustainable Development is founded.

1999—"Battle in Seattle" massive street demonstrations against the World Trade Organization meeting in Seattle, Washington.

2000—Thirtieth anniversary of Earth Day.

Glossary of Terms

Aquifer is a layer of rock, gravel, or sand that contains or conducts underground water.

Biodegradable refers to things that decay through the action of living organisms.

Biopower is the generation of electricity from specially grown organic materials or organic wastes.

Carrying capacity refers to the upper limits of Earth's ability to support life in a sustainable manner without degrading its resources.

Climatologist is a scientist who studies climate conditions.

Closed loop systems are self-contained and generally self-sustaining.

Closed-loop recycling is the process of collecting an item such as a bottle and processing it back into another bottle.

Composting is the natural process of decomposition and recycling of various organic materials into a humus-rich soil amendment called compost.

Continental shelf is the part of a continent that is submerged in relatively shallow seas.

Coral reef is a ridge or part of a shallow area of sea floor near the sea's surface made up of the calcium-containing remains of millions of tiny coral animals, red algae, and mollusks.

Defaunation is the removal of large segments of bird and mammal populations from forests by local hunters looking for food to feed their families with.

Degradable plastics are designed to eventually break down and disintegrate due to bacterial action or exposure to sunlight.

Downshifting is a voluntary decision to cut back on your work hours, or to take a new, lower-paying job in exchange for more time to spend with family or other parts of your life that are more important to you.

Ecological footprint is the measure of area needed to supply national populations with the resources and area needed to absorb their wastes.

Ecology is the set of relationships between organisms and their physical environment.

Ecosystem is a community of living organisms in which there is constant interchange between its various parts.

Ecotourism is travel to places to learn about the culture and natural history of that location while not damaging its environment. It also usually involves trying to help the local economy and the local population.

El Niño refers to the periodic appearance of unusually warm water in the eastern and central Pacific Ocean along the equator. This can cause unusual and often undesirable shifts in weather systems around the planet.

Electrolysis is a process that produces chemical changes by passing an electric current through a nonmetallic electric conductor, such as water.

Embodied energy refers to the amount of energy needed to produce any product initially.

Ethanol is a gasoline-fuel additive made from corn.

Fossil fuel is an organic, energy-rich substance formed from the long-buried remains of prehistoric life.

Frugal means not wasting things.

Greenhouse effect is the heating of the atmosphere that results from the absorption of solar radiation by certain gases, especially carbon dioxide and methane.

Humus is a dark, organic material in soils produced by the decomposition of organic matter.

Hydrologic cycle is the perpetual cycle in which water evaporates from lakes and oceans, forms clouds, falls as rain or snow, and then flows back into the ocean and lakes.

Hydrologist is a scientist who studies water.

Industrial ecology is the use of ecological thinking in industrial settings.

Irradiated foods are subjected to radiation exposure—or high-speed electrons—to kill microorganisms that cause spoilage.

Kilowatt hour is 1,000 watts of electricity used for one hour.

Leachate is the liquid (often toxic) solution created when water percolates through a landfill.

Manifest Destiny was the widely held belief that the territorial expansion of the United States was not only inevitable but also divinely ordained.

Methanol, also known as "wood alcohol," can be used as a substitute fuel for gasoline.

Net metering enables electrical customers to sell back electricity at a retail price to the main power grid, by spinning their meter backward when their photovoltaic system is generating more then they are consuming.

Obesity, or excessive body fat, occurs when the food energy you eat exceeds the food energy you use.

Organic foods are grown without chemicals that can harm the land and water.

Pesticide is any agent that is used to kill or control insects, weeds, rodents, fungi, or other organisms.

Photosynthesis is a process by which plants and other organisms use light to convert carbon dioxide and water into a simple sugar. This provides the basic energy source for almost all organisms.

Planned obsolescence is the deliberate design of products to wear out or break down in a fairly short period of time.

Primary reuse is when something is reused for its original purpose.

Rationing is the restriction of the consumption of products and supplies, often during wartime.

Recycling is the collection of waste materials and reprocessing them into new materials or products, which are then sold again.

Regeneration center is a central location where various skilled repair technicians are encouraged to go into business to provide a wide range of repair capabilities for a community.

Resin is a sticky substance from which most plastics are made.

Secondary reuse is when something is used for some other purpose than what it was originally designed for.

Source reduction refers to reducing the quantity of waste, which in turn lessens the amount of material that enters the waste stream in the first place.

The Three Rs of the environmental movement are reduce, reuse, and recycle.

Typhoon is a hurricane that occurs in the Western Pacific and China seas.

Urban sprawl is the outward spread of built-up areas caused by their expansion into large suburbs.

Voluntary simplicity is a lifestyle movement that generally stresses very low consumption, careful spending, and a deep concern for a variety of ethical, moral, environmental, and spiritual issues.

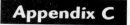

Further Reading

Books

Dacyczyn, Amy. *The Tightwad Gazette: Promoting Thrift as a Viable Alternative Lifestyle.* New York: Villard Books, 1993.

Elgin, Duane. *Voluntary Simplicity: Toward a Way of Life That Is Outwardly Simple, Inwardly Rich.* New York: William Morrow, 1993.

Hawken, Paul. *The Ecology of Commerce.* New York: HarperCollins, 1993.

Hawken, Paul, Amory Lovins, and L. Hunter Lovins. *Natural Capitalism: Creating the Next Industrial Revolution.* Boston: Little, Brown and Company, 1999.

Johnson, Huey D. *Green Plans: Greenprint for Sustainability.* Lincoln, Nebraska: University of Nebraska, 1995.

Leopold, Aldo. *A Sand County Almanac.* New York: Ballantine Books, 1991 (reissue).

Marsh, George Perkins, and David Lowenthal, ed. *Man and Nature.* Cambridge, Massachusetts: Harvard University Press, 1973 (originally published in 1864).

Nash, Roderick. *Wilderness and the American Mind.* New Haven, Connecticut: Yale University Press, 1986.

Pahl, Greg. *The Unofficial Guide to Beating Debt.* Indianapolis, Indiana: IDG Books Worldwide, 2000.

Rulghum, Robert. *All I Really Need to Know I Learned in Kindergarten: Uncommon Thoughts on Common Things.* New York: Villard Books, 1993.

Saltzman, Amy. *Down-Shifting, Reinventing Success on a Slower Track.* San Francisco: HarperCollins, 1991.

Schor, Juliet. *The Overspent American.* New York: Basic Books, 1998.

Schumacher E.F. *Small Is Beautiful: Economics as If People Mattered.* New York: HarperPerennial, 1989.

Thoreau, Henry David, and J. Lyndon Shanley, ed. *Walden.* Princeton, New Jersey: Princeton University Press, 1989.

Yago, Jeffrey R. *Achieving Energy Independence—One Step at a Time.* Gum Spring, Virginia: Dunimis Technology, 1999.

Online Publications

Better World Zine

www.betterworld.com

A terrific online magazine that deals with issues that relate to the environment, society, and your wallet.

BioCycle Journal

www.environmental-expert.com/magazine/biocycle

An excellent online journal of composting and recycling, also available in a printed version.

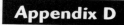

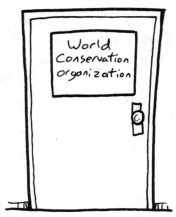

Groups, Organizations, and Other Resources

Alternatives to Violence Project
AVP/USA
821 Euclid Avenue
Syracuse, NY 13210
713-747-9999
www.avpusa.org

AVP is an international association of volunteer groups working to encourage nonviolent lives in prisons, communities, and schools through community building, respect, cooperation, and trust.

American Council for an Energy-Efficient Economy
1001 Connecticut Avenue, NW, Suite 801
Washington, DC 20036
202-429-0063
aceee.org

This group focuses on issues related to energy policy and energy efficiency.

American Farmland Trust
1200 18th Street, NW, Suite 800
Washington, DC 20036
202-331-7300
www.farmland.org

American Rental Association
www.ararental.org

The ARA's Web site contains a wealth of information on the organization and its members, as well as some handy household tips.

American Wind Energy Association
122 C Street, NW, Suite 380
Washington, DC 20001
202-383-2500
www.awea.org

The AWEA promotes wind energy as a clean source of electricity for consumers around the world.

Buy Recycled Business Alliance
brba.nrc-recycle.org

A group of organizations committed to increasing the purchase of recycled content products.

Center for a New American Dream
6930 Carroll Avenue, Suite 900
Takoma Park, MD 20910
301-91-3684
www.newdream.org

A nonprofit membership-based organization that helps individuals and institutions reduce and shift consumption to enhance the quality of life and to protect the environment.

Center for Resource Solutions
P.O. Box 29512
San Francisco, CA 94129
415-561-2100
www.green-e.org

This nonprofit organization has established the Green-*e* Renewable Electricity Certification Program.

Certified Forest Products Council
www.certifiedwood.org

An independent, nonprofit, voluntary initiative committed to promoting responsible forest-products-buying practices throughout North America in an effort to improve forest management practices worldwide.

Communities by Choice
433 Chestnut Street
Berea, KY 40403-1510
859-985-1763
www.communities-by-choice.org

A national network of individuals and communities committed to learning and practicing sustainable development.

Compost Resource Page
www.oldgrowth.org/compost

An online source of information about composting, which includes basic and advanced composting information, tips, products, and services, and links for additional information.

Context Institute
www.context.org

Context Institute explores how human society can become sustainable, and has served as a catalyst for voluntary change toward a more humane and sustainable culture. Best known for their journal, *In Context: A Quarterly of Humane Sustainable Culture*, now available on their site.

Co-Op America
1612 K Street NW, Suite 600
Washington, DC 20006
1-800-58-GREEN
www.coopamerica.org

A national nonprofit organization, providing the economic strategies, organizing power, and practical tools for businesses and individuals to address today's social and environmental problems.

Defense Reutilization and Marketing Service
www.drms.dla.mil

An interesting source of a staggering array of surplus military items.

Directory of U.S. Food Cooperatives
www.prairienet.org/co-op/directory.html

Online listing of food cooperatives.

EarthFirst!
Home of the EarthFirst! Journal
P.O. Box 1415
Eugene, OR 97440
541-344-8004
www.earthfirst.org

Founded in 1979, EarthFirst! is a grassroots, activist-based environmental movement rather than an organization.

Eco-Source Network
www.ecosourcenetwork.com

A comprehensive Web site that connects you with industry experts, searchable online directories, forums for information exchange, and numerous other resources related to responsible travel.

Eco-Village Information Service
www.gaia.org

Features information covering all aspects of eco-villages, including the social, infra-structure, ecological, and spiritual. Also the Eco-village network and green resources.

Electric Auto Association
National EAA Headquarters
60 Alan Drive
Pleasant Hill, CA 94523
www.eaaev.org

A nonprofit educational organization that promotes the advancement and wide-spread adoption of Electric Vehicles.

Energy Star Programs
1-888-STAR-YES
www.energystar.gov

A collaboration between the U.S. Department of Energy, the Environmental Pro-tection Agency, and many manufacturers, designed to prevent pollution by helping consumers buy products that use less energy.

The EnviroLink Library
library.envirolink.org

This site claims to be the most comprehensive resource of environmental information available on the Internet.

Environmental Defense

www.edf.org

Founded in 1967 as the Environmental Defense Fund, this nonprofit focuses on a broad range of regional, national, and international environmental issues.

Environmental Protection Agency

1200 Pennsylvania Avenue, NW
Washington, DC 20460
202-260-2090
www.epa.gov

Friends of the Earth

1025 Vermont Avenue, NW
Washington, DC 20005
202-783-7400
www.foe.org

Frugal Living Resources

www.igc.apc.org/frugal

The purpose of EcoNet's Frugal Living Resources section is to provide information sources for better, healthier, more satisfying living with less.

Global Action Plan for the Earth
P.O. Box 428
Woodstock, NY 12498
914-679-4830
www.globalactionplan.org

A nonprofit environmental education organization that promotes and supports the development of environmentally sustainable lifestyles worldwide.

Greenpeace

702 H Street NW
Washington, DC 20001
1-800-326-0959
www.greenpeaceusa.org

Green Seal

1001 Connecticut Avenue, NW
Suite 827
Washington, DC 20036-5525
202-872-6400
www.greenseal.org

An independent, nonprofit organization dedicated to protecting the environment by promoting the manufacture and sale of environmentally responsible consumer products.

International Institute for Sustainable Development
161 Portage Avenue East
Sixth Floor
Winnipeg, Manitoba
Canada R3B 0Y4
204-958-7700
iisd.ca

National Association of Exchange of Industrial Resources
560 McClure Street
Galesburg, IL 61401
1-800-562-0955
www.naeir.org

National Audubon Society
700 Broadway
New York, NY 10003
212-979-3000
www.audubon.org

The mission of the society is to conserve and restore natural ecosystems, focusing on birds and other wildlife for the benefit of humanity and the planet's biological diversity.

National Renewable Energy Laboratory
www.nrel.gov

The U.S. Department of Energy's laboratory for renewable energy and energy-efficiency research, development, and deployment.

Negative Population Growth
1717 Massachusetts Avenue, NW
Suite 101
Washington, DC 20036
202-667-8950
www.npg.org

A national organization that advocates a smaller and sustainable United States population.

New Road Map Foundation
P.O. Box 15981
Seattle, WA 98115
206-527-5114

An all-volunteer, nonprofit organization based in Seattle that promotes frugality and a sustainable future for the world.

Pennsylvania Resources Council
3606 Providence Road
Newtown Square, PA 19073
Attn: Michele
610-353-1555
www.prc.org

Publisher of the 1998 Buyers Guide to Recycled Products. To get a copy, send $4 (PA residents) or $6 (nonresidents) to the address.

People-Centered Development Forum (PCD Forum)
iisd1.iisd.ca/pcdf

An international alliance of individuals and organizations dedicated to the creation of just, inclusive, and sustainable human societies through voluntary citizen action.

Rails-to-Trails Conservancy
RTC National Headquarters
1100 17th Street, NW
10th Floor
Washington, DC 20036
202-331-9696
www.railtrails.org

A nonprofit organization dedicated to creating a nationwide network of public trails from former rail lines and connecting corridors.

Recycler's World
Recyclenet Corporation
P.O. Box 1910
Richfield Springs, NY 13439
519-767-2913
www.recycle.net

A Web site of the Recyclenet Corporation, this is a worldwide trading site for information related to secondary or recyclable commodities, by-products, used, and surplus items or materials.

Resource Renewal Institute
Fort Mason Center, Pier One
San Francisco, CA 94123
415-928-3774
www.rri.org

RRI was founded in 1983 to study and promote green plans.

Scientific Certification Systems (SCS)

1-800-ECO-FACTS

www.scs1.com

Among its many activities, this company's environmental division certifies a wide variety of claims related to environmental achievement in the product-manufacturing sector.

Sierra Club

85 Second Street
Second Floor
San Francisco CA, 94105-3441
Phone: 415-977-5500
Fax: 415-977-5799
www.sierraclub.org

The Simple Living Network

www.slnet.com (also www.simpleliving.net)

For those who are serious about learning to live a more conscious, simple, healthy and earth-friendly lifestyle. Includes the Web of Simplicity, featuring a massive 3,000-page Web site loaded with step-by-step ideas, a free e-mail newsletter, lists of support groups and study circles around the world, links to other earth-friendly Web sites, and more.

The Sustainable World Web Site

www.sustainable-world.com

If you liked *The Complete Idiot's Guide to Saving the Environment,* check out this site for additional, up-to-date information and the latest links for helping to create a sustainable world. This site also has more books and articles by Greg Pahl.

Union of Concerned Scientists

UCS National Headquarters
2 Brattle Square
Cambridge, MA 02238-9105
617-547-5552
www.ucsusa.org

An independent nonprofit alliance of 50,000 concerned citizens and scientists across the country committed to build a cleaner, healthier environment and a safer world.

WasteWise

1-800-EPA-WISE

www.epa.gov/wastewise

A free, voluntary program sponsored by the Environmental Protection Agency that helps organizations eliminate municipal solid waste, while benefiting their bottom line and the environment.

The World Conservation Union
www.iucn.org

Created in 1948, the IUCN, with headquarters in Switzerland, is one of the world's largest conservation-related organizations.

World Wide Fund for Nature
www.panda.org

One of the world's largest and most experienced independent conservation organizations.

Worm Digest
www.wormdigest.org

An online resource for information about vermicomposting (earthworm composting).

Retailers

Bio Pac, Inc.
www.the-body-shop.com

An international chain with 1,500 outlets around the world, which encourages reuse by offering discounts when you bring back your empties for refilling of their personal-care products.

Tom's of Maine
P.O. Box 710
Kennebunk, ME 04043
207-985-2944
www.tomsofmaine.com

Manufacturer of safe, effective, natural personal-care products.

Index

H